Valiant or Virtuous?

GENDER BIAS IN BIBLE TRANSLATION

Valiant or Virtuous?

GENDER BIAS IN BIBLE TRANSLATION

Suzanne McCarthy

Edited by
Jay Frankel, Christy Hayhoe, and Ruth Hayhoe

WIPF & STOCK · Eugene, Oregon

VALIANT OR VIRTUOUS
Gender Bias in Bible Translation

Wipf & Stock
An Imprint of Wipf and Stock Publishers
199 W. 8th Ave., Suite 3
Eugene, OR 97401

www.wipfandstock.com

PAPERBACK ISBN: 978-1-5326-7663-5
HARDCOVER ISBN: 978-1-5326-7664-2
EBOOK ISBN: 978-1-5326-7665-9

Manufactured in the U.S.A.   JUNE 14, 2019

About the author:

Suzanne McCarthy grew up in an evangelical Christian family in Toronto, Canada. She completed an honors degree at the University of Toronto in Classical and Modern Languages, and pursued French-language biblical studies at Institut Emmaüs in Switzerland. Her MA thesis was on the syllabary of the indigenous Cree people. Suzanne authored a popular blog on biblical translation and gender, and was also a poet (https://www.blogger.com/profile/07033350578895908993). She died of breast cancer in 2015, while completing this book.

About the editors:

Jay Frankel, Suzanne's husband, is a clinical psychologist based in New York. He organized Suzanne's chapters thematically and oversaw the editing of this book. Christy Hayhoe, Suzanne's niece, is a professional editor based in Toronto and was responsible for all aspects of editing this book. Ruth Hayhoe, Suzanne's older sister, is a professor at the University of Toronto. She arranged a set of focus groups to obtain feedback on the chapters after Suzanne's death and supported all aspects of the preparation of this book for publication.

Before I came to write

I thought before I came to write
That words would be like rock.
You choose a piece and turn it
And heave it into place.

Each word must fit the rest
And suit the space and shape
Then each single solid word
Will be set
For posterity

Until a path is built
Both flat and smooth
Firm beneath the feet
And people will walk on it
Surely.

But I found that words are like water
Running in the creek
You can dip your hands and cup your palms—
Or open your fingers and let the words run out
And rejoin the stream.

Soon with fingers dripping
And dipped again
Into the stream of language
Words coincide with thought
For brief moments
And become consumable.

I didn't know that words
were just water
Trapped momentarily
and then let go.

Table of Contents

List of Abbreviations for Bible Translations

CEB: Common English Bible

ESV: English Standard Version

GNB: Good News Bible

HCSB: Holman Christian Standard Bible

NASB: New American Standard Bible

NET: New English Translation

NLT: New Living Translation

NIV: New International Version

NRSV: New Revised Standard Version

RSV: Revised Standard Version

TNIV: Today's New International Version

Introduction

by Jay Frankel

IN JUNE 2013, SUZANNE McCarthy, my fiancée and soon-to-be wife, learned that the breast cancer she had fought off the previous year, and that we had hoped was gone, had returned. Believing her time to be very limited, she devoted herself in the months following to writing the book that had been taking shape for years in her mind and in her blog posts.

Her plan was to write a book that explored and exposed a *systematic bias* in interpretations of the Bible's teachings, a bias that is unacknowledged—and in some cases even supported—by conservative Christian theologians. These influential theologians seek to advance the view that according to God's plan, men are inherently suited to be leaders in the home, church, and community, while it is natural and right for women to submit to men's leadership. The view that men and women differ in their essential nature in these ways is called *gender essentialism*, and those who believe that relationships between men and women should be complementary and hierarchical rather than egalitarian are called *complementarians*.

Complementarian theologians have undertaken these efforts against a background of the growing influence of feminist attitudes, the expansion of women's leadership roles, and the increase in egalitarian relationships between men and women among evangelicals in English-speaking North America. They root the authority for their "male-headship" theology both in subjective readings of the Bible's stories and in systematic errors that are present in the translations of many modern Bibles—including many errors that are very basic—that support their subjective readings. They present their incorrect biblical interpretations as an accurate rendering of God's word, and advance their own perceptions of men's and women's separate roles in the home and church by presenting them as God's plan, revealed in

xi

scripture. Suzanne's critique in this book focuses on exactly how these false representations are employed to bolster a view of the church and home that requires women to be subordinate and submissive. Suzanne counters the false claims of these complementarians with facts.

The male-headship movement has been spearheaded by the influential Council on Biblical Manhood and Womanhood (CBMW).[1] Its members include some of the most prominent evangelical Christian leaders in North America. This group has conducted a campaign to influence publishers not to produce, and booksellers not to sell, Bibles that are sometimes called "gender neutral." In fact, these Bibles are more accurately translated than the versions that are approved for use by such evangelicals, and are called "gender accurate" by those who use them.

Suzanne's daughter, Helen, then 24 years old, was very much on Suzanne's mind when she began to write this book. Suzanne hoped to reach Helen and other young Christian women like her, who were at the point of contemplating a life pathway and committing themselves to a life partner. Suzanne wanted to protect them from the dangers she had seen some evangelical women of her own generation fall prey to. Suzanne's fear was that by reading mistranslated Bibles and hearing mistaken interpretations of the Bible's stories, these young women would be silenced in their marriages, become submissive, and acquiesce to far-too-limited roles within their churches and larger communities. They might well believe that God's plan required them to forego making full use of their gifts or expressing their humanity in the ways most suited to who they were as individuals. Suzanne was concerned that both men and women would read these inaccurate translations and "proceed to construct their doctrinal thinking from this," as she says in chapter 13.

Suzanne understood that a theology that is oppressive on paper has effects that can be subtle or even relatively harmless in the real world, in relationships where genuine mutual respect prevails. However, she also knew that such a theology can be used to justify great harm and to put women into situations in which they accept serious mistreatment.

Suzanne herself grew up in a vibrant evangelical family in Toronto. She was the second youngest of eight children, and attended various evangelical churches over the course of her life. She spent many years in high school and at university studying biblical languages—ancient Hebrew, Aramaic and Syriac, Classical and Hellenic Greek, and Latin—as well as modern

1. http://cbmw.org/about/mission-vision/

languages such as German and French that have played an important role in the history of Bible translation over the past millennium. She was also trained in the specialist area of written language systems, which was the subject of her MA thesis. Suzanne was an expert in Bible translation. For many years, she was also an active and popular blogger who researched the details of various Bible translations and argued against theologians across the cultural divide. Many of the theologians she opposed had a higher academic standing than her own, but their actual knowledge was far less than hers.

Suzanne's writing was grounded in who she was as a person—in her loving nature, her humility and kindness, and her dignity and courage. These qualities were deeply rooted in her and were obvious to all who knew her, whether in person or though her writing. They allowed her to endure considerable adversity in life without ever becoming hardened. They remained unchanged even in the terrible final stages of her illness, and as she faced her life's end. These qualities, I believe, produced an unobstructed, honest vision, and granted a certain moral authority to Suzanne's perspective—an authority even beyond that which came from the extensive knowledge and crystal-clear thinking she brought to bear on her subject matter. (Although I suspect that, characteristically and sincerely, she would claim no special moral authority for herself.)

Suzanne's writing is open-hearted and down to earth, as she herself was. She invites the reader into a welcoming space, and accompanies the reader in looking at technical concepts in a way that makes them both clear and compelling—yet without oversimplification. She introduces stories—from the Bible, the history of Bible translation, and her own life—that illuminate her subjects. Suzanne has written a rare book that is both scholarly and a pleasure for non-specialists to read.

Suzanne lived for two more years before succumbing to her illness. During that time, ideas that had ripened over the previous decade poured out into chapter after chapter. She matured her first drafts through blog posts and notes and, in their later stages, largely in her head. For example, during a car ride through the countryside of upstate New York, after Suzanne spent several minutes gazing silently at passing hills and forests, I asked what she'd been thinking about. Her answer: "I'm writing chapter 7." Indeed, her first drafts would be born beautifully formed after long and often silent gestation, and only required a little tidying up.

Unfortunately, Suzanne never managed to write the introduction to her book. However, her notes for it and the conversations we held as her ideas evolved made it possible for me to frame the substance of her book in a way that I think she would find acceptable. Since I do not share Suzanne's expertise in this subject matter, cannot guess how she would have introduced her book, and lack the elegant simplicity of her writing style, I cannot write the introduction she would have written.

The Organization of This Book

Suzanne critiques the complementarian misrepresentation of the Bible in three ways, which correspond to the three main sections of this book. Section 1, which consists of chapters 1 to 4 and focuses largely on the Old Testament, is about *gender attributes*. In this section, Suzanne examines which qualities the Bible assigns to men and which it assigns to women. Complementarian Christians see God as having created men with active qualities and women with passive ones; for example, women are portrayed as beautiful, while men are portrayed as strong. However, Suzanne shows how these complementarians miss the fact that in the Bible, men and women are depicted with exactly the same attributes. (Biblical men and women also fill the same roles in biblical narratives, as will be discussed in Section 2.) Both Esther and Joseph were beautiful, and Ruth was described as strong. Although desire is viewed by complementarians as a male quality, the biblical Eve felt desire.

Wisdom and its related qualities of understanding and rationality are often said to be essentially male according to the authority of the Bible. In contrast, relationality and nurturance are said to be female. However, as Suzanne demonstrates, biblical narratives do not specifically reserve any of these qualities to one gender or the other.

Chapters 5, 6, and 7, which comprise section 2 of this book, focus on *gender roles*. What does the Bible actually say, in its original languages, about women in the Bible taking on the role of protector and provider? Are only men suited to be the protectors and defenders of others, or the providers for their families, as complementarian theologians assert? In fact, Esther was a savior of her people, just as Joseph was. Lydia and Phoebe were providers for and protectors of the Apostle Paul. What does the Bible, in its original languages, say about women being teachers? Can women be leaders? Can they be founders of families and of peoples? Suzanne explores what the Bible *really* says about these questions.

In all the chapters of section 2 and, to some extent, in all the chapters of this book, Suzanne explores how inaccurate translation is used to support the essentialist view of gender attributes and gender roles. For example, the Hebrew word for "strength," *chayil*, is translated in some Bibles as "valiant" when applied to men and "virtuous" when applied to women—although it is the very same Hebrew word: *chayil*! These Bible translations choose an English word that minimizes the strength of these biblical women. (In fact, all the chapters in section 2 also examine what the Bible has to say about women's strength.) As another example, the Hebrew word for "helper" is sometimes translated as "help meet" when applied to women, thus suggesting that the woman is subordinate to the man she is helping; however, the original Hebrew word is actually identical to the word used in the Bible to describe God being a "helper" to His people—hardly a situation in which the helper is subordinate! Clearly, the use of this word does not imply that women are subordinate to men. Similarly, when the Greek word *prostatis* is applied to Phoebe in the Bible, it is translated as Phoebe being a "great help" to Paul; however, *prostatis* can also mean "leader," "defender," or "benefactor." The stature and status that this word confers on Phoebe could never be guessed by a reader of most English Bible translations.

In chapter 7, Suzanne takes up the issue of pronouns. In certain sentence constructions, English requires third-person pronouns, while ancient Greek does not. As a result, certain Bible translations from Greek to English add pronouns such as "he" and "his," thus attributing gender to passages that are not gendered in the original. These *added* "he's" and "his's" have been taken as proof by some complementarians that God intends certain roles (like that of provider) to be only for men.

By examining biblical narratives and correcting biased translations, Suzanne demonstrates that the roles complementarian theologians would limit to men, citing the authority of the Bible, were often fulfilled by women in the Bible as well. Biblical women defy stereotypes, lead communities, build cities, go to war, and interact with others without their husbands' involvement. Suzanne also documents how Christian women have taken on leadership roles in the church since the earliest days of Christianity.

Section 3, which includes chapters 8 to 13, is about the translation of *gender terms*. Do biblical words in the original Hebrew and Greek that have often been translated as *man* include women as well? Do the original words for *brother, father,* and *son* include sisters, mothers, and daughters? In May 1997, a group of twelve complementarian Christian leaders agreed on gender guidelines for Bible translations (i.e., the Guidelines for Translation of Gender-Based Language in Scripture, referred to as the Colorado Springs Guidelines in this book and elsewhere[2]), and campaigned against Bibles that did not adhere to these guidelines. For example, the guidelines said that the ancient Greek word *adelphoi*, the plural of the word for brother, should be translated as "brothers" and not as "brothers and sisters." In fact, *adelphoi* is explicitly used in ancient Greek texts to refer to the names of pairs of brothers and sisters, such as Cleopatra and Ptolemy, or Orestes and Elektra. Therefore, the literal translation of this word into English *must* include men and women, as *adelphoi* does in the original Greek. The systematic errors that populate the Colorado Springs Guidelines—such as its directive about how the word *adelphoi* must be translated—have been used to advance a theology of male headship that limits the roles women can play in Christian communities. In chapter 8, Suzanne assesses several of these gender translation guidelines against evidence from the ancient Greek.

The three main sections of this book are followed by a briefer section 4, consisting of chapters 14 and 15, that focuses on the *gender of the divine*. Chapter 14 discusses a series of translation errors dating from the third century BCE that led to masculinizing the portrayal of God in the Bible. Finally, chapter 15 documents a shift that occurred within one early Christian tradition, away from an initial view of the Holy Spirit as feminine.

2. CBMW, "Guidelines"; the Colorado Springs Guidelines can also be read online at http://www.bible-researcher.com/csguidelines.html or http://www.keptthefaith.org/docs/CSG.pdf.

Section 1

Gender Attributes

CHAPTER 1

Strength

A good wife who can find? She is far more precious than jewels.

(PROV 31:10, RSV)

I ATTENDED A WEDDING with my family in the Pacific Northwest last summer. On the day of the wedding, we drove out of town on a country road to a large house situated in a field of dry grass and surrounded by ponderosa pines. We parked and made our way—some of us in spike heels and others in flip flops—down the gravel driveway to the rough lawn where chairs were set up. Strains of a cello drifted through the trees as we took our seats. A dozen young men in gray cotton slacks and blue shirts, and a dozen bridesmaids in short chiffon dresses in shades of mint, lemon, and sand, flanked the bride and groom. The clouds threatened rain and the wind sifted through the pines and gently lifted the hems of the soft frocks.

The ministry leader spoke warmly of the bride and groom, about their faithful Christian lives, and about their commitment and leadership qualities. He described the groom in biblical language as a "mighty man of valor." Next, a dozen young men, with one arm raised to the sky, stepped forward in unison and a cheer rang out, three times: "a mighty man of God."

Then the leader spoke in equally laudatory terms of the bride, using a biblical turn of phrase once again: "a virtuous woman of God." Before turning to the bridesmaids to signal their turn to cheer, however, he hesitated. He paused, wavered, and then altered the cheer. The bridesmaids stepped forward and with one arm raised, cheered three times for "a noble woman of God." This beautiful young couple, with both partners suited for leadership, was married to the cadences of rich biblical prose and the sighing of the wind in the pines. It was an exuberant, over-the-top, evangelical Christian wedding.

But what caused the hesitancy and self-correction on the part of the leader when he came to address the bride, after he had spoken of the groom in no uncertain terms as a "mighty man of God?" Why did he feel compelled to redefine the language he used for the bride? It was not that he was unfamiliar with the vocabulary of the Bible; rather, it may have been the fact that the word choice varies greatly from one Bible translation to another, and that this variation is especially marked in passages dealing with women.

A man who is called in Hebrew an *ish gibbor chayil*, or *gibbor chayil*, is often called a "mighty man of valor" or a "valiant man" in English Bibles. However, the *eshet chayil*, the woman of Prov 31, is called a "virtuous woman," an "excellent wife," or "a noble woman."[1] Although the vocabulary for men and women is similar in Hebrew, it differs in most English Bibles. In the Jewish Publication Society translation, however, *eshet chayil* is translated as "woman of valor," a phrase that matches "man of valor."

In fact, most Bible translations rarely translate a word in Hebrew or Greek into the same particular word in English every time, particularly when it comes to gender. It is common for men and women who are given the same attributes in the Hebrew Bible to be described using different attributes in the English Bible. In the words of Al Wolters, a respected Hebrew scholar who wrote about Prov 31[1]:

> The subject of this song is called an *eshet chayil*, a term which has been translated in many different ways, but which in this context should probably be understood as the female counterpart of the *gibbor chayil*, the title given to the "mighty men of valour" which are often named in David's age. The person who is celebrated in this song is a "mighty woman of valour."

Even though this analysis of the Hebrew language is well known to scholars, the woman in Prov 31 is not called a "woman of valor" in any of the major evangelical Bible translations. Even though the same Hebrew word, *chayil*, is used to describe the mighty men of David's army[2] and the woman in Prov 31, the same English word is never used in both cases. Rather, *chayil*

---

1. Wolters, *Song*, 9.

2. 2 Sam 23

is usually translated as "valor" when describing men and as "virtue" or "excellence" when describing women.

This style of translation appears to align with the view of some English translators regarding the appropriate way to describe the two genders in English. In earlier translations, the word *chayil* used to be translated as "virtuous," for women; more recently, it may be translated as "noble" or "excellent," while men are still described as "valorous" or "valiant." However, even this more recent translation bears no relation to the Hebrew poetic style, which describes both men and women as *chayil* or "valiant."

At first glance, one might suspect English Bible translators of obvious gender bias. However, the story behind this style of translation is much longer and more varied than the history of English Bibles. It is worth taking a look at how these translations came about.

The Greek translation of the Hebrew Bible, called the Septuagint, was completed a couple of centuries before the Christian era. In this translation, the woman of Prov 31 and Ruth[3] (the only other woman in the scriptures who is called *chayil*) were both described using the Greek word *andreia*, or brave. The word *andreia* is an adjective derived from the Greek word *aner*, meaning "man," "warrior," or "citizen." The adjective does not mean "manly" or "masculine," but rather "brave" or "courageous." In the same way, the adjective *chayil* in Hebrew does not refer specifically to a male, although when used as a noun, *chayil* often refers to the military or to a prominent or leadership role in society. God is described as *chayil* in the Psalms. It is clear that women can be *chayil* as well. So, in the Greek translation, the desired wife was valiant, and a match for her husband.

The next stage of Bible translation was into Latin. This translation, called the Vulgate, was made in the late 4th century.[ii] It was the work of the Christian scholar Jerome and the wealthy Roman widow Paula, who financed his project and worked alongside him in learning Hebrew and drafting the translation. Over the centuries, this translation became the preferred text of the Roman Church. In this translation, the *eshet chayil* of Prov 31 became *mulier fortis*: "woman of strength."

However, in the book of Ruth, Jerome translated the word *chayil* into *virtus*, or virtue, so the phrase became a "woman of virtue." The Latin word *virtus* had a wide range of meanings that encompassed manliness, excellence, character, worth, and courage. In Roman mythology, Virtus was the deity of bravery and military strength, and the personification of Roman

---

3. See the book of Ruth.

virtue (*virtus*). In fact, the word *virtus* was derived from the word *vir*, meaning "man." In English, however, "virtue" typically means "chastity" or "discretion"—a far cry from bravery and manliness.

Another Latin translation that influenced the English Bible translators was that of Pagninus, a Dominican scholar who printed his Latin Bible in 1528. He characterized Ruth as a *mulier virtuosa*, possibly meaning "distinguished" or "excellent"—it is difficult to know in retrospect—or perhaps just "virtuous" as we know it. In any case, the word *chayil* in regards to Ruth was subsequently translated as "virtuous" in English, giving the impression that virtue in the form of "chastity" and "discretion" is the chief attribute for a worthy woman. Yet the narrative makes it clear that Ruth was recognized as *chayil* for her bravery in traveling without the protection of a man to a foreign nation, and for providing for her widowed mother-in-law.

Boaz, the wealthy landowner, an *ish gibbor chayil*, who seeks Ruth as his wife, addresses Ruth: "And now, my daughter, do not be afraid; I will do for you all that you ask, for all the assembly of my people know that you are an *eshet chayil*."[4]

English has a preference for different vocabulary for men and women. However, readers of the Bible need to be aware that when men and women are described in the Bible using different vocabulary, this is a feature of the English language, and in no way reflects the original languages that the Bible was written in. Hebrew contains no adjectives that are used to describe only men and not women, or vice versa. Boaz was a valiant man and wanted a valiant wife—a wife who would be a good match for him.

It may be more accurate to describe this phenomenon of different vocabulary for men and women as a gender bias within the English language. It can be considered as simply an inexact transfer of meaning from the Latin *virtuosa* to the English virtuous, which are *faux amis*—words that appear to have the same meaning across languages but don't. One can say that this effect is not through a conscious decision by the translators to discriminate against women, but is rather a consequence of language change and incidental translation error. However, others may disagree and find reason to suggest that some of the Bible translators at the time of the Reformation or later deliberately wished to distance women from the attributes of bravery or valor.

In any case, the tradition developed that women would be described as virtuous and men as brave or valiant; and many have attributed to this

4. Ruth 3:11

pattern a divine design of men being one thing while women are another. It is important to establish, first and foremost, that this differential design of men and women cannot typically be found in the adjectives used in the original languages of the Bible. Men and women are both beautiful; and men and women are both strong and brave.

How might the word *chayil* have been translated into English if a woman had translated the Bible? In fact, some Bible translations were authored by women. One of the most interesting translations is that of Julia E. Smith,[5] who translated Ruth 3:11 as follows: "And now, my daughter, thou shalt not fear; all which thou shalt say, I will do to thee; for all the gate of my people will know that thou art a woman of power."

Here, Smith uses "power," which is a literal translation of *chayil*. However, for some reason, she retained the traditional "woman of virtue" in Prov 31.

Smith's Bible, which was published in the United States in 1876, is worthy of note as the first English translation of the whole Bible that was completed entirely by a woman. It is an extremely literal translation, as Smith attempted to translate from the Hebrew without introducing interpretation or bias on the part of the translator. This method of translation resulted in many awkward and sometimes incomprehensible passages. In her preface, Smith declares that "never has the sense of the Original Tongue been altered."[6]

Aside from her gender, Smith's translation was a landmark Bible in that it was the only new Bible translation undertaken by an individual in the United States in the 19th century. Charles Thomson produced the first translation of the Greek Septuagint in 1808. In England, one of the few translations done in the 19th century was by J. N. Darby, in 1878, and the only translation done in the 18th century was by John Wesley. Curiously, both of the abovementioned American translations were printed by women. Charles Thomson's Bible was printed by Jane Aitken, who took over the family printing business when her father died. Although the name of Smith's printer is unknown, Emily Sampson, a biographer of Smith, says:

> It is not only the first translation of the Bible by a woman, but it is … the first work "set up" by a type-setting machine; and this machine is itself run by a woman—and another woman does the

---

5. Smith, *Holy Bible.*
6. Smith, *Holy Bible*, preface

proof reading. Everything connected with this Bible seems to be on a new and original plane.[7]

In contrast, Charles Thomson, who worked from the Septuagint, which uses the word *andreia* for Ruth and for the woman of Prov 31 (a word that unequivocally means "brave" or "courageous"), did not break with the King James tradition and translated *eshet chayil* as "a virtuous woman."

Looking back, we must ask how women have been impacted by the fact that *eshet chayil* has been translated into English for several centuries as "a virtuous woman" rather than as "a woman of power." How often have modesty and chastity been valued above strength as a female attribute, even though Prov 31 speaks explicitly of the strength of a woman's arms? Even today, this picture has hardly changed, as many major Bible translations do not include women in the committee of translators. Noted exceptions are the *Gender-Sensitive Torah*, which was edited by Athalya Brenner, and the inclusion of Karen Jobes in the New International Version (NIV) translation team.

Over the centuries, a few women have been agents in Bible translation, and have been active in translating and printing the original text of the scriptures. However, it is more common for women to experience the biblical text as something that acts upon them by setting standards of otherness and difference.

---

7. Smith, *With Her Own Eyes*, 62.

CHAPTER 2

Beauty

Leah's eyes were weak, but Rachel was beautiful and lovely.

(GEN 29:17, RSV)

MY DAUGHTER HAS JUST returned from several months working on organic farms, before returning to university. She is the image of beauty to her mother, as she should be. Henna-tinted auburn hair falls in smooth but unbrushed ripples over her shoulders, framing her sun-browned face. She is tall, with strong shoulders and arms sculpted by months of animal husbandry, milking goats, making cheese, kneading bread, and riding bareback. She glows with health and inner harmony. Even as a child, she had the talent of controlling our dominant husky pup, and on a childhood visit to a farm, she nurtured the baby goats. Now she can herd pigs into a barn, milk the nanny goats, hug the billy goats, and gallop across the fields riding bareback. It is her fearlessness and sense of control that calms the animals—a combination of strength and confidence.

My daughter reminds me of one of the young women in the Genesis narratives, Rachel:[1] living a pastoral life outdoors and growing brown, strong, and active. Rachel herded sheep and carried water pots. Artists over the years have portrayed Rachel as particularly beautiful, tall, and confident, either carrying a shepherd's staff or pot, or standing straight with bare arms shaped by a physically demanding lifestyle. Jacob is often portrayed

---

1. The story of Rachel starts in Gen 29.

in paintings with his head leaning on her shoulder, looking at her with longing. I imagine that part of Rachel's beauty was her relationship with the outdoors and with animals. If she thrived on that life, it would have filled her with the happiness that makes the skin glow and the spirit overflow with joy.

Rachel's beauty is significant not only for what it brings to her life, but for how it affects the role she plays as mother and ancestor to a line of beautiful people in the Hebrew Bible. Beauty is used repetitively to single out a main character and to foreshadow events in their life; the advantages and pitfalls of beauty drive the narrative. In contrast to what we may be led to suppose from reading the Bible in English, or from reading modern Christian views on men and women, the beautiful people in biblical Hebrew narratives are both men and women, in similar proportion. Sarah, Rachel, Joseph, Moses, Saul, David, Abigail, Bathsheba, Absalom, Tamar, and Esther are all described by a similar phrase in Hebrew: "beautiful in form and beautiful in face."

In recent years, with the growing emphasis among certain Christians on gender differences, some Bible teachers have gone so far as to say that the sexes are different in that women were created to reflect the grace and beauty of God, and men to reflect His strength and self-sacrifice. This is more than just a vague observation; rather, it is usually a statement about how men and women are "wired" or "designed." Some say that there is a deep spiritual lesson to be drawn from "man's desire to enjoy beauty and woman's desire to be beautiful." Men are the agents, those who experience beauty, whereas women are the objects of this enjoyment. In this framework, men have the active role and women the passive role, according to how we were created by God. According to this interpretation, any deviation from this pattern contravenes how God intended us to be.

Men and women are considered to be essentially different in respect to beauty and strength, in this reading of the Bible. In his recent popular books on gender, John Eldredge[2,iii] writes that women reveal beauty, while men seek action and adventure. Women wish to be the beauty that is rescued, and men wish to rescue beauty. Vulnerability is sometimes also said to be a specifically feminine trait, and is contrasted with male strength.

In fact, these ideas cannot be found in biblical narratives, or anywhere in scripture. A quick reading in the original language reveals that men and women are equally beautiful, with all the pros and cons, the influence and

2. See Eldredge, *Wild at Heart* and Eldredge, *Captivating Revised.*

vulnerability, that this entails. In the Hebrew Bible, men and women are equally attributed with features that inspire emotion in others: They are equally the object of love and desire, of jealousy and passion. Likewise, men and women are equally the ones who seek out and rescue, who initiate and drive intimate relationships.

Rachel is described as being shapely and beautiful. She is beautiful in form and beautiful in appearance—*yefat toar* and *yefat mareh*.[iv] For Rachel, her beauty meant that she was uniquely and especially loved by her husband. Rachel is one of the few women in the Bible about whom it is said that her husband married her for love. Jacob was instructed to look for a wife among his cousins, and was committed to this goal, but when he saw Rachel, his immediate reaction was one of passion, not reason: He kissed her and then he wept. Fortunately for him, she was also his cousin; unfortunately, she had an older sister who had to be married first.

Rachel's story includes many plots and subplots; in brief, Jacob asks for her in marriage but is deceived by her father, and is married to Rachel's older sister, Leah, instead. He is then allowed to marry Rachel as his second wife. He loves only Rachel, but it is many years before she has children. Her sister and their servants have many other children by Jacob. In giving birth to her second child, Rachel dies. Jacob's love and attention, his signal focus, is then transferred to Rachel's older son, Joseph,[3] and is demonstrated by his gift of an elaborate multi-colored coat. Joseph is described as beautiful—*yafeh toar* and *yafeh mareh*. When used to describe Joseph, this phrase is usually translated into English as "handsome and well-built" or "strong"; however, the Hebrew words are identical to those that are used for Rachel: "beautiful in form and beautiful in appearance." The words differ only in their use of the masculine grammatical gender. Joseph has inherited his mother's beauty.

Joseph's beauty, and the singular devotion of his father, bring on him a series of unfortunate events. His brothers are jealous of him and want to kill him, but eventually leave him stranded in a pit. Traders pull him out, and save him to sell as a slave, as he is beautiful and will fetch a good price. Potiphar, an official in Egypt, buys him and elevates him to be a steward in his house. Joseph's beauty continues to drive the narrative: Potiphar's wife falls in love with him and wants to sleep with him. When he resists, she accuses him of sexual assault and Joseph is thrown in jail. He gains an influential ally in prison, and is later released and lives to become a high

---

3. The story of Joseph starts in Gen 30.

official in Egypt. When a famine brings starvation to his homeland, Joseph provides his family with food, and thereby becomes the savior of the fathers of the tribes of Israel.

Reading the English Bible, it is easy enough not to focus on the detail of Joseph's beauty, since it is translated into idiomatic English as "handsome and well-built" or "strong." While this translated language fits the gender patterns that are present in the English language, it does not reflect the underlying Hebrew; as a result, Joseph's beauty is easily skimmed over by those reading his story. In contrast, in the Qur'an,[4,v] Joseph's physical appearance draws more attention: He is described as "beautiful," and his story is expanded to emphasize his beauty. The women of the city question Potiphar's wife regarding her unsuitable desire for a slave, so she invites them to a banquet and gives them knives to cut the fruit. When she parades Joseph before them, they are so distracted that they cut their fingers; they admit that he is beautiful—an angel, even. His beauty is irresistible.

In concert with this brief episode in the Qur'an, an extensive body of literature was developed in Greek, Hebrew, Arabic, Persian, Urdu, Punjabi, and Bengali, recounting the tale of Yusuf—that is, Joseph—and Zulaika, Potiphar's wife. This literature variously represents the themes of adultery, a woman's erotic desire, and the longing of the female soul for male beauty. In some versions, Yusuf and Zulaika even manage to get married. Within this tradition of love poetry, there is no particular notion that beauty is an essentially feminine attribute, and that the pursuit of beauty belongs to the masculine gender. The concept of the soul being feminine in its pursuit of beauty and transcendence—of an experience that is beyond the concrete reality of our lives—is persistent in Middle Eastern literature. The modern Western bias of men and women is essentially different in this respect, in that beauty is presented as a feminine attribute, and pursuit or agency are presented as predominantly masculine attributes. In our tradition, the man is commonly shown as the one who loves or desires; however, this perspective is culture-bound and is not based in any way on the text of the Hebrew Bible.

Not long ago, I stood in the Accademia Gallery in Florence, gazing at Michelangelo's David: the smooth marble, sculpted limbs, and powerful hands. This statue of a young man is considered one of the most beautiful art objects ever created. In the Renaissance, the spotlight was on male beauty, rather than female. Things have changed considerably since then!

4. Surat Yusuf 12:30–32

In the mystical tradition, the soul is represented as feminine in its search for the divine or transcendent; that is, in its search for something other than the physical world. In the tale of Yusuf, Zulaika desires a man whom she perceives to be beautiful. This situation thus represents the worthy desire of the soul as it seeks a spiritual experience—something beyond the material plane. Erotic love represents the longing of the soul for the transcendent or divine; for something unattainable that is missing in our daily experience. In this literature, the female or feminine aspect is the one who seeks beauty, and the one who is beautiful is masculine.

Ps 42[vi] in the King James Bible contains a similar example in Hebrew poetry. This psalm was translated as follows: "As the hart panteth after the water brooks, so panteth my soul after thee, O God." The word used is "hart," a male deer. However, the Hebrew word that was translated here as "hart" can be more accurately translated as "doe," a female deer. The New English Translation of the Greek Septuagint uses the Greek word for "doe" in a parallel construction with the soul, a word that is also feminine in Hebrew: "Just as the doe longs for the springs of water, So my soul longs for you, O God."[5]

Here, the word usage in the original Hebrew suggests to the reader that the ancient Hebrews and early Greek translators were comfortable thinking of the soul in feminine terms.

Readers may fail to appreciate how the soul can be seen as feminine seeking beauty in the masculine aspect, if men in the Bible are never called beautiful but are only called handsome. In the English language, "beauty" is an abstract value like "wisdom" and "strength," and is commonly referred to as an intangible quality that humans desire. "Handsomeness," on the other hand, never plays this role in the English language, so a connection cannot be made between the "handsomeness" of a male character and a transcendent value such as "beauty." However, in many other languages, this connection is automatic because the same word for "beauty" is used for both genders. In using distinct vocabulary for men and women, English differs from most other languages. However, language matters if we want to understand the poetry and literary shape of the Hebrew narratives.

Another biblical hero whose life is altered because of his beauty is Moses.[6] His mother sees that he is a beautiful child. To protect him from the Egyptians, who were killing male Hebrew babies, she places him in a

---

5. Ps 42:1

6. The story of Moses starts in Exod 2.

reed basket waterproofed with tar and has his older sister watch over him. The princess of Egypt finds Moses, perhaps finding a beautiful baby more difficult to resist than a less attractive one, and adopts him as her son. Once again, beauty plays a role in establishing a Jewish child of lowly status in a position of power and influence in Egyptian society. Like Joseph, Moses eventually becomes a savior of his people.

The next group of beautiful people in the Bible live during the time of King David,[7] and include David himself. In modern English translations, David is described as "fine-looking" and "a man of good presence" with "beautiful eyes." Although these expressions are slightly different than the one used for Rachel and Joseph, the implications are the same. David is beautiful and inspires emotion in many people.

In the story that introduces David into the dynastic narrative, Samuel the prophet is told by God to anoint one of the sons of Jesse as king. Samuel goes to Jesse's home in Bethlehem and is presented with Jesse's sons in birth order. He rejects each one. Finally, Jesse admits that the youngest son is out tending the flock. The youngest son, David, is brought home; Samuel anoints him and then leaves. Later, an evil spirit attacks the current ruler, King Saul, and his servants look for a skilled musician to soothe his spirit. David is brought to Saul and plays the lyre for him, bringing Saul relief from his melancholy. The narrative states that Saul loves David greatly, and makes him his armor bearer. When discussing this episode, in which David plays a relatively passive role as the object of a search for a new heir apparent to the throne, the Bible scholar Robert Alter describes David as a "male Cinderella left to his domestic chores instead of being invited to the party."[8,vii] Tending the sheep is a task for a younger child, whether male or female. Rachel, the younger sister, was also out with her father's herd at the beginning of her story.

The next story about David also has echoes in European and Western folklore: A giant threatens the community, and the king offers wealth and the hand of his daughter in marriage to whoever can kill him. David, a very young man with no battle experience, now comes out of obscurity on his own initiative to conquer the giant and win the day with his wits and resourcefulness. He sets aside the armor he is offered, and slays the giant with his slingshot. Saul offers him the hand of his older daughter, Merab, in marriage; however, David expresses his unworthiness and declines.

7. The story of David starts in 1 Sam 16.
8. Alter, *The David Story*, 87.

These two stories present strongly contrasting versions of David in terms of gender role. In the first story, David is sought out: He is the object, not the driver, of the action. First, David is the object of the search by the prophet Samuel for the next king; and second, he is the object of the search by Saul's servants for someone to play the lyre for Saul. Through the beauty of his music, David charms the king's senses and relieves his depression. David influences the situation indirectly, by stimulating the senses and revealing beauty through music. He becomes the object of Saul's great love, and plays a role that can be seen from the Western perspective as feminine and passive. In this story, it is Saul's experience that matters, not David's.

In the second story, David takes the initiative. He is not sought out by others, but rather volunteers for an adventure. Coming once again from his father's remote fields, David offers to play the combatant's role in a life-threatening encounter with a giant warrior. His success leads to his receiving the adulation of the people, and puts him in direct conflict with the king as a possible heir apparent to the throne. This turns the king's love for him into jealousy and resentment. Here, David plays a typical masculine role.

The contradictory nature of David's character, which is presented in these stories—the poet versus the musician; charming others with his beauty, versus being an aggressive warrior who is ready for combat—continues throughout his life.

In any narrative, it is common to find a clear contrast between the passive and active roles that people can play. However, in David's case, these contradictory portrayals exist within a single individual, and reveal the dual aspects of David's personality as both a poet and a warrior. By extension, this duality suggests that the Bible attributes both agency and receptivity to men as characteristics that are natural to that gender. Adele Berlin[9] describes the dual personality of David in these words: "What has not been observed is that there is also an alternation in the narratives between David as main character and David as subordinate character, and that these correspond roughly to the public and private domains."

As David's story continues, more members of the royal family are described as loving him, attracted not only by his exploits but also by his beauty and personal magnetism. Saul's son Jonathan[10] loves David, and his "heart is knit to him." Jonathan makes a pact with David, and protects him against his father's scheming. He undertakes considerable risk to save

9. Berlin, *Poetics and Interpretation*, 33.
10. The story of Jonathan starts in 1 Sam 16:1.

David's life, even though it is clear that David is his rival for the throne. Jonathan repeatedly demonstrates his love for David by giving him his own clothes and weapons.

It is only at Jonathan's funeral, much later, that we are told of David's feelings for Jonathan. However, even then, David only says about Jonathan that "your love to me was wonderful, surpassing the love of women." David's statement is more a recognition of the love that Jonathan had for him than an expression of his own love for Jonathan. We are led to believe that David did return Jonathan's love—he kissed Jonathan and wept with him—but it is clear that Jonathan, as a prince, took the initiative in the relationship.

Following Jonathan's declaration of love and commitment, Michal,[11] Saul's younger daughter, also declares her love for David and asks her father if she can marry him. Taking initiative does not necessarily mean that Michal is acting outside of the expected behavior of a woman in her society; rather, it is a reflection of the fact that her relationship with David is defined more by social class than by gender. Michal is a princess, and David is a commoner. She proposes marriage.

Like Rachel, David is one of the few people in the Hebrew narratives about whom it is explicitly written that the prospective marriage partner wishes to marry for love. Michal also takes risks and plays a role in David's survival of Saul's intrigue, ultimately helping David to become the next king. However, David does not take leadership immediately, and in his subsequent retreat and absence from court, Saul gives Michal to another man, Paltiel. When David later establishes his monarchy, he demands that Michal, the royal princess, be returned to him. Paltiel follows her in tears, mourning the loss of what we must assume was an intimate and loving relationship.

It is hard to tell whether David ever considered Michal's feelings and returned her youthful love, or whether her main function in David's story is to provide him with a legitimate claim to Saul's throne. Michal criticizes David in a later incident, complaining about his behavior in dancing with the commoners in a procession in front of the Ark.[12] For that disrespect, the Bible tells us that she will never bear children. Perhaps David does not have marital relations with her again. She never appears as David's loved and trusted companion, in spite of her protection and influence in his rise to power.

11. The story of Michal starts in 1 Sam 18:20.

12. 2 Sam 6:20

Saul, Saul's servants, Jonathan, Michal, and the people of both Judah and Israel all love David, propelling his ascent to the throne. But David is never said to return their love. David does subsequently marry two beautiful women, Abigail and Bathsheba. Although he initiates these relationships, it is not clear whether he truly loves either of them. When we finally do read that David loves someone, it is his son Absalom,[13] who is described as another person of exceptional beauty—*yafeh bekal*—"most beautiful of all." This is the person David loves.

David's children, Absalom and Absalom's full sister Tamar,[14] are among the next generation of beautiful people. Their beauty makes them the objects of desire and adulation, but brings tragedy rather than triumph. Absalom is described as more beautiful than anyone else in the nation, with thick, heavy hair that he cuts and weighs once a year. Tamar, his sister, is also exceptionally beautiful, and attracts the attention of her older half-brother Amnon, David's oldest son. Amnon is said to love Tamar, but we later understand that while he desires her physically, he has no respect for her. He schemes to trap Tamar and isolate her alone with him in order to assault her. Amnon pretends to be sick and asks his father, David, to have Tamar prepare a meal for him[viii] in the privacy of his room. He sends everyone else away and rapes her, after which he turns away from her in disgust. Tamar cries out and makes the crime public, but neither David nor Absalom avenge her at that time. She retires to live with Absalom. Although Tamar is a princess, she has no power due to her position. Rather, her beauty makes her the object of lust and assault and brings her only tragedy.

Two years later, Absalom does avenge Tamar by killing Amnon. Because of the time lapse, the murder of Amnon may also be motivated by Absalom's desire to dispose of an older brother and an heir to the throne. Absalom's beauty is then instrumental in helping him to develop a strong following in the nation. He captures the hearts of the people and rebels against his father's authority, with the intent of taking the throne. However, David continues to love Absalom in spite of his plotting and treason. Warriors who are loyal to David finally kill Absalom when they find him hanging from the branches of a tree, where he was caught by his heavy hair—a feature of his beauty—as he was riding through the woods on a donkey. David mourns the death of his beautiful son, whose main intent was to

13. The story of Absalom begins indirectly, with the story of his sister Tamar and brother Amnon, in 2 Sam 13:1, and continues from verse 23.

14. The story of Tamar starts in 2 Sam 13:1.

depose him from the throne, and cries: "My son, my son, if only I had died instead of you."[15]

For David and Absalom, personal beauty is key to creating a following among the people and to building a group of loyal supporters. Beauty makes them the object of not only love, loyalty, and admiration, but also passion, desire, jealousy, and aggression. For Absalom, beauty brings him to an untimely end, as his heavy hair traps him and enables his enemies to kill him. For the princess Tamar, beauty brings assault and despair.

Esther[16,ix] is probably the person in the Bible who is best known for her personal beauty. She is said to be *yefat toar tovat mareh*,[x] in a near echo of the expressions used to describe Rachel (*yefat toar yefat mareh*) and Joseph (*yafeh toar yafeh mareh*). Although these expressions vary slightly, there is no gender distinction beyond the grammatical gender endings. The word *tov* (good-looking) is used to describe Saul and David; it is also used to describe Queen Vashti, as well as the maidens who are intended for the harem in Esther's story. *Yafeh* (beautiful) and *tov* are both used indiscriminately for men and women.

Like Joseph, Esther is a Jew of lowly status who is imprisoned at a foreign court. In both cases, their beauty promotes their survival and makes them an object of desire—with all the vulnerability and advantages that this entails. Ultimately, their beauty attracts allies and leads to promotion to a high position. Joseph saves his family, the founding fathers of Israel, from famine; Esther saves the Jews of Persia from annihilation. These two individuals are "victim-saviors" of the Jewish people, both propelled to power by their personal beauty. Although they begin as victims of circumstance, they risk their lives and use their wisdom and sound judgment to turn the tide of history for their own people.

In one sense, Esther and Joseph play the same role in their stories: that of a powerless individual who is chosen for a powerful position because of her or his beauty and personal attributes of charm, wisdom, and restraint. Nonetheless, Esther's story is bound by the reality of Persian gender politics. Her role as savior of the Persian Jews must be shared with her uncle Mordecai. He is the one who will become second to the Emperor in the kingdom.

The context for Esther's story is well established. She lives in Persia, where wives must strictly obey their husbands and cannot speak for

15. 2 Sam 18:33
16. See the book of Esther.

themselves. She begins by obeying her uncle and adopted father, Mordecai. However, as the story develops, Esther takes her own risks, makes her
own decisions, and develops her own strategy. She speaks out beyond the
bounds of the politically enforced gender constraints, and takes her life in
her own hands. Esther has personal beauty and natural wisdom, and thus
mirrors Joseph, Moses, and David. Although she has the same characteristics as the men, she cannot fill an official role that was denied to women in
that ancient society.

Political position only goes so far for women in the Bible. On the
one hand, women of royal households rescue beautiful males. The princess of Egypt adopts Moses; Michal marries David, saves his life, and aids
his ascent to the throne. However, Michal is put aside for Bathsheba, who
becomes the next queen mother, and the princess Tamar is raped and aban-
doned. The attributes of women—their beauty and wisdom, their rhetoric
and influence—mirror those of men in the Hebrew narrative. Nonetheless,
women in the Bible are often victims of their society's gender restrictions.
However, a second look demonstrates that men in the Bible are also ren-
dered victims and vulnerable due to their personal beauty. Some succumb,
such as Absalom, while others, such as Joseph, Moses, and David, come
through their trials and victimization to emerge as leaders.

In the Hebrew Bible, beauty often marks the main character, the central person in the story, and is the instrument by which this person inspires
not only love and desire, but also jealously on the part of others. Although
this person is the main character, at times he or she plays a subordinate role
in the action by becoming the object of other people's pursuit. This gath-
ering of people around the central character propels the action. Beautiful
people in the Bible are typically the object of other people's obsession and
desire, but are rarely said to love others. Beauty puts them at the center of
the plot, but accentuates their vulnerability. It would not be out of place to
regard the beautiful people of the Hebrew Bible as glowing with strength
and health; however, in the narratives, beauty often indicates sexual or psy-
chological vulnerability for both men and women. These men and women
inspire desire, which changes their lives. For some, beauty places them in
a particular political situation, setting them up for a unique and powerful
role in their own adventure, and ultimately in the history of Israel. For others, it brings tragedy and grief.

Throughout these narratives, the women are constrained by the
rules of ancient society: Rachel must obey her father, Michal is played as a

political pawn by David, and Esther obeys Mordecai. On the other hand, class plays a role. The princess of Egypt adopts Moses, Potiphar's wife attempts to seduce Joseph, and Michal chooses to marry and protect David. Esther, the queen, speaks out for her people and saves her nation.

In one book in the Hebrew Bible, the Song of Solomon, beauty and desire are intensely and explicitly mutual. Although most Bible translations celebrate this mutuality in love-making, many translations continue to mask the Hebrew words that are used for men and women. Compare these two translations. The first reflects the gender-based English language system and the second is a more literal translation of the Hebrew.

> *New English Translation (NET) Bible:*[17]
> The Lover to his Beloved:
> Oh, how beautiful you are, my beloved!
> How beautiful you are!
> Your eyes are like doves!
> The Beloved to Her Lover:
> Oh, how handsome you are, my lover!
> Oh, how delightful you are!
> The lush foliage is our canopied bed;[18]
>
> *Common English Bible (CEB):*
> [Man]
> Look at you—so beautiful, my dearest!
> Look at you—so beautiful! Your eyes are doves!
> [Woman]
> Look at you—so beautiful, my love!
> Yes, delightful! Yes, our bed is lush and green![19]

In the first translation, the New English Translation (NET) Bible, the male is called the "lover"—that is, the actor, or giver of love; and the female is called the "beloved"—that is, the object, or receiver of love. However, these words do not reflect any underlying meaning in the Hebrew text. Translating the words into English in this way, when the original Hebrew words do not indicate who is active and who is passive, suggests that men are

17. Free online Bible published at https://bible.org/netbible.
18. Song 1:15–16
19. Song 1:15–16

naturally active in love and women are naturally passive—something that the Hebrew text in no way suggests. In fact, Hebrew verb forms are gendered and normally indicate when a female is speaking or when a male is speaking. Since we cannot do this in English, most translations now add labels to clarify the female and male speaking parts of the poem. In addition to these labels, the NET Bible contains references within the text itself to the "lover" and the "beloved"; however, these two words in Hebrew are better understood as "companion" and "sweetheart." The original contains no indication whatsoever that the man is playing an active role while the woman plays a passive role. These words are used equally for both genders. The NET Bible also calls the woman "beautiful" and the man "handsome," in spite of the fact that the same word—*yafeh*—is used in Hebrew for both the man and the woman. The NET Bible therefore masks the fact that the same language is used for both men and women. By gendering the language in ways that do not reflect the original Hebrew meaning, certain English translations mask the mutuality and reciprocity of this love poem.

The second translation, the Common English Bible (CEB), presents a more literal rendition of the Hebrew, and translates the same word in Hebrew into the same word in English, regardless of gender. Both the man and the woman are *yafeh*—beautiful—and the man and woman are not assigned active ("lover") or passive ("beloved") roles. In this translation, the passage communicates a clear contradiction to the idea that man alone is the pursuer and active lover, and that the woman's role is to be the beautiful object and receiver of love. She is an active pursuer of her lover, and he at times also pursues her.

In spite of existing rigid social gender roles, Hebrew narratives and poetry demonstrate that beauty is an attribute that is shared by men and women alike, and that both men and women pursue beauty. Nothing in these stories justifies the recent claims being made by contemporary Christian authors that according to the scripture, the characteristics of beauty and invitation versus those of strength and agency are distributed to women and men, respectively, in a non-overlapping fashion. The next chapter investigates these claims in a more detailed manner. There is no indication in the Hebrew narratives that men have the more active role and women the more passive role in love relationships. Although women in the Bible often play their parts with an initial assent to the social expectations that were placed on females at that time, they typically play out roles that are interchangeable with those of men. However, perhaps more surprising to us today is the prominence that male beauty plays in the Hebrew Bible. Beauty is not an exclusively, or even predominantly, feminine trait in the Bible. A reading of the Hebrew words reveals that beauty is as often attributed to men as to women in the Bible.

Translations that diversely render *yafeh toar* and *yafeh/tov mareh* as "beautiful" for women and "handsome" or "good-looking" for men are following a standard translation technique in which the word that would be most suitable in English is chosen. However, these translations mask the fact that Rachel, Joseph, Esther, and the lovers in the Song of Solomon are described in almost the exact same words in Hebrew. They render opaque the very language that indicates to the reader that these people have something in common. Many translations into contemporary English, as appropriate as they may be in some ways, mask the fact that the original Hebrew does not support the notion that men and women have naturally different traits by gender, a notion that some contemporary Christian thinkers claim to be rooted in the Bible. It is not a universal principle in the Bible that men and women differ in the attribute of beauty; rather, the Hebrew word for beauty is translated into two different English words, based on gender. This is an issue that is specific to the English language, and should not shape theology.

CHAPTER 3

Wisdom

She opens her mouth with wisdom,
and the teaching of kindness is on her tongue.

(PROV 31:26, RSV)

DESPITE ALL GOOD INTENTIONS, grammatical gender is an aspect of language that cannot be translated. In Hebrew and Greek, as in French and other European languages, all nouns have gender. In Hebrew, Latin, and French, nouns are either masculine or feminine, and all objects, including tables and chairs, houses and books, trees and rocks, have gender. In Greek and German, nouns are masculine, feminine, or neuter. However, as words transfer from one language to another, they often do not keep the same gender. For most items, gender is language specific. One of the best examples of this is the word for "spirit," which is feminine in Hebrew and Aramaic, neuter in Greek, and masculine in Latin. Of course, some abstract nouns do retain the same gender in different languages.

Wisdom happens to be a feminine word in Hebrew (*hokmah*), in Greek (*sophia*), and in Latin (*sapienta*). More than any other abstract noun in the Bible, wisdom is personified, and appears as a woman. In Prov 1:20–21:

Wisdom cries out in the street;
in the squares she raises her voice.
At the busiest corner she cries out;
at the entrance of the city gates she speaks:

In Prov 8:1–3:

> Does not wisdom call,
> and does not understanding raise her voice?
> On the heights, beside the way,
> at the crossroads she takes her stand;
> beside the gates in front of the town,
> at the entrance of the portals she cries out.

Wisdom is also personified in the *Wisdom of Solomon,* a book written in Greek that is part of the Deuterocanon. (This literature of the Hebrew nation is positioned between the books of the Old Testament and the New Testament; it is included in Roman Catholic and Eastern Orthodox Bibles, but not in evangelical Bibles.) Here, wisdom is personified as the bride and consort of Solomon: "I loved her and sought her from my youth; I desired to take her for my bride, and became enamored of her beauty."[1]

In the book of Luke, wisdom is also personified as a mother: "Nevertheless, wisdom is vindicated by all her children."[2] Later, Jesus himself is called wisdom: "Therefore also the Wisdom of God said, 'I will send them prophets and apostles, some of whom they will kill and persecute.'"[3] (In Matt 23:34, these words are spoken directly by Jesus.) Still later, the book of Corinthians says: "…but to those who are called, both Jews and Greeks, Christ the power of God and the wisdom of God."[4]

This personification of an abstract noun is a metaphorical device that depends on a feature of a word that is found in the original language— that is, it stems from the grammatical gender of the word. Although the personification itself can be translated, the underlying motivation—the grammatical gender—for the personification of wisdom as a woman is not visible in English. It is similar to punning, which occurs frequently in the Hebrew Bible. Two punning pairs in Hebrew are found in Gen 2. Adam is formed from the soil (*adamah*) and woman (*ishsha*) is formed from man (*ish*). These words may simply be used because they form a linguistic pattern in the original language. Sound features like these become invisible in translation, but have a strong influence on word choice and poetic devices. Grammatical gender is similar. It is a linguistic feature of the original

1. Wis 8:2 (RSV)
2. Luke 7:35
3. Luke 11:49
4. 1 Cor 1:24

language that is used to create a certain effect. It is important to realize that these linguistic features are not universal and do not translate across languages. It is hard to see how they would reflect an underlying reality, but they do provide impetus for expressions of spirituality.

In one sense, wisdom as a woman, or "Woman Wisdom," is simply a poetic device. Folly as a woman, or "Woman Folly," is another female entity in Proverbs that acts as a counterpart to Woman Wisdom. She represents a different value that men can choose: licentiousness. It is as if men are projecting their own desire for wisdom or their own moral depravity onto different female figures. However, the book of Proverbs presents another wise woman: The ideal yet human woman of Prov 31 is also characterized by wisdom. In this way, the figure of Woman Wisdom is transformed via concrete and vivid detail into a fully human character.

This characterization of wisdom as a woman can be interpreted in several different ways. In one interpretation, wisdom is a feminine virtue, or a feminine essence, that has been present with God since creation. Women can find in wisdom a feminine divine and an equal partnering of masculine with feminine. In this view, wisdom is other than man; she is a divine essence, but is also the real-life companion of a man.

In a contrasting interpretation, Woman Wisdom is simply a metaphor for the virtue that men love. Men are presumed to pursue wisdom as a man pursues his lover. In this interpretation, wisdom is really a masculine attribute; it is understood as being either a pure and spiritual mistress of a man, or an actual representation of the man's ideal self. Wisdom is not woman as a discrete individual; rather, wisdom is represented as a woman in order to portray the sense that wisdom is the ultimate object of male desire. In this interpretation, a man wishes to possess the abstract quality of wisdom.

Both of these interpretations of Woman Wisdom seem to be quite possible from the text. However, although both have long traditions, these interpretations are based on metaphor and do not actually indicate that the attribute of wisdom is relegated to one sex or the other.

A third important tradition is one that recognizes that wisdom was with God in creation and in this sense prefigures Christ. In the Christian scriptures, *sophia*, the Greek translation of the Hebrew word for wisdom, *hokmah,* is used frequently in association with Christ. Another Greek word also stands for wisdom. In John's Gospel, the *logos* was in the beginning with God.[5] Here, a masculine noun is used to correspond with the masculine

---

5. John 1:2, where the Greek word *logos* is usually translated as "the Word"

nature of Christ. In the Hebrew scriptures, the consort of God in creation is the feminine *hokmah*; in the Christian scriptures, it is the *logos*, the masculine Christ. On one level this is wordplay; on another level, gender nuances can be taken very seriously. It appears that the Hebrew *hokmah* could not lead naturally into *sophia*, the Greek word for wisdom, since Christ apparently could not be associated with a grammatically feminine word.

Conversely, in the Jewish discipline of Kabbalah, wisdom and understanding, or *hokmah* and *bina*, were both with God in the beginning: "The Lord by wisdom founded the earth; by understanding he established the heavens."[6] For Kabbalists, *hokmah* is masculine and *bina* is feminine. In this framework, grammatical gender has no relationship to metaphorical gender. Thus, although grammatical gender does have a very important role to play in biblical literature, it does not reveal universal truths; rather, it is a part of the form of the language. Women do not have a special relationship with wisdom simply because wisdom is personified as a woman in the Bible.

Switching from poetic and philosophical passages to named individuals in the narratives, Eve[7] is the first person who desires wisdom: "The woman saw that the tree was beautiful with delicious food and that the tree would provide wisdom, so she took some of its fruit and ate it."[8] In this case, a different word is used for wisdom in Hebrew—*sekel*; this word is considered to be a close synonym to wisdom that is associated with prudence or insight.

The serpent, referred to as the most intelligent of all living creatures, reasons with Eve. Looking at the Hebrew words used to describe this situation allows us to reject the usual translations, which present a scenario in which a woman is confronted by "a crafty beast." Doesn't she see that he is a crafty beast? In fact, the Hebrew says that the serpent was the most "insightful" of all the "living creatures of the field" that the Lord had made. There is no negative connotation to the word "insightful"; if anything, it is used because it sounds like the word for "naked," which is found in the last verse of chapter 2. In Hebrew literature, the same sounds and words are often repeated. Like the serpent, Adam and Eve are called "living creatures." Thus, Eve is confronted by an "intelligent living creature" who offers her

---

6. Prov 3:19
7. The story of Eve starts in Gen 2:4.
8. Gen 3:6 (CEB)

the means to become *sekel*, that is, "prudent" or "wise." According to Prov 19:14, "A prudent wife (*sekel/maskelet*) is from the LORD."

The serpent is able to persuade Eve that if she eats the fruit, she will be like God and will know good and evil. Although this story associates woman with wisdom, it does so in a morally ambiguous way. Eve is the first of the two humans to utter recorded dialogue: She enters a debate, and displays agency and rational thought. However, the story ends in disaster. Nonetheless, most biblical characters after Eve (both male and female) are portrayed positively for seeking wisdom. In fact, they are commanded to do so.

In contrast, Adam eats the fruit in order to maintain his relationship with Eve, and ultimately his relationship with God, who gave Eve to him: "The woman you gave me, she gave me some fruit from the tree, and I ate."[9] It was not just the woman, but the woman *that God had given him* who Adam needed to remain connected to. He makes a decision based on his desire to remain in his relationships with his wife and with God—or at least, so he says.

In view of the fact that both men and women are later exhorted to seek wisdom, this story presents a paradox. Throughout the Hebrew Bible, humans are told to seek wisdom. However, the story of Adam and Eve seems to show that seeking wisdom is a temptation that draws humans away from God's clear commands and prohibitions. Surely, Adam and Eve were created with the abilities and tendencies to act in the way that they did. How could they have acted in this way if they were not created with this disposition? Would Eve have desired wisdom if humans had not been created with the tendency to desire wisdom? And would Adam have obeyed Eve if humans had not been created with the desire to maintain relationships with their partners?

The evangelical theologian and author Wayne Grudem, a member of the Council on Biblical Manhood and Womanhood (CBMW), and a vocal spokesperson for gender essentialism, understands the story in the following way:

> God gave men, in general, a disposition that is better suited to teaching and governing in the church, a disposition that inclines more to rational, logical analysis of doctrine and a desire to protect the doctrinal purity of the church, and God gave women, in general, a disposition that inclines more toward a relational, nurturing

9. Gen 3:12

emphasis that places a higher value on unity and community in the church. Both emphases are needed, of course, and both men and women have some measure of both tendencies. But Paul understands the kinder, gentler, more relational nature of women as something that made Eve less inclined to oppose the deceptive serpent and more inclined to accept his words as something helpful and true.[10]

However, the text clearly says that the serpent was the most intelligent of all God's creatures. Eve was deceived because of the intellect and logic displayed by the serpent, and because of her desire for wisdom—not because she was less rational than Adam and more susceptible to being deceived. It was certainly not because of Eve's kinder and gentler nature, nor because she placed a higher value on unity and community. Rather, Eve was motivated by a desire for beauty and wisdom.

Adam did not assess the serpent's argument at all; instead, he behaved in a way that would maintain harmony in his relationship with Eve, and by extension would also maintain his communion with God. Adam was relational, and was inclined to accept the fruit without hesitation. If Eve had in fact been created to be relational over and above being a seeker of wisdom and beauty, would she have been attracted by the argument of the serpent? Would she not have been inclined to maintain unity and community with her fellow human? Was it her so-called "relational nature" that made Eve susceptible, as Grudem claims, or was it her single-minded desire for knowledge and beauty, as well as her sense of agency?

One might say that both Adam and Eve behaved in contradiction to their created dispositions, but there is nothing in the text that suggests this. Nor is this Grudem's argument. He says that Eve behaved in accordance with her kinder and gentler nature, and her created disposition to value unity and community. However, this viewpoint is not found in the text. Eve *broke* the existing unity and harmony, whereas Adam tried to preserve them. Perhaps Eve portrays the precursor of Woman Wisdom later in the Hebrew Bible, and signals the close literary connection between woman and wisdom in the Bible. However, the idea that men are more rational and women are more relational is simply not present in the creation narrative.

Although wisdom and rationality are not identical, Grudem uses rationality and a disposition towards logical analysis as prerequisites for leadership in the Christian community. In the Hebrew Bible, wisdom

---

10. Grudem, *Evangelical Feminism*, 72.

(*hokmah*), which is often paired with understanding (*bina*), are prerequisites for leadership. Moses gives this instruction at the beginning of Deuteronomy: "Choose wise, understanding, and experienced men, according to your tribes, and I will appoint them as your heads."[11] This instruction is to establish commanders and officers at different levels throughout the tribes; in the next verse, there is an instruction for judges to judge righteously. Thus, although the two concepts of "wisdom and understanding, or discernment" and "a disposition for the rational, logical analysis of doctrine" are not necessarily identical, they are presented as the basic requirements for filling a leadership role. This verse is usually translated with the word "men," but some recent translations have used "individuals" instead. (This is repeated in Exod 18:21, where the phrase *anashim chayil*, "valiant people," is used.)

It seems clear in this context that Moses is speaking about males: He is referring to men who will be tribal leaders. However, the Hebrew word is *anashim*, which is the plural not only for *ish* (i.e., "man" or possibly "individual"), but also for *enosh* ("man" or "human" in general). Therefore, the Hebrew does not explicitly refer to men as purely males; rather, this interpretation is left to the context. In the passages on circumcision, the text is always explicit as to gender, and the phrase always means to circumcise the "males": "Then Abraham took Ish'mael his son and all the slaves born in his house or bought with his money, every male among the men of Abraham's house."[12]

Here, the phrase "every male among the men" explicitly refers to the *zakar* (males) among the *anashim* (men) of Abraham's house. If *anashim* explicitly and unquestionably only referred to males, this phrasing would have been unnecessary. Nonetheless, the context appears to indicate that in Deuteronomy, Moses was referring to males, although he does not explicitly specify that the leaders and judges must be males.

Grudem, along with others in the Council on Biblical Manhood and Womanhood (CBMW), believes that the New Testament passage of 1 Tim 2:12[13] explicitly specifies that only males may be leaders in the church and in the home, for two reasons: first, because Adam was born first; and second, because Adam was less likely to be deceived than Eve because he was

---

11. Deut 1:13 (RSV)

12. Gen 17:23

13. "I do not permit a woman to teach or to assume authority over a man; she must be quiet." (NIV)

less relational in disposition and therefore less likely to be influenced by others. These theologians are under the impression that it is a recognized scientific fact that men are more rational and logical than women, and that women are more relational than men.

Statistics from older studies exist, and are still considered valid by some, that indicate that men on average have slightly higher IQ scores than women; however, IQ statistics are famously fluid over time and space. At present, on the basis of a recent analysis of multinational studies, women are shown to have crept ahead in IQ by a hair's breadth. In the area of visual-spatial intelligence, the results of recent math Olympiads demonstrate that for a few ethnic groups, females outrank males. Some studies of hedge fund leadership also demonstrate that women outperform men, albeit very slightly, both in this area and in broader financial management, an area where success is easily quantifiable. The claim to greater analytic and rational skills as an immutable male attribute does not reflect current studies, nor does it reflect any Bible passage that I am aware of. Thus, best practice would currently indicate having mixed-gender leadership.

There is also no objective measure that demonstrates that the relational nature of women, whether it is greater than that of men or not, detracts from leadership capabilities. Historical studies of justice-oriented decision-making and care-oriented decision-making have shown a significant gender gap. However, now that studies are being controlled for occupation and are varied by age and culture, gender is shrinking into the background as a salient feature. In certain leadership roles, both men and women access justice orientation and care orientation in ways that are consistent with that role. Although statistics comparing male CEOs with housewives may display a significant gender gap, studies of male and female managers conclude that there is no statistically significant gender gap.

However, the real test is not whether modern scientific research establishes certain gender differences in the attributes that are required for leadership; the real test is whether these differences can be found anywhere in the Bible. If we consider the story of Adam and Eve to be ambiguous, if not counterproductive, in demonstrating that men have a disposition towards rationality (a leadership essential), whereas women have a disposition towards relational emphasis, then what about the rest of the Hebrew Bible? Who are the wise people of the Hebrew Bible, and are they only men?

There are three different domains in which people of the Hebrew Bible are wise. The first is the area of technical skills required in the production of goods. The second is the area of public leadership—that is, being a ruler of a nation or community, or being a court advisor. The third is in the home—that is, being a wise parent and teacher of children. Examples of wise people are given in the Bible for each of these areas. Are these people both men and women, or only men?

During the building of the tabernacle,[14] there are references to those in the community who are "wise-hearted" in certain skills: the men in weaving and metal work, and the women in dying and spinning linen and goat's hair. Later, weaving becomes the domain of women; however, in the work on the tabernacle, men's names are mentioned in association with weaving. Although specific gender roles did exist, some tasks in the home-based economy at that time were shared by men and women. Working the ground with a hoe and animal husbandry were two areas that were shared by men and women alike in the Bible. Food preparation and the spinning and dying of linen and wool were in the female domain, whereas metal work and plough agriculture belonged to men. There was no concept of men being economically productive versus women acting primarily in a reproductive role. Women filled both a reproductive and a productive role in the home. Men also worked within the family unit. Later, during the monarchy of Israel, both women and men filled specialized labor positions. Both men and women were "wise-hearted" or "skilled."

The first time "wise men" are mentioned in terms of leadership occurs in the context of Pharaoh's court. Pharaoh's advisors are called "wise men."[15] There is also a female equivalent of the wise man: In the court of Sisera's mother, there are "wise princesses,"[16] who are attendants that advise the queen mother. This is not a role that is restricted to men.

Solomon[17] was the most notable wise man in the Hebrew Bible. As king of the nation of Israel, he prayed to God, and God gave him wisdom and understanding to render justice to the people, to write proverbs, and to classify trees and animals. The Queen of Sheba[18] came to question Solomon to see if he was as wise as his reputation suggested. The Queen of Sheba was a monarch who interacted with Solomon as an equal. Like Solomon, she was a seeker of wisdom and a prosperous ruler.

14. The building of the tabernacle begins in Exod 35.

15. Gen 41:8

16. Judg 5:29

17. Solomon's rule begins in 1 Kgs 3:1.

18. 1 Kgs 10:1

On a smaller scale, during the reign of King David, two women had the position of "wise woman" for their communities. One was the wise woman of Abel,[19] and the other the wise woman of Tekoa.[20] In the story of the wise woman of Abel, the town is being besieged because a rebel has taken refuge within the walls. The wise woman asks Joab, the general, why he is building a rampart against the city wall; he asks for the fugitive rebel to be turned over, and states that in return he will withdraw from the city. The wise woman responds that the head of the rebel will be thrown from the city wall; she then tells the people of the city to follow her instructions. This woman is the spokesperson, decision-maker, and leader of the city. The wise woman of Tekoa fills a slightly different role in her association with Joab. She becomes his spokesperson in an attempt to reason with King David. She is the one who goes head to head with the king, although Joab tells her what words to use.

The fact that these two women are listed as "wise women," and the absence of any comment on this being an unusual circumstance, suggests that the people of Israel did not consider that having a wise woman contravened any instruction from God that community leadership had to be male only. In the time of the Judges, two more female judges are described: Deborah[21] and Jael.[22] Only Deborah is usually mentioned as a judge; however, in Judg 5, Deborah lists Jael as a judge as well, singing, "In the days of Shamgar, son of Anath, in the days of Jael, caravans ceased, and travelers kept to the byways."[23]

In addition to these two wise women and two female judges, several women were named prophets. One was Hulda,[24] who was consulted by King Josiah's advisors regarding the book of the law, the Torah. Another was Noadiah,[25] a prominent prophet who opposed Nehemiah. Other female prophets are Miriam,[26] Isaiah's wife,[27] and Anna.[28] We do not have a

19. 2 Sam 20:16

20. 2 Sam 14:2

21. The story of Deborah starts in Judg 4:4.

22. The story of Jael starts in Judg 4:17.

23. Judg 5:6

24. 2 Kgs 22:14

25. Neh 6:14

26. Exod 15:20

27. Isa 8:3

28. Luke 2:36

full record of the worthiness of some of these women. However, we know that Deborah was considered to be a "mother in Israel," and that during her time, the land had rest for forty years. The wise woman of Abel also refers to a "mother in Israel":

> Then she said, "They used to say in the old days, 'Let them inquire at Abel'; and so they would settle a matter. I am one of those who are peaceable and faithful in Israel; you seek to destroy a city that is a mother in Israel; why will you swallow up the heritage of the Lord?"[29]

In both cases, the expression a "mother in Israel" seems to reinforce the validity of the leadership role of women. There is no question that these women are worthy and are fully respected by the men with whom they interact.

However, Grudem, who determined on the basis of Eve's behavior in the Garden of Eden that women are too relational and nurturing for leadership (in that they have a kinder and gentler nature than men), concludes that no women may be in a leadership role in the church:

> [I]t seems that 1 Timothy 2:14 is saying that men are better suited for the task of governing and of safeguarding the doctrine of the church. This does not mean that women *could not* do this task and do it well, at least in certain cases. But it does mean that God has both established men in that responsibility and has given inclinations and abilities that are well suited to that responsibility.
>
> Yet we must be cautious at this point. We should not say, "since Paul's reasoning is based on different general tendencies in men and women, there will be some unusual women who can be elders because they don't fit the generalizations but reason and relate more like men." We should not say that because Paul does not say that; he prohibits *all women* from teaching and governing the assembled congregation, not just those with certain abilities and tendencies.[30]

If women may serve as city leaders, judges, and prophets in the Hebrew Bible, and if all women are prohibited from teaching and governing in Christian congregations, then the status of women has decreased considerably from pre-Christian times to the time of the early church. Not only are women prohibited from leadership, but they are also no longer considered

---

29. 2 Sam 20:18–19

30. Grudem, *Countering the Claims*, 39 (Kindle Edition).

to be endowed in the same measure as men with the abilities and disposition that make a person suitable for leadership. What has changed? In what way have women's innate gifts for leadership diminished with the coming of Christ? Or is this the real meaning of Paul's letter? Does Paul really mean that now that we have salvation in Christ, women may no longer lead? This is a huge question facing the church, and relevant passages of the New Testament will be discussed in later chapters.

It is enough to note here that the Hebrew Bible does not contain just one or two wise women in leadership. There were queens, court advisors, city elders, judges, and prophets. Some were successful and some were not, like the men they were surrounded by. However, women in the Old Testament had the prerequisite attributes for leadership and were decision-makers and administrators of justice.

The remaining domain where wisdom is important is the home. Parents, both mother and father, are told to pass on the teaching of the ancestors to their children. Children are told to honor, revere, and obey both their father and their mother. Both father and mother are involved in decision-making regarding the children. In some stories, the father goes ahead without consulting the mother, as when Abraham takes Isaac to the mountain to sacrifice him.[31] In another story, Rebekah[32] makes decisions without Isaac's consent, but the result fulfills God's prophecy to her. In the story of Samson,[33] both mother and father are equally involved. In Proverbs, both parents are mentioned as the instructors of their children: "Hear, my child, your father's instruction, and do not reject your mother's teaching."[34] The woman of Prov 31 "opens her mouth with wisdom and the teaching of kindness is on her tongue." This woman is celebrated for both her strength and her wisdom. When "kindness" is mentioned in relation to this woman, it does not mean a purely female trait or feminine disposition. The Hebrew states that she opens her mouth in *hokma* (wisdom), and that the *torah* of *hesed* (the law of covenant love, God's law) is on her tongue. There can be no stronger words of worthiness for being a leader and decision-maker in the family.

The implication of these passages is that both men and women are equally suited for leadership in society, in the Christian community, and in

31. Gen 22:2

32. This story about Rebekah starts in Gen 27:13.

33. The story of Samson starts in Judg 13:1.

34. Prov 1:8

the home. Although women appear in the role of decision-maker less often than men, and are restricted in many ways in the stories in which they do appear, there is no comment on their unsuitability for the task of leading because they are women. The incidents cited here suggest a smooth and untroubled communication between men and women—between Solomon and the Queen of Sheba, Joab and the wise woman of Abel, Hulda and Josiah's advisors, and so on. Deborah runs into some resistance with Barak,[35] and there is a sense of some friction there because it was the job of a male to be the leader in war, whereas Deborah was a judge. Nonetheless, the outcome of Deborah's story is forty years of peace—no small feat!

In a last note, it must be acknowledged that in the Hebrew Bible, women do not play a role as leaders in war. They do participate in war in a covert fashion, and they do contribute to war efforts. Jael kills Sisera,[36] the wise woman of Abel makes strategic decisions, Rahab shelters the spies[37] and saves the lives of all her family, and Judith kills Holofernes.[38] However, women are not leaders in war. The nagging question here is whether all men are created with a disposition to wage war. This seems to be countered by the evidence in the Hebrew narratives. Solomon was not a warrior, and Jacob was not even a hunter. Did God have war in mind when he created men and women in the Garden of Eden? Is waging war one of the areas in which a leader must have wisdom? It seems from the biblical narratives, and from history as we know it, that only some leaders are warriors, not all.

Wisdom is the quality of having specialized skills, knowledge, and experience, and of being able to give sound advice and administer justice. It is also the quality that is necessary for building a home and providing for a family. The wise man built his house on a rock,[39] and the wise woman also builds her house.[40] In my Sunday School, we sang at great length about the wise man who built his house on a rock, but there is no song about a wise women building her house. Similarly, we learned about Solomon but never about the wise women of Tekoa and Abel. We weren't taught about Hulda, and we never asked who the women elders were in our congregation. Secretly, of course, the men in our church did consult women, but in a way

---

35. Judg 4:8
36. The story of Jael and Sisera starts in Judg 4:21.
37. The story of Rahab and the spies starts in Josh 2:1.
38. Jdt 13:12
39. Matt 7:24
40. Prov 14:1

that seemed to imply they didn't want to make it public. Wise men know that women are also wise. Rational men know that women are rational in equal measure. They also know that being relational and taking the welfare of the family into consideration is equally the job of men and of women. But it is necessary to say this out loud.

CHAPTER 4

Desire

To the woman he said, "I will greatly increase your pangs in childbearing;
in pain you shall bring forth children, yet your desire shall be for your
husband, and he shall rule over you."

(GEN 3:16, NRSV)

WHEN MY SISTER AND I were in our early teens, we received a lesson in desire. An elderly great aunt was living with us, and Mother was responsible for her care. My father would take her on holidays every once in a while, and Mother's Cousin Cathy would come and look after the great aunt for a week or two. Cousin Cathy was a widow in her late 60s whose husband had died of premature Alzheimer's; even at the best of times, however, he had been neither congenial nor much of a provider. We were told to be kind and polite to Cousin Cathy and to put up with her obsessively frugal ways.

Cousin Cathy was also an artist, and everywhere she went, she carried a rolled-up bundle of canvases. She would spread them out and show us beaches and palms of the Caribbean where her daughter was a missionary doctor, or the lemon yellow sky on the ocean horizon in the Aleutian Islands. Cathy loved beauty.

We eventually began to get the notion that some very amusing conversation was going on between the great aunt and Cousin Cathy. Cathy would retreat from the great aunt's room with a blush on her face, and would deny that anything had happened. We soon began listening to their conversations. Cathy had a "beau," and the great aunt made sure we all knew about it.

We eventually met Cousin Gilbert, who happened to be some kind of second cousin who had met Cousin Cathy at another relative's funeral. We kids were sure that Gilbert must have been at least eighty. But we did know that he was awfully good company. Gilbert was interested in all of us, was generous and loving with Cathy, and was very funny. He had eyes that twinkled and a personality to go along with it.

The next time that Cathy came to relieve my mother, she took over the sewing room, laid out a filmy white fabric in excessive folds on the table, and began to cut out the pattern for her bridal negligee. We followed her progress, from the front-opening housecoat to the also front-opening nightgown, in mixed wonder and puzzlement.

Not long after, Cathy and Gilbert were married by the roses in our backyard. Tall Cousin Gilbert folded his long legs into Cathy's VW beetle, and they drove off to the Maritimes for their honeymoon. On their way back, they were to stay at our place for one night before driving on to the West Coast and home.

Mother was away again, and we girls were responsible for getting the guest room ready. The couple did not arrive that night, so we went off to bed. In the morning, I checked the empty guest room, shrugged my shoulders, and went downstairs to get breakfast. As I clanged around the kitchen, the two of them emerged from the basement. They had slept in the single cot on the floor in my absent brother's rather minimalist bedroom downstairs.

I exclaimed in dismay that the guest room had been all ready, but Gilbert replied that they didn't want to bother us so late, and that the single bed had been quite adequate for the two of them, who wanted to be close anyway. Cathy blushed and simpered. I only saw them a couple more times, but I was happy to speak at Cathy's funeral many years later. She was a woman who knew how to love beauty, life, and her new beau.

Since then, I have been at several weddings of older couples, and I have found that the traditional teaching that the wife is subordinate to the husband is not included in the vows and sermon. It does not seem as if this concept has resonance among those marrying late in life. They seek companionship, not hierarchical order, and desire is not absent. A friend once commented to me that her 85-year-old father and his partner were behaving just like teenagers. The longing to be part of a couple, to know and be known by someone, does not disappear. It may be replaced by a community of loving friends, for many who do not remarry. With that in view, we must look at what is arguably one of the most difficult verses in the Bible about desire, at least for women.

In the Hebrew Bible, this one line may have had more effect on Christian views on marital relations than any other. It stands out for the wide variety of ways it has been translated and interpreted. In Gen 3:16, the line "and thy desire shall be to thy husband and he shall rule over you," from the King James Bible, has been translated in three contrasting ways. For many centuries, it was translated as "you will return to your husband," or "you will be under the power of your husband." Then, for several centuries, it was translated as "your desire will be to your husband." Today, the exact opposite of the first version has recently appeared: "you will want to control your husband." How can a verse be made to mean the opposite of its original translation? And which translation can we trust?

First, "desire" fits well into Gen 3, where Eve has just been tempted by her appetite, her admiration for beauty, and her desire for wisdom. She is responding to the exact elements—beauty and wisdom—that men and women will pursue throughout the Hebrew narratives. In addition, Eve has just been given the task of frequent pregnancies, in a world of broken relationships and laborious subsistence farming. She desires more. She longs for intimacy and transcendence, beauty and wisdom; she also longs for children, who will validate her existence. The notion that Eve experiences longing is not hard to imagine.

In the familiar translations of the King James tradition, the complete verse reads:

> Unto the woman he said,
> I will greatly multiply thy sorrow and thy conception;
> in sorrow thou shalt bring forth children;
> and thy desire shall be to thy husband,
> and he shall rule over thee.[1]

The King James Bible is remarkable in its restraint and in its fidelity to the original vocabulary. But it is also a translation that has existed relatively recently, from 1528 till now. There is a complex history regarding desire for the preceding translations, as well for those that follow.

The Hebrew word *teshuqa*, which is translated in the King James Bible as "desire," is found only three times in the Hebrew Bible: in Gen 3:16,

1. Gen 3:16

regarding what Eve feels towards her husband; in Gen 4:7, regarding sin towards Cain (or, in some early translations, regarding Abel towards Cain); and in Song 7:10, regarding how the lover feels towards his sweetheart. In the Aramaic tradition and in the rabbinical literature, *teshuqa* was usually considered to mean "desire," and this tradition persisted into medieval Hebrew commentary.

However, in the Greek Septuagint, which was translated around 200 BCE, *teshuqa* was understood in a completely different way; and this translation exerted an influence on the Latin Vulgate, which was the predominant Christian text until the 1500s. For the two passages in Genesis, the Hebrew word *teshuqa* was translated into Greek using words that meant "a turning" or "to return to." For example:

> And to the woman he said,
> "I will increasingly increase your pains and your groaning;
> with pains you will bring forth children.
> And your recourse [return] will be to your husband,
> and he will dominate you."[2]

This translation has the rather elegant effect of the *adam* being taken from the *adamah* (the ground), and the *ishsha* (woman) being taken from the *ish* (man); then the woman's "return" is to the man, and the man "returns" to the ground. The lines then read:

> . . . with pains you will bring forth children.
> And your return will be to your husband,
> and he will dominate you.
> By the sweat of your face you will eat your bread
> until you return to the earth from which you were taken,
> for you are earth and to earth you will depart.[3]

Considering that the Jewish translators into Greek may not have known the original meaning of the Hebrew word *teshuqa,* this translation creates a satisfying parallelism from a literary point of view, and certainly fits the context. It is a viable interpretation. Their translation of Gen 4:7 reads, "his/its recourse/return is to you," which possibly means that Abel would return to his subordinate position as Cain's younger brother, and Cain would rule over him. Their translation of Song 7:10 reads, "and his attention is for me."

2. Gen 3:16
3. Gen 3:16

The next stage of translation was into Latin. Jerome's Vulgate became the standard Bible from the 4th to the 16th century. In the Vulgate, the three occurrences of *teshuqa* were translated in slightly different ways:

> *et sub viri potestate eris,*
> *et ipse dominabitur tui.*
> [and thou shalt be under thy husband's power,
> and he shall have dominion over thee.][4]

> *sed sub te erit appetitus ejus,*
> *et tu dominaberis illius.*
> [but the lust thereof shall be under thee,
> and thou shalt have dominion over it.][5]

> *Ego dilecto meo, et ad me conversio ejus.*
> [I to my beloved, and his turning is towards me.][6]

In spite of the difference in vocabulary, a common idea runs through these translations. The one who is the subject of the verb (whether Eve, sin, or the lover), is "under" or "in the thrall of" the other: It is a position of subordination. The woman is under the authority of her husband. It is difficult to find this exact meaning in the original Hebrew, and in the Nova Vulgata today, this phrase has been changed to *et ad virum tuum erit appetitus tuus* (and your appetite will be to your husband).

One of the difficulties in trying to find a common meaning in the two passages in Genesis is that the line in Gen 4 referring to Cain is difficult to translate. The word *teshuqa* requires a masculine reference, possibly Abel, in "his desire is for you." Sin, on the other hand, is a feminine word. This is problematic, and the lack of agreement between the ending on the word *teshuqa* and "sin" suggests that the original version of the line is unknown. If Abel returns to Cain, and Cain rules him, then it makes some kind of sense that Cain murders Abel. But if sin returns to Cain, and Cain rules over sin, it is odd that Cain rises up and kills Abel. Nonetheless, it is the latter translation that appears most often. In this passage, Cain is the one being addressed, and is told that sin is returning to or desires him, and that he will rule over it. However, Cain does not, in fact, overrule sin; he

4. Gen 3:16
5. Gen 4:7
6. Song 7:10

murders his brother. Later, Cain is also told that the soil will be difficult to work. So there are two separate aspects of the curse on Cain.

For Eve, the fact that she "returns to" or "desires" Adam, and that he will rule over her, is a part of her own suffering from the fall. The two passages are not parallel. Even though we can try to compare the phrasing in Gen 3 with the phrasing in Gen 4, we can see that Eve is not easily compared to "sin," as the supposed agent of the word *teshuqa*. Sometimes, there is repetition, alliteration, or wordplay in the Hebrew for which the deeper meaning is opaque. It is perhaps not possible to know exactly how these two passages relate.

In any case, the Latin Vulgate is still the standard translation of the Roman Catholic Church, and the Septuagint remains the official text of the Greek Orthodox Church. Neither of these texts include the word "desire." "Desire" came into Bible translations during the Reformation in a rather roundabout way. In the 15th and 16th centuries, Christian Hebraists committed time to studying Hebrew in depth, often with rabbis or with Jews who had converted to Christianity due to circumstances at the time. One of the outstanding Hebrew scholars of the late 15th and early 16th centuries was an Italian Dominican scholar, Sanctus Pagninus, who had originally been interested in Kabbalah, and had produced a detailed Hebrew lexicon. He was then commissioned by Pope Leo to make a new translation of the Hebrew Bible into Latin. Such a translation would validate the position of the Roman Catholic Church by demonstrating that it was faithful to the original Hebrew.

Pagninus' translation was printed in 1528, and was considered by Jewish scholars to be a careful and respectful translation of the Hebrew into Latin. Unfortunately, it was considered by its Latin readers to be stilted and unnatural in its language, and it never superseded the Vulgate. However, it was widely revised by later scholars, and reprinted, and often appeared along with the original Hebrew text. Coverdale, who published the first complete Bible in the English language, explicitly stated that Pagninus' translation was one of the four Bibles that he used, along with the Latin Vulgate and Luther's and Zwingli's Bibles. It is considered likely that all the translators into the English language would have had access to and been influenced by the Pagninus translation. It is also likely that Luther and Zwingli were aware of this Bible and referred to it at times. By 1535, other Latin translations were available that had been influenced by Hebrew commentary, and were used by the early translators of the Bible into the modern languages of Europe.

For the first time in the history of European Bibles, the Hebrew word *teshuqa* was translated into Latin as *desiderium* in Gen 3 and in the Song of Solomon, and as *appetitus* in Gen 4. It was then reasonably translated into German by Zwingli as *lust*, "desire," and by Luther as *verlangen*, "longing." Tyndale translated *teshuqa* into English as "lust," although his use of the word "lust" also referred to a general desire for truth and godliness. Tyndale writes: "If we ask we shall obtain, if we knock he will open, if we seek we shall find, if we thirst, his truth shall fulfill our lust."[7]

One example of the rabbinical tradition that interpreted *teshuqa* as "desire" is the commentary of the 11th century Jewish scholar Rashi:

> And to your husband will be your desire: for intimacy, but, nevertheless, you will not have the audacity to demand it of him with your mouth, but he will rule over you. Everything is from him and not from you.[8]

The text that Rashi mentions for comparison, Ps 107:9, reads, "For he satisfieth the longing soul, and filleth the hungry soul with goodness." In this verse, "longing" is a desire for the goodness of God, and does not refer to sexual desire. Rashi's interpretation portrays women in a dependent position in relation to a husband, but not in a pejorative position.[xi]

Finally, we come to Gen 3:16, where Adam and Eve [and the snake] are punished. It seems to me that Rashi must have received input from his daughters when explaining Eve's penalty. He states that "multiplying her toil/sorrow" of childbearing refers to the burdens and worries that a mother, more so than the father, is subject to when raising children; her "pain in pregnancy" means the discomfort that pregnant women often experience; while "anguish in childbearing" describes the painful birth pangs themselves. As the author Maggie Anton puts it:

> So while it may go too far to describe Rashi's commentaries on Genesis as "feminist," for a man of the 11th Century, he appears to hold a more sympathetic view of women than other medieval theologians. Did his daughters influence him in this? I certainly hope so.[9]

7. Tyndale, *Obedience*.

8. Rashi, *Complete Tanach*, Gen 3:16.

9. Anton, "Hebrew Text," under the entry for November 5, 2009.

Although Anton does not comment here on Rashi's treatment of *teshuqa*, she makes the claim that in contrast to some passages in the earlier Talmudic tradition, Rashi did not promote a negative view of women.[10]

However, the introduction of the word "desire" into the English Bible tradition meant that a Bible citation could now be used to attribute troublesome sexual desire to women. Men had additional ammunition for declaring women to be the problem in issues of sexual relations. One rather extreme example is the interpretation by the Hebrew scholars Keil and Delitzsch:

> The woman had also broken through her divinely appointed subordination to the man; she had not only emancipated herself from the man to listen to the serpent, but had led the man into sin. For that, she was punished with a desire bordering upon disease (*teshuqa* from *shuq* to run, to have a violent craving for a thing), and with subjection to the man.[11]

It is no wonder that in response to the use of the word "desire" for *teshuqa* some would prefer the original Greek translation "return."

Katherine Bushnell was a medical missionary of the 19th century who worked with women and children in China, and later in the United States, as a public activist to free women enslaved in prostitution. She became convinced that male translators of the Bible had introduced bias into the text, and set out to demonstrate her case in a series of lessons delivered by correspondence. This issue of a woman's "desire" or "lust" was particularly poignant to Bushnell, who was active in petitioning the law to intervene in the cases of hundreds of women being held in forced prostitution in Wisconsin lumber camps, and under British rule in India and Hong Kong. She certainly found the interpretations that emphasized the "lust" of women to be morally repugnant—when, in reality, she saw women who were being held as slaves to men's sexual demands. Bushnell argued that "return" had been the original meaning, and that the sexualization of the passage was damaging to women and gave men an excuse for the violence and sex slavery that she saw.[12]

However, in her book *Gender and Grace*, Mary Stewart Van Leeuwen interprets desire as longing, in a similar manner to Rashi, but does not associate this meaning with subordination: "Woman is being warned that

10. Anton, *Rashi's Daughters.*

11. Keil and Delitzsch, "The Pentateuch."

12. Bushnell, *God's Word.*

she will experience an unreciprocated longing for intimacy with the man."[13] "Longing" is also the preferred translation of Robert Alter, a respected contemporary Hebrew scholar.

"Longing" is a word that can describe the desire for something that is lost, unavailable, or broken in some way. It is a desire whose fulfillment is denied. This word fits very well into a context where frequent pregnancies and difficult childbirth threaten the life of mother and child, and where intimacy between husband and wife has been hijacked by conflict. It fits well within the narrative in which Eve has just been tempted by her appetite, love of beauty, and desire for wisdom. These desires, particularly those for beauty and wisdom, are typical and worthy desires of men as well. There is no particularly feminine aspect to desire.

Perhaps Eve does not represent the weakness of women, but instead represents the attributes of humankind; perhaps she stands for all of humanity, as she expresses a longing that is common to both men and women: for knowledge and wisdom, for intimacy and life, for beauty and transcendence. Eve does not escape Adam's fate, but must share equally in tilling the ground. She also shares in his mortality—his return to the soil; she too dies. Adam may also share in Eve's fate, in experiencing sorrow over children dying young, in all the problems of child rearing, and in knowing an unfulfilled longing for both intimacy and transcendence.

Those who see non-overlapping gender roles in this text may forget that in agricultural societies that do not use ploughs and draft animals, tilling the soil belongs equally to men and women, and often defaults to women. Carol Meyers suggests that the first line of Gen 3:16 should read "toil and conceptions." Women must work the soil and (at least historically) experience frequent pregnancies as well.

However, there is one more permutation in the history of the translation of the word *teshuqa*: the shift from "desire" to "control." This newer interpretation proposes that whereas the ancient woman was under the power and authority of her husband, the modern women is in revolt and is trying to control her husband. Although this interpretation is now widespread, it is only found explicitly as a translation in the text of two popular Bibles. "You will want to control your husband," is found in the New English Translation (NET) at Bible.org, and "And you will desire to control your husband," is in the New Living Translation. The NET Bible provides a note saying that this interpretation is consistent with the use of the word

13. Stewart Van Leeuwen, *Gender and Grace*, 44.

teshuqa, or "desire," in the Song of Solomon, because in that case, according to the NET Bible notes, the man is trying to "have his way sexually with the woman. He wants to possess her." In one fell swoop, the NET Bible obliterates the joy and beauty of the mutual relationship found in the Song of Solomon. It is all about the man "having his way" with the woman.

But "desire to control" is also the preferred understanding of Wayne Grudem, editor of the English Standard Version and author of *A Systematic Theology*, who wrote in reference to an article published by Susan Foh:[14] "Susan Foh has effectively argued that the word translated 'desire' (Heb. teshûqah) means 'desire to conquer,' and that it indicates Eve would have a wrongful desire to usurp authority over her husband."[15]

This translation of *teshuqa* is a far cry from Calvin's commentary. Calvin maintains that *teshuqa*, or "desire," is the same meaning as the original Latin of the Vulgate: that Eve is "under the authority of her husband" rather than "wants to control" her husband:

> The second punishment which he exacts is *subjection*. For this form of speech, "Thy desire shall be unto thy husband," is of the same force as if he had said that she should not be free and at her own command, but subject to the authority of her husband and dependent upon his will; or as if he had said, "Thou shalt desire nothing but what thy husband wishes." As it is declared afterwards, Unto thee shall be his desire.[16]

It is difficult to resist the notion that the new interpretation, which is usually attributed to Foh, and which has been made popular within the last few years, is tailored to fit the situation in which men find themselves today. Regarding this new interpretation, "desire to control," Foh writes as the basis of her thesis:

> Experience corroborates this interpretation of God's judgment on the woman. If the words "and he shall rule over you" in Genesis 3:16b are understood in the indicative, then they are not true. As Cain did not rule over sin (Genesis 4:7b), so not every husband rules his wife, and wives have desires contrary to their husbands' and often have no desire (sexual or psychological) for their husbands.[17]

14. Foh, "Woman's Desire," 376–83.
15. Grudem, *Systematic Theology*, 464.
16. Calvin, *Calvin's Complete Commentary*.
17. Foh, "Woman's Desire," 382.

Whether these conditions are true or not for women now, or at any time in history, has no bearing on a discussion of a passage that was written in the patriarchal society of ancient Israel. If there was a sense that the husband did rule his wife in ancient Israel, then we have no business extrapolating back from our own social circumstances, that this is "not true." In a society where every women wanted to bear children, in spite of the difficulties involved, sexual desire was not out of place. Whether this desire is a longing for intimacy, childbearing, meaning in life, or beauty and wisdom, it is hardly valid to argue that the word *teshuqa* cannot mean desire, just because some women today have no "desire" for their husbands.

Foh also argues her point by comparison with Gen 4:7. She writes: "As the Lord tells Cain what he should do, i.e., master or rule sin, the Lord also states what the husband should do, rule over his wife."[18]

Besides the fact that the interpretation of Gen 4:7 is extremely difficult due to the non-agreement of *teshuqa* with "sin," there is also the fact that in Gen 4:7, God is addressing Cain in the statement that he should rule "over it or him." In Gen 3:16, God is addressing Eve, so this is not an instruction addressed to Adam to rule over Eve. However, this refers to an increased dependence on her husband as a consequence of her frequent pregnancies, linked with her desire. The parallel is unfounded.

Unfortunately, Foh's interpretation, which is now widely popular in conservative Christian circles, has provided a basis for a practical teaching on marriage relations and domestic abuse. Recently, Bruce Ware, a theologian who is associated with gender essentialism, puts it this way:

> As most complementarians understand it, Gen. 3:15–16 informs us that the male/female relationship would now, because of sin, be affected by mutual enmity. In particular, the woman would have a desire to usurp the authority given to man in creation, leading to man, for his part, ruling over woman in what can be either rightfully-corrective or wrongfully-abusive ways.[19]

In a sermon at Denton Bible Church on June 22, 2008, Ware preached these words:

> The very wise and good plan of God, of male headship, is sought to be overturned as women now, as sinners, want instead to have their way, instead of submitting to their husbands, to do what they would like to do, and seek to work to have their husbands fulfill

18. Foh, "Woman's Desire," 381.
19. CBMW, "Summaries."

their will, rather than serving them; and their husbands on their part, because they are sinners, now respond to that threat to their authority either by being abusive, which is, of course, one of the ways men can respond when their authority is challenged. Or more commonly by becoming passive, acquiescing and simply not asserting the leadership they ought to as men in their homes and churches.[20]

The teaching goes like this: God created marriage as an authority-submission relationship. Eve's sin represents her rebellion against male authority. The husband responds by being abusive. The behavior of the wife "leads" the husband to behave in an abusive way. The blame for violence in the home, therefore, is placed firmly on the shoulders of the woman, who by her association with Eve is naturally understood to be seeking to overturn male headship. Men in turn must "assert" their rule over their wife; in Ware's words: "Eve's desire will be to rule illegitimately over Adam ... and in response Adam will have to assert his rightful rulership over her."[21]

Gen 3 is a passage that might appeal to the heart of each of us. It places problematic human desires within a garden: the desires for fruit, beauty, wisdom, intimacy, and family—all desires that God puts in the human heart. However, with his interpretation, Ware transforms this passage into a justification for a man to assert rulership over his wife.

"Desire" translates but does not interpret the Hebrew original; it invites the reader into the text. The word "desire" leads into a wide variety of themes in the Hebrew narratives. Is it only the wife who desires? No; we know that both men are women are beautiful, and both are objects of desire. Both men and women desire wisdom and beauty; sexual desire is mutual; and erotic desire represents the soul's desire for the divine and for transcendence. We know that the Hebrew Bible includes the Song of Solomon, and we are free to take the mutual eroticism in this book literally or figuratively. We know this, but some Bible translators seek to obscure this knowledge.

---

20. Visit http://www.dennyburk.com/bruce-ware%E2%80%99s-complementarian-reading-of-genesis/ for an audio recording of this sermon.

21. CBMW, "Satisfied and Complementarian?"

Section 2

Gender Roles

CHAPTER 5

Champion and Defender

I commend to you our sister Phoebe, a deacon of the church at Cenchreae,
so that you may welcome her in the Lord as is fitting for the saints,
and help her in whatever she may require from you, for she has been a
benefactor of many and of myself as well.

(ROM 16:1-2, NRSV)

As I WRITE, I am sitting in the early morning sun with my coffee, scanning the pages of a cherry-red cloth-bound book that was printed in about 1925—although it has no recorded date. The title *The Enterprise* is embossed on the front in gold gilt script, below a pasted-on black-and-white photograph of the staff of the Canadian Baptist Mission in India. I keep pausing to reread bits and pieces of the story, which fascinates me; it tells about my own hometown, Toronto, and in particular about certain young women who attended Trinity College at the University of Toronto at the end of the 19th century.

Pearl Smith graduated from Trinity College in Toronto in 1895, just two years after her brother, Everett Smith—both training to work as doctors in India. She received her medical training through the Ontario Women's Medical College, which, apart from one other training college in Kingston, was the only place in Canada for women to get medical training until 1906, when the University of Toronto admitted women into the medical school. The Women's Medical College closed at that point, but three years later, a group of prominent Toronto women formed a committee to establish the Women's College Hospital in order to more fully address the medical needs of women, in terms of both medical care and full medical training.

However, for Pearl Smith in the 1890s, no hospital in Toronto had yet accepted a woman in the position of medical intern. Fortunately, St. Michael's Hospital, founded by the Catholic Sisters of St. Joseph in 1892, was happy to promote women's participation and offered her a position as an intern, and she completed her necessary hospital training there. So Pearl Smith was, in fact, able to go to India as the first Canadian woman doctor trained in a hospital internship. On arriving in India, she married her fiancé, Rev. Jesse Chute, who committed a large part of his time to supporting her work—her late-night emergency calls to remote villages, and her never-ending lineups of patients waiting to be treated on the verandah. He soon built a hospital for her growing practice, which was the only medical aid in the area, and did much of the physical labor himself. Ironically, Dr. Pearl Chute, as a missionary wife, did not receive an income or stipend for her work.

In 1876, the Women's Society of Western Ontario was in the process of being formed at the Jarvis St. Baptist Church; from the first, it was led by a female president. In 1882, the Society sent its first missionary to India. During the next few years, the Women's Society funded and sent many single women to India. The Society and its work was not unchallenged by some men, and by suggestions that such work was not suitable for the "weaker sex." However, one woman missionary wrote a paper on the validity of women touring alone as evangelists and teachers, and another woman received funding from the Leprosy Mission to establish and run a new leprosy asylum. Women stepped into full leadership roles and defended their right to do so. For the most part, as these women proved their competence, they gained the approval of their male colleagues. In 1900, the Women's Society sent Dr. Gertrude Hulet as its first doctor, and many female doctors followed. Women founded and administered hospitals and training schools for local teachers.

In 1906, Dr. Jessie Allyn was sent from Toronto by the Women's Society to work in the same locale as Dr. Everett Smith, but with the aim of providing medical aid specifically for women. Not long after arriving, she was asked to attend the childbirth of the Rani of Pithapuram and delivered the Rani's son, who was the heir of the Raja of Pithapuram. In return, the Rani provided funds and ongoing patronage for a Women's Hospital and Home for Nurses. In 1918, Dr. Ida Scudder established a medical school to train local female doctors. Although there had certainly been some initial resistance to the independent work of single women missionaries, an overall theme of "women's work for women" evolved, along with the acknowledgement that women were working alongside men as full and equal partners. The Canadian women, in their turn, trained Indian women to participate as equals in the medical work.

During this era, young Christian women were at the forefront of the feminist movement, as they sought professional training in medicine as part of the first cohort of Canadian women to be trained in this field. These women were supported by a mission society that was founded and administered by women, for women. They experienced what could be called "institutional completeness." Women leaders supported women to become women leaders in turn. In India, these women acted on the same principle, as they provided facilities for the Indian women they worked with to become fully trained medical doctors with their own full professional competence. The Canadian women in India functioned as equals to men and opened up opportunities for local women to function as their equals. People interacted on the basis of each person having equal human potential and equal possibilities for achievement without predetermined boundaries.[xii]

Interestingly, the medical field was at that time interpreted by male missionaries as the ideal place for feminine virtues to be expressed, because it was suited to the nurturing nature of women; however, this perception had not previously been the case. In fact, these women had to fight the male establishment for entry into the medical profession, which was viewed as a masculine domain. Women founded separate training colleges for women and had to prove themselves before being allowed entry into the medical profession. Only after the success of female doctors was established was their full participation reinterpreted as belonging within the domestic and, therefore, female domain.

A slightly different pathway emerged in regard to religious training. Women trained in biblical studies and went as missionaries to India, where they set up separate training schools for "Bible Women." However, these female missionaries were usually excluded from the seminaries, which were the domain of men. Across Asia, including China and India, Bible Women became the counterparts of the male-trained native ministers. Bible Women were often single women or widows who traveled to remote villages on their own, specifically to teach women and children. However, when they were the only Christian presence in an area, as often occurred, Bible Women also evangelized, taught, and held services for the general population, men included. This practice was common in many pioneering areas, and was certainly the case on the North American frontier. Bible Women thus filled similar functions as the male clergy, but without recognition or financial support.

Happily, some men did accept the full involvement of women in these fields. For example, Dr. Tympani urged the women of the Jarvis Street Baptist Church in Toronto to found a Women's Missionary Society of their own. Pearl Smith's husband, Jesse Chute, decided not to train as a doctor himself, but instead spent considerable time supporting his wife's medical practice and building a hospital for her work. Rev. Orchard, one of the authors of *The Enterprise*, celebrated the inclusion of women alongside men in the fullest sense, as equals. He wrote as much when describing the "Apostolate of Women," and recognized the role of women missionaries as equal in every sense to the work of the men.

The Hebrew Bible tells us that the first woman was created to be the "help meet" for the first man.[1] Popular modern translations offer a variation on this theme. Some say "a helper suitable for him" or "fit for him." Owen Strachan, the former president of the Council on Biblical Manhood and Womanhood (CBMW), interprets this phrase as saying that women may only function as a support to a male-led ministry. In Strachan's words:

> Most fundamentally, godly women should serve the local church by supporting, helping, encouraging, and affirming the ministry of the elders as the elders promote the gospel in the church and the world . . . Men have been created and commanded to lead the church's mission, expose Scripture, shepherd, and give oversight. Women have been created and commanded to submit to the church's mission and to buttress the ministry produced by the male leaders. At the most basic level, this involves encouraging and affirming their elders, embracing "support" ministries, and modeling a spirit of affirmation and encouragement wherever possible.[2]

Of course, it is possible to understand establishing and administering teaching hospitals and Bible Women training schools as a "support"

1. Gen 2:18
2. Strachan, "Genesis of Gender."

ministry. However, in the 1890s, this work was undertaken by women who were trained by schools that were founded by women, and who were sent by a Women's Society. They worked on their own; they were the leading personnel in setting up hospitals and training centers. Their initial goal was to help women. In India at that time, not only were all doctors male, but up until the late 1800s, male doctors did not see female patients. Female doctors did not go to the mission field to support the work of the male elders or to contribute to a male-led ministry; they went to help their sisters. This was all done in an era when medical services and biblical studies were considered to be the exclusive domains of men. For the most part, men did not consider this medical work to be a "supporting" role, or a "buttressing" of a ministry under male elders, but rather a pioneering work that was challenging to both men and women.

However, it was often single women who were more willing to take on this work, because male missionaries often had pregnant wives or young children in need of a medical infrastructure. Women did, in fact, "lead, expose scripture, shepherd, and give oversight." Although they certainly did submit to the church's ministry, they did not "buttress a ministry produced by the male elders." They did not "encourage and affirm" a male-led ministry, but rather threw themselves into establishing new ministries, leprosy asylums, hospitals, schools, and training institutions, under the auspices of a female-led mission society.

Of course, we might argue that although these women missionaries functioned as equals in the medical domain, which was eventually viewed as an extension of the domestic sphere and thus suitable for women, they were restricted in a formal sense from full recognition as clergy. However, on examination of Genesis 2, we must admit that God created women with a general competence, and not specifically one that was divided into spheres and domains. Women were either fully competent from the start, and were fully required to take on initiative and leadership, or they were not. One cannot divide up the original garden environment into the spheres of home, workplace, and the church. Either women are not equal to men in their leadership design, or they are.

Regardless of what has been said by theologians about the essential difference between men and women, women did undertake the same kind of work as men, and produced successful institutions and ministries. They demonstrated equal leadership acumen, fortitude, and agency as men who were in similar positions. They underwent equal hardship and sacrifice, often giving up any hope of marriage and family for themselves, in order to spend a lifetime providing medical services and Bible training to others. These women followed the example of scripture regarding full commitment to God and to their fellow human beings; they alleviated suffering and proclaimed the Gospel.

Around this time, Helen Montgomery, a young women from Rochester, NY, became licensed to preach in the 1890s, although she was never ordained. Montgomery often led the service when the minister was absent. She was the top in her class in Greek studies; as an experienced Bible teacher, she went on to translate the New Testament into a new and more readable version for the young people in her Bible classes. Eventually, Montgomery became the president of the Northern Baptist Convention and the first female president of any denomination in North America.

Given that Christian women have not functioned solely as a support to a male-led ministry, theologians continue to explore the meaning of the phrase in Genesis 2 that describes the woman as a "helper" suitable for the man. The expression "help meet" or "suitable helper" is a translation of two Hebrew words: *ezer,* meaning "help," and *kenegdo,* meaning "like" and "in front of" or "opposite"[3] to a person. Theologians promoting male leadership look for evidence of subordination in one or the other of these two words. Subordination is sometimes cloaked in the word "complementary." The man is first defined as the leader, and the woman is then defined as the "complement" to the man, and therefore a follower.

However, the Bible uses the Hebrew word for "helper" (*ezer*) in two other contexts: first, for God as the one that humans call on for help; and second, for a human ally in war. For example, Eliezer's name means "God is my help." Obviously, the word *ezer* in this context does not mean that God is Eliezer's subordinate assistant; rather, God rescues him when he is in need or danger. Here, *ezer* names the one who supplies aid or succor to an individual who is in danger or in need of rescue. While acknowledging that God is called our "helper," the theologian Andreas Kostenberger discusses how the word *ezer* applies to women:

> Moreover, in the case of woman, Genesis 2 does not teach that she may merely *act* as the man's "helper" when she so chooses but rather that serving as the man's "helper" sums up her very reason for existence in relation to the man. Being the man's "helper" is

3. In a positional sense

the purpose for which the woman was created, as far as her wifely status is concerned.[4]

Here, Kostenberger argues that God acts as a helper to humans, but that this is not his reason for existence; it is only one of his actions. However, for a woman, helping is her exclusive purpose for existence.

In *Systematic Theology*, Grudem indicates that God is subordinate to man when he acts as man's helper. However, woman is always and only man's helper, and therefore is always subordinate to man. In the *Journal for Biblical Manhood and Womanhood*, Dorothy Patterson writes:

> For example, the phrase used by the writer of Genesis (Heb., *ezer kenegdo*, literally "helper like unto himself"), defines the way the woman functions or how she does her assignment, i.e., as a helper, while the rest of the phrase makes clear that she is equal, like, and in the image of God just as the man from whom and for whom she was created (Gen 1:27; 2:18–23).[5]

In fact, it is unreasonable to argue that the Hebrew word *ezer* means that someone is subordinate in any way. It is only by explicitly restricting women to the role of helper, and therefore depicting them as people who do not have their own agency—where "agency" refers to setting their own goals and making their own decisions—that women are relegated to the subordinate role. Kostenberger derives these restrictions from elsewhere in the Bible, and limits women's ministry to whatever domains may be defined, or redefined (as the medical profession was), as the "domestic sphere": "It may be that Paul used the phrase "childbearing" in 1 Tim 2:15 as a shorthand for the woman's involvement in the domestic sphere."[6]

Tom Schreiner uses a passage in 1 Cor 11 to say that women should not take on any roles defined as "male leadership roles," or else they will lose their femininity:

> [T]he arrogation of male leadership roles by women ultimately dissolves the distinction between men and women . . . Paul rightly saw, as he shows in this text, that there is a direct link between women appropriating leadership and the loss of femininity.[7]

---

4. Kostenberger and Jones, *God, Marriage*, 25.
5. Patterson, "Equal in Being," 73.
6. Kostenberger, "Saved Through Childbearing?"
7. Schreiner, "Head Coverings," 139.

Such efforts by theologians to rein women in, keep women within a certain culturally defined "domestic sphere," or keep women out of what are defined as "male leadership" roles in contemporary culture ultimately raise a serious question: When woman is called *ezer* in Hebrew, does the word imply subordination? If *ezer* means subordinate, why are other verses in the New Testament required to reinforce the teaching of subordination? Did early female readers of the Hebrew Bible clearly understand that the term *ezer* restricted them to a subordinate role?

Since *ezer* cannot provide firm evidence for the subordination of women, some Bibles translate the next Hebrew phrase, *kenegdo,* to define women as the "complement" of man. For example, the Holman Christian Standard Bible (HCSB) translates Gen 2:18 as "I will make a helper as his complement." Grudem puts it this way: "She was created as one who differed from him, but who differed from him in ways that would exactly complement who Adam was."[8] That is, woman is defined as the complement, or as the opposite of whatever man is defined as; because the woman is the complement, she must be the follower. Among others, Bruce Ware argues that because man was created first, he is the leader; the woman must then be under his authority as his helper.

> Notice that God created woman after the man (Genesis 2:7, 21–23) in order for the woman to be a helper to the man (Genesis 2:18). This means that while the man and the woman are completely equal in value before God (Genesis 1:27), the woman is under the man's leadership and authority since she was created after him, to be a help to him.[9]

Regarding the phrase *kenegdo,* John Walton says, "most interpreters find in this phrase whatever they come to it looking for."[10] Other translations read: "a help like unto himself," "a suitable companion to help him," "a companion for him, who corresponds to him," "a helper comparable to him," and "a helper as his partner." Robert Alter translates *kenegdo* as an "a sustainer beside him":

> The Hebrew 'ezer kenegdo is notoriously difficult to translate. The second term means alongside him, opposite him, a counterpart to him. "Help" is too weak because it suggests a merely auxiliary function, whereas 'ezer elsewhere connotes active intervention on

8. Grudem, *Biblical Foundations,* 32.

9. Ware, *Big Truths,* 91.

10. Walton, *NIV Application Commentary,* 176.

behalf of someone, especially in military contexts, as often in the
Psalms.[11]

Here, Alter gives a fairly literal translation that reflects the use of *ezer* elsewhere. This word can mean someone offering succor or aid, or a life-giver
or sustainer; and it can refer to a divine being or a peer. It is only in Gen 2
that anyone suggests that *ezer* denotes a subordinate. The phrase *kenegdo*
appears only in this one place in the Hebrew Bible, and is a compound of
a word meaning "like" or "equal" and "in a physical location in front of or
opposite to oneself." The woman is an *ezer*, but not someone who helps
from a position of greater strength as God does; rather, she is someone who
is equal, a partner, not going in front of a person, and not following behind
a person, but as an equal alongside or beside the other person. Woman is
not the inferior or the superior; she is a person who is suited to be an equal
partner to the man.

Another woman in the Bible is often called a helper. Many translations
say that Phoebe, the servant of the church at Cenchrea, was a "great help" to
Paul. But what does the Greek actually say? Not that. In the Greek, Phoebe
was a *diakonos* (deacon) of the church of Cenchrea, and was a *prostatis* of
Paul. The word *prostatis* has a wide range of meanings, and can be used to
refer to a patron, leader, benefactor, or defender of someone else. Several
women were known for their works of *prostasia*. In Corinth, the tombstone
of a Lycian woman named Junia Theodora (not the Junia of the Bible, but
another Junia) states that she was recognized for works of *prostasia*, or
patronage, on behalf of her fellow Lycians. Junia Theodora was wealthy,
influential, and independent, and was granted a gold crown and a portrait
in recognition for her works.

Tation the daughter of Straton was a Jewish benefactress. She built a
synagogue out of her own funds and was rewarded with a gold crown and
a front seat in the synagogue.[xiii] A person who was known as a *prostatis*
(female) or *prostates* (male) was an independently wealthy person who
funded others who were less well-off (usually those of their own ethnic
background). Some of these benefactors went on to become the president,
ruler, or high priest of their province or federation. *Prostatis/prostates* was
a function that belonged to the influential and ruling class. Opramoas was
a famous Lycian benefactor who served as both ruler (Lyciarch) and high
priest for the Lycian League or Federation of Lycia in Turkey, which was
at that time a province of Rome. Opramoas paid for the education of both

11. Alter, *Five Books*, 22.

boys and girls, provided widespread relief, endowed funeral funds, and gave dowries for young girls, among other things. Being a benefactor was usually a road to power.

However, Phoebe, Paul's associate, is usually called a "great help" in English—just like Eve. But how else are the words *boethos* (the Greek translation for *ezer* and the word used for Eve) and *prostatis* (the word used to describe Phoebe) used? In fact, in the early Christian Church, Clement of Rome recorded a prayer to Christ: "This is the way, beloved, in which we found our salvation; even Jesus Christ, the high priest of our oblations, the champion (*boethos*) and defender (*prostates*) of our weakness."[12]

When used to describe Christ, *boethos* (*ezer*) and *prostates* are translated as "champion" and "defender," not as "a help" and "a great help." Although these are the same words in Greek, most translators do not view them as appropriate ways to refer to women. There are a few exceptions: In the late 1800s, Joseph Rotherham produced an unusual and highly literal translation of the Bible called the *Emphasized Bible*. Rotherham's translation reads:[xiv]

> And I commend to you Phoebe our sister—being a minister [also] of the assembly which is in Cenchreae; In order that ye may give her welcome in the Lord in a manner worthy of the saints, and stand by her in any matter wherein she may have need of you; for, she also, hath proved to be a defender of many, and of my own self.[13]

In 1921, Helen Montgomery translated the same verses as follows:

> I commend to you our sister Phoebe, who is a minister of the church at Cenchrae. I beg you to give her a Christian welcome, as the saints should; and to assist her in any matter in which she may have need of you. For she herself has been made an overseer to many people, including myself.[14]

Women need to see themselves represented fairly in scripture. Unfortunately, we cannot assume that most popular Bible translations represent women fairly. I wish it were otherwise. Rotherham and Montgomery, both strong scholars, agree on this: that Phoebe was named a "deacon" or "minister" (*diakonos* in Greek) of the church of Cenchrae, and was not just a

---

12. Clement, *Epistle to the Corinthians*, 36:1.

13. Rom 16:1–2

14. Rom 16:1–2

servant. Phoebe was a wealthy and influential person, the carrier of Paul's letter, and a benefactor of many. Women need a Bible that presents women as they really are: as those who can be the benefactors of others. Women are not followers of men; like male benefactors, we are the benefactors of both men and women.

I am proud to live in Vancouver, where the Vancouver Foundation is one of the largest community funds in North America. The Vancouver Foundation was founded by a woman, is currently led by a woman, and receives substantial legacies from wealthy women.[xv] It is a fund for all, and has a particular focus on street-involved people. The Vancouver Foundation is a good example of who women were in the Bible and of who they are today—not followers and supporters of male-led efforts, but people who initiate, establish, and administer major projects. At least, this is who we *ought* to be as Christian women today.

CHAPTER 6

Her Mother's House

She will be the mother of nations; kings of peoples will come from her.

(GEN 17:16)

ONE OF THE MOST enduring themes in the Hebrew Bible is the conception and safe birth of a son to carry on the family line. The biblical text
abounds with fathers who have sons and myriad descendants. Women are
less frequently mentioned; this is the reality of a patriarchal society. The
genealogies are traced through the males, the family lives in the husband's
home locale, and the sons inherit. In the Hebrew Bible, sons create a nation
unto God, and men are simply mentioned more often than women. But
women are a vital part of the story.

Offspring do not come exclusively from the man, nor are most conceptions the result of a husband initiating intercourse with his wife. Language
has sometimes confused this issue with words that are "false friends"—
words in different languages that look as if they have the same meaning but
don't. One of these words occurs frequently in the King James Bible: the
word "seed." This word is translated into Greek as *sperma*, and into Latin
as *semen*. Men have seed, which refers not only to their physical emission,
but also to descendants. Men are promised descendants. It seems unlikely,
then, that the Bible would refer to a woman's seed.

This has led to one verse that refers to the "laying down of seed" being
somewhat rearranged. Heb 11:11 has been translated in the King James
Bible and in many other traditional translations as follows: "Through faith

also Sara herself received strength to conceive seed, and was delivered of a child when she was past age, because she judged him faithful who had promised."[1] Or, "By faith, even though Sarah herself was barren and he was too old, he received the ability to procreate, because he regarded the one who had given the promise to be trustworthy."[2]

When "he" is mentioned in this case, it refers to Abraham—because it must, presumably, be Abraham who has received the ability to procreate. In other words, some translations have inserted Abraham into the text because of the belief that a woman cannot "lay down seed." The case in Greek is puzzling: Although Sarah is the subject of the sentence, the verb preceding "seed" seems to refer to the male activity of "planting/laying down seed." Therefore, the NET Bible has reconfigured the verse to make Abraham the agent of the activity, whether begetting or procreating, rather than Sarah.

However, the Greek verb doesn't actually have to refer to either planting semen or begetting children as a father; it can also refer to the act of laying down the foundation of a nation of descendants. Some Bibles in other European languages have taken this option. For example, a Swedish Bible translates this into English as: "Through faith even Sara, even though too old, received power to become founding-mother for a descendant."[3]

Instead of assuming that the Greek verb refers to depositing semen, this phrase could mean that Sarah has laid the foundation for a nation of descendants. The Greek word *sperma* certainly refers to the descendants or offspring of women in the Hebrew Bible. In this case, Sarah would be recognized as a founding mother, the one who laid down the foundation.[xvi]

In the Hebrew Bible, Eve has "seed": "And I will put enmity between thee and the woman, and between thy seed and her seed; it shall bruise thy head, and thou shalt bruise his heel."[4]

And God promises Sarah "seed": "And the angel of the Lord said unto her, I will multiply thy seed exceedingly, that it shall not be numbered for multitude."[5]

---

1. Heb 11:11 (KJV)
2. Heb 11:11 (NET Bible)
3. Heb 11:11 (*Svenska*)
4. Gen 3:15
5. Gen 16:10

Rebekah was also to have "seed": "And they blessed Rebekah, and said unto her, Thou art our sister, be thou the mother of thousands of millions, and let thy seed possess the gate of those which hate them."[6]

In each of these cases, "seed" means descendants. Each of these women were promised descendants. Eve was promised a descendant who would crush the serpent, and Sarah and Rebekah were promised a nation of descendants.

There are other references to the seed of women, both good and bad, in the Hebrew Bible:

> And if the woman be not defiled, but be clean; then she shall be free, and shall conceive seed.[7]

> But draw near hither, ye sons of the sorceress, the seed of the adulterer and the whore.[8]

In a slightly different phrase, the Hebrew Bible says that Judah and Elkanah were "given seed," meaning a descendant, by Tamar and Hannah, respectively. Therefore, several women are established as the mothers of peoples, nations, or tribes. Eve was the mother of everyone living, Sarah and Rebekah were the mothers of all Israelites, and Tamar was especially important as the mother of the tribe of Judah, to which both David and Jesus belong. Tamar is mentioned in Jesus' genealogy along with Rahab, the mother of Boaz, and Ruth, the mother of Obed, the father of Jesse. Thus, Rahab and Ruth were direct ancestors of David.

Another aspect of these Hebrew narratives relating to conception is that the women were not passive. Leah told Jacob that she had bought him for the night; Ruth snuck under Boaz's blanket; Hannah wept, prayed, and argued; and Tamar disguised herself as a prostitute and slept with her father-in-law. Even after a son was born, the mother often had significant control over his future. Rebekah made sure that Isaac inherited, Ruth gave Obed to Naomi, and Hannah gave Samuel to the temple. In none of these cases does the father appear to have prior authority over his own son.

Occasionally too, we get a glimpse of women having their own homes. Women in the Bible do not always talk of their father's house; sometimes they mention their mother's house. Rebekah went to her mother's house

---

6. Gen 24:60
7. Num 5:27–29
8. Isa 57:2–4

64

before leaving to marry Isaac; she was then taken by Isaac into his mother Sarah's tent, which was vacant since Sarah had died. In this society, some women, although perhaps only the wealthy ones, had space allotted to them. These women were in charge of their own servants and belongings; they had a domain of authority.

Naomi tells her daughters-in-law to return to their mother's house, but Ruth declines in order to stay with Naomi. When biblical women talk among themselves, this is their normal manner of speech. Genealogies list the father's house, but among women, there is more flexibility. Some daughters deal directly with their fathers, as Achsah did when she asked for more land from her father Caleb.[9] Other women refer to their mother's house, as the lover does in the Song of Solomon.[10] Both male and female children interact with and appeal to the authority of both their mother and father. Jacob gained his birthright through the actions of his mother. Isaac also had his birthright reinforced when God told Abraham that he must obey Sarah and send Hagar and Ishmael away.

Some women gained their own property; for example, Achsah inherited a field, but was also able to negotiate with her father for land that had water available. The daughters of Zelophehad,[11] the daughters of Job,[12] and the wealthy Shunammite woman[13] who dwelt with her husband among her own people also inherited land from their father's family. One women was said to have built three towns:

> And the sons of Ephraim . . . Ezer, and Elead, whom the men of Gath *that were* born in *that* land slew, because they came down to take away their cattle. And Ephraim their father mourned many days, and his brethren came to comfort him. And when he went in to his wife, she conceived, and bare a son, and he called his name Beriah, because it went evil with his house. (And his daughter *was* Sherah, who built Bethhoron the nether, and the upper, and Uzzensherah.)[14]

In the Hebrew narrative, God placed certain women in the role of establishing a nation, tribe, town, or family; this was an acceptable role. If women

9. See Josh 15:16–19.
10. See Song 3:4 and 8:2.
11. See Num 27.
12. See Job 42:15.
13. See 2 Kgs 8:1–6.
14. 1 Chr 7:20–24

were so important in procreating, giving birth to a nation, and establishing the genealogy of King David and ultimately of Jesus, why are these women seldom referred to as our mothers or ancestors in the Bible? Where are the founding mothers in the text?

If we investigate the same phenomenon that we have reviewed in the other chapters regarding the masculine plural of words for people, we may be able to evaluate whether the Greek and Hebrew words translated so frequently as "fathers" may also refer to "mothers." Let us revisit Sarah—in this case, Sarah's funeral. Abraham was living among strangers and needed a place to bury Sarah. In acquiring a burial place for Sarah, Abraham was establishing a burial site for his own family that was independent of his origins. He and Sarah were the founders of a nation, and the progenitors of the nation of Israel. Abraham made a point of paying full price for a field with a cave, surrounded by trees, called the cave of Machpelah.[15] This site was near Hebron, where David was crowned king many centuries later. It was here that Sarah was buried, and Abraham wept. When Abraham died, his sons Isaac and Ishmael buried him alongside Sarah.[16] Isaac and Rebekah were also buried there, as was Leah.[17] Rachel had died near Bethlehem; although she was the great love of Jacob's life, he was not buried with her.

Here is the narrative of Jacob's death in the English Standard Version (ESV), and then again in the New Revised Standard Version (NRSV). Note that, in the first line of one translation, Jacob asks to be buried with his fathers, while in the other translation, he asks to be buried with his ancestors:

> ESV: "I am to be gathered to my people; bury me with my fathers in the cave that is in the field of Ephron the Hittite, in the cave that is in the field at Machpelah, to the east of Mamre, in the land of Canaan, which Abraham bought with the field from Ephron the Hittite to possess as a burying place. There they buried Abraham and Sarah his wife. There they buried Isaac and Rebekah his wife, and there I buried Leah—the field and the cave that is in it were bought from the Hittites." When Jacob finished commanding his sons, he drew up his feet into the bed and breathed his last and was gathered to his people.[18]

15. See Gen 23:3–20.
16. See Gen 25:9.
17. See Gen 49:29–32.
18. Gen 49:29–33 (ESV)

NRSV: "I am about to be gathered to my people. Bury me with my ancestors—in the cave in the field of Ephron the Hittite, in the cave in the field at Machpelah, near Mamre, in the land of Canaan, in the field that Abraham bought from Ephron the Hittite as a burial site. There Abraham and his wife Sarah were buried; there Isaac and his wife Rebekah were buried; and there I buried Leah—the field and the cave that is in it were purchased from the Hittites." When Jacob ended his charge to his sons, he drew up his feet into the bed, breathed his last, and was gathered to his people.[19]

Who is it that Jacob wants to be buried with? Is it really only his fathers, or is it the fathers *and mothers* in his family, Abraham and Sarah, Isaac and Rebekah, and his wife Leah? The Hebrew word for "father" is *ab*, and the plural is *avot*. Does *avot* always mean "fathers," or does it sometimes also mean "fathers and mothers"? Are "mothers" often intended to be included in the word *avot*? Perhaps all the kings of Israel, who are said to have "slept with their fathers," were actually buried in plots that included their mothers as well. Perhaps it would be just as true, and in line with what the author meant, if this phrase was translated "he slept with his ancestors."

Today, *avot* works both ways. It is sometimes used in a traditional way, such as in *pirkei avot*, which is translated as "Chapters of the Fathers." In Israel today, however, homes for the elderly are called *beit avot*—meaning "house of elders," in the sense of a retirement home. In fact, *avot* is the normal way to refer to one's ancestors, both male and female. The footnote in the Hebrew lexicon affirms that *avot* means "ancestors or founders," in case there were any doubt. Abraham and Sarah, and Isaac and Rebekah, and Jacob and Leah and Rachel were the founding ancestors of the nation of Israel.

The use of *avot* varies in the Hebrew Bible. The qualitative adjective "male" sometimes indicates that only male adults are referred to by the Hebrew word *avot*: "...by the house of their fathers, with the number of their names, every male by their polls."[20] In this case, *avot* is intended to refer to males only; however, the text also uses the adjective "male" to disambiguate and make it clear.

Here is another occurrence of *avot*: "And I brought your fathers out of Egypt: and ye came unto the sea; and the Egyptians pursued after your

19. Gen 49:29–33 (NRSV)
20. Num 1:2

fathers with chariots and horsemen unto the Red Sea."[21] Is it offensive if this passage were instead translated like this? "When I brought your ancestors out of Egypt, you came to the sea; and the Egyptians pursued your ancestors with chariots and horsemen to the Red Sea."[22]

Let's not forget the role of Miriam, who led a band of women singing and drumming on their hand drums, saying: "Sing ye to the Lord, for he hath triumphed gloriously; the horse and his rider hath he thrown into the sea."[23] We don't know if Miriam ever married and had children, but surely she was one of the ancestors, one of the foremothers of the nation of Israel.

This pattern continues in the New Testament, in John 6:21: "Our fathers did eat manna in the desert; as it is written, He gave them bread from heaven to eat."[24] Perhaps it should be understood that "our ancestors, both male and female" ate manna in the wilderness. "Ancestors" is used in both the NRSV and the 2011 New International Version (NIV). In Greek, the word used here is the plural of the Greek word for "father"—*pater*. The plural of *pater*, *pateres*, appears to be used to refer to a group of people including men, women and children—that is, the ancestors of the children of Israel. Although this might appear to be a false argument at first, in fact, the lexicon of classical Greek does list "ancestors" as one possible meaning of *pateres*.

This makes perfect sense when it comes to this verse: "By faith Moses, when he was born, was hid three months of his parents."[25] This verse also uses *pateres*, but nobody doubts that this word refers to Moses' parents— both his mother and his father. In fact, it was actually Moses' mother who proactively hid Moses, and it was Miriam and the princess of Egypt who ensured his survival.[26]

Every Bible translation committee must decide whether to translate into "the God of our fathers" or "the God of our ancestors." They must decide whether God made a covenant with the "fathers" or with the "ancestors." The Hebrew word *avot* and the Greek word *pateres* are ambiguous. In Hebrew, when exclusively male activities such as circumcision or readiness for battle are discussed, the adjective for "male" is often used to

21. Josh 24:6 (KJV)

22. Josh 24:6 (NRSV)

23. Exod 15:21 (KJV)

24. John 6:21 (KJV)

25. Heb 11:23

26. Exod 2:1–10

qualify words that were commonly used for "men"—whether *avot, banim,* or *anoshim.*

The English language has a set of words that are inclusive of men and women, such as "children" and "ancestors." It is not common English usage to call our parents of both sexes "fathers" or to call our children of both sexes "sons." And yet the Guidelines for Translation of Gender-Related Language in Scripture (also known as the Colorado Springs Guidelines, and referred to as such in this book)[27], which were drafted by Wayne Grudem and agreed upon in Colorado Springs at the Focus on the Family headquarters, specifies this: "'Father' (*pater, 'ab*) should not be changed to 'parent,' or 'fathers' to 'parents,' or 'ancestors.'"[28]

What this seems to mean is that *avot* and *pateres,* the plurals of *ab* and *pater,* cannot be translated as "parents" or "ancestors." Of course, the English Standard Version (ESV) does not suggest that Moses has two fathers, so it does indeed translate *pateres* as "parents"—but only in that one place, Heb 11:23. Both mother and father might act to protect a child, and that should be acknowledged, but usually the word *pateres* is reserved by the ESV to refer to "fathers" only. We are not made aware that this term *pateres* often refers to both parents, or to all our ancestors. Although the Greek lexicon includes the meaning "parents," the Colorado Springs Guidelines do not refer to or acknowledge any lexicons.

Once again, the Hebrew *avot* and the Greek *pateres* are ambiguous. Sometimes they refer to men lined up for battle, or to men inheriting land for their tribes and families. At other times, the *avot/pateres* are those who are rescued from Egypt, and clearly included men, women, and children. The *avot* are also those who pass on traditions or teachings to their children; above all, they are those with whom God has a covenant.

What does the Bible say about how traditions are passed on? Does God, in fact, instruct women to teach the Torah[29] to their children? "Hear, my child, your father's instruction, and do not reject your mother's teaching."[30] This verse puts the teaching of the father and the mother on an equal level. The word for "teaching" here is *torah,* the law. Mothers are to teach their

27. CBMW, "Guidelines." The Colorado Springs Guidelines can also be read online at http://www.bible-researcher.com/csguidelines.html or http://www.keptthefaith.org/docs/CSG.pdf.

28. CBMW, "Guidelines," B3.

29. I.e., the first five books of the Hebrew scriptures (the first five books of the Christian Bible as well)

30. Prov 1:8

children *torah*. Children, in return, are to obey their mothers equally with their fathers—there is no hierarchy here. A later warning states: "The eye that mocketh at his father, and despiseth to obey his mother, the ravens of the valley shall pick it out, and the young eagles shall eat it."[31] So the traditions that God's children are to follow are the traditions and teaching passed down by the fathers and mothers, not only the fathers. Paul said that he "...profited in the Jews' religion above many of my equals in mine own nation, being more exceedingly zealous of the traditions of my fathers."[32]

However, we know that Paul's companion, Timothy,[33] was instructed by his mother Eunice and his grandmother Lois; children in Paul's time were raised in the tradition and teaching of both their mothers and fathers. Perhaps Paul meant that he was zealous of the traditions of his *ancestors*, both mothers and fathers. This translation is found in the NRSV: "I advanced in Judaism beyond many among my people of the same age, for I was far more zealous for the traditions of my ancestors."[34]

Translating *avot* or *pateres* as "ancestors" instead of "fathers," and creating the phrases "traditions of our ancestors" or "faith of our ancestors," opens up space for both men and women to explore the faith of female ancestors. Both men and women should read not only the spiritual writings of the men in their tradition, but also the spiritual writings of women. They need to know the full tradition, not just the male-oriented tradition. Fortunately, many people are now working on recovering the writings of women in the church. This would be even more encouraging if we could read in the Bible of the traditions of our ancestors, with the understanding that this referred to the traditions and teaching of both mothers and fathers.

One remaining context for *avot* and *pateres* remains: This is with the word "covenant." Was God's covenant with Abraham, Isaac, and Jacob, or was it first with Abraham and Sarah, and then Isaac and Rebekah, and so on? On the one hand, the covenant was sealed with circumcision, a male ritual practice. On the other hand, God spoke directly to Sarah and Rebekah. These women did not hear God's words from their husbands, but directly from God. And God used their actions directly, without mediation by the male of the house, to fulfill His purposes. Sarah's and Rebekah's

---

31. Prov 30:17
32. Gal 1:14
33. See 1 and 2 Timothy.
34. Gal 1:14 (NRSV)

husbands did not have control or final decision-making authority over the blessings and inheritance of their sons Isaac and Jacob.

In addition, God changed Sarah's name as well as Abraham's.[35] God's promises were made directly to the descendants of Sarah and Rebekah, as well as to the descendants of Abraham and Isaac. The task of the women in the covenant was not circumcision, but childbirth, which was accomplished through faith in God.[36] God made a covenant with Abraham and Sarah, with Isaac and Rebekah, and with their descendants, the children of Israel, for all time. God swore this covenant to the *ancestors*.

Jewish women have been active for a long time in recovering the traditions and teachings of their foremothers, or female ancestors. One particular example is found in the life of Bertha Pappenheim, who is now considered to be the founder of social work among European Jews. Pappenheim was born in Vienna in 1859, and began her career as a social worker in Frankfurt, where she founded the league of Jewish Women in 1904. She worked with orphans, set up infant-feeding programs, set up schools for girls, and set up programs for prostitutes and unwed mothers; she also fought against sex slavery. Pappenheim strongly advocated an Orthodox Jewish faith-based education, but also an education that would prepare women for independence from men in adulthood. The women she worked with needed to be able to earn a living and become independent of abusive marriage and sex slavery.

True to her instincts, Pappenheim became a translator of the traditions and writings that she felt that Jewish women needed. She also taught at the Free Jewish House of Learning, which was run by Martin Buber and Franz Rosenzweig in Frankfurt, and was familiar with their work in translating the Hebrew Bible into German and developing an authentic Jewish literature in the German language.

First, Pappenheim translated Mary Wollstonecroft's revolutionary work from 1792, *A Vindication of the Rights of Woman*. She then went on to translate the *Tzena Urenah* from the 16th century, also known as the Yiddish Women's Bible. Although Pappenheim recognized that the *Tzena Urenah* was a modified version of the Hebrew Torah, it was the text that Jewish women had been raised on for several centuries. She wanted to be familiar with the texts that had inspired the moral and spiritual courage of her Jewish foremothers. She wanted the women around her to be aware that

35. Gen 17:15
36. 1 Tim 2:15

71

they were a part of a centuries-old heritage of Jewish women helping their families survive. Pappenheim also translated a selection of stories called *The Women's Talmud*. In addition, she wrote poetry, plays, and a novella, some under a male pseudonym.

Perhaps her most significant translation was that of the memoirs of Gluckel of Hameln, who may have been an ancestor of Pappenheim. The memoirs are the handwritten diary of a Jewish businesswoman who lived in Hamburg in the 17th century. Gluckel described her life as a widow and as a mother of fourteen children; she also ran a factory, traveled all over Europe for trade purposes, and managed her own accounts. Gluckel's memoirs afford a rare and unique glimpse into life in northern Germany in the 17th century. Unfortunately, later in life, after a period of financial success, Gluckel married again, and her husband lost both his fortune and his wife's.

Bertha Pappenheim wanted women to be fully trained in the Orthodox Jewish tradition, and to be familiar with the courage and enterprise of their foremothers. She wanted Jewish women to know that they had both economic power and spiritual influence in the family. She also wanted women to be educated in the feminist writings of modern women. Pappenheim wanted the Hebrew Bible, the Yiddish Bible, the history and traditions of her foremothers, and the teachings of modern feminism, to be available in German for the education of the prostitutes, rescued sex slaves, single mothers, and cast-off orphans she was responsible for.

Who was Bertha Pappenheim, and where did this tremendous drive come from? Where did she get the clarity and means to follow through on the needs of so many destitute young women? Born into a wealthy family in Vienna, Pappenheim was kept at home and was not allowed a university education like her brother. Whether for that reason or due to other circumstances in the home, she developed a mental disorder and was treated by Joseph Breuer, a colleague of Freud. Pappenheim became the patient, referred to as "Anna O.," who was the focus of one of the first published cases of psychoanalytic treatment. Was she cured by this treatment? She never referred to it for the rest of her life, although she expressed disapproval of the psychoanalytic process.

Bertha Pappenheim knew what it meant to be treated as a passive female who was expected to display nurturance and response, in contrast to men, who had agency and power. She wanted more for women, and dedicated her entire life to the rescue and rehabilitation of orphans, girls, and women for whom the traditional model of a patriarchal house and home had failed. Pappenheim was one of the pioneering Bible translators; she believed that educating women in the text and traditions of the foremothers was in keeping with the tenets of feminism.

CHAPTER 7

Worse than an Unbeliever

Anyone who does not provide for their relatives, and especially for their own household, has denied the faith and is worse than an unbeliever.

(1 TIM 5:8, NIV)

I HAVE A WIDE circle of women in my life: sisters, friends, colleagues, neighbors, and so on. When we get together, we sometimes talk about where you can still buy sewing notions, linen fabric, and other things that were a part of our past but are harder to find now. We depend on the Internet and on checking in with other women to find stores with the right yarns, fabrics, patterns, and paints. Sometimes we talk about herbs; sometimes we discuss whether cardinals are taking over the backyards of eastern North America. We share the latest book titles and discuss the economy.

But most of all, we share our concerns, commitments, and responsibilities for our families: our children, parents, and siblings. About half of the women in my circle are either single or are the primary breadwinners in their family, and most of us are approaching retirement. We have continuing commitments to provide for our families, both children and parents. In the most difficult of cases, I know some women who have not just one, but two children with significant disabilities. Looking down the road and planning for their care is just as pressing as dealing with them now. These children are young adults who would normally be out of the home by this point, but they remain dependent.

Some of us have children who are still in college or just getting settled in full-time employment; some of us have grandchildren, while others have parents who require increasing care. One friend, a lawyer, bought a house, renovated a basement apartment for herself, and had her parents move in upstairs. I called her on a Saturday morning recently to find that she was out helping her ex's ex, who is disabled by long-term alcoholism, to sort out her papers and get ongoing care set up. This friend also has a son with a disability, although he has been successful in getting a good education and now has a young family of his own. His mother paid for the specialized education he required. However, of all these amazing women, the one who sets the most powerful example is a retired nurse, a friend of a friend, who has taken in her ex-husband who is dying of cancer, and has committed to care for him for as long as necessary.

I can't compete with these women, although I too visit a financial planner, organize my banking, estimate what my kids will need to finish college, and so on and so forth. The fact is that we are all providers, even those who have not worked outside the home. Stay-at-home women are also involved in planning and keeping things going, and also must stay alert regarding family needs. So when we get together, the most important thing we talk about is the welfare of our family, and how we can organize ourselves to be competent providers as well as caregivers for the weaker members of our family, even into retirement. We know this responsibility belongs to us.

It's not that I don't honor men as providers, particularly those who plan the support of their families and organize their lives around it. I do see men who sacrifice or compromise the high points of their career for their families. But I see that although *both* men and women do this, men are more often recognized in the role of provider. To be most effective, providing is ideally a partnership undertaking, even though earning the primary wages often falls to one or the other of a couple. Later in life and moving towards retirement, death, divorce, illness, or unemployment often leave one person, whether the husband or the wife, as the primary provider. As adult human beings, we are all given the responsibility to provide, according to what has been given to us in terms of our own strength. We can't abdicate from this obligation just because we are women.

A couple of years ago, I visited a new mission church that was just getting established in the poorer end of town. The congregation was a mixture of young and old; most were single, and some had difficult backgrounds and lacked some of the niceties of life. I had heard that the young intellectual pastor, who had recently arrived from London, England, was doing a great job there. My son was happy to attend this church, and wanted me to come one Sunday—so I did. The sermon was on 1 Tim 5:8: "If anyone does not provide for his relatives, and especially for his immediate family, he has denied the faith and is worse than an unbeliever."[1]

The pastor chose his words carefully, pointing out that although this verse was addressed to men at the time that it was written, women are also providers now and are familiar with these responsibilities. He explained that this instruction now applied to everyone.

I was a little surprised. Yes, this preacher understood that this use of the masculine pronoun "he" represented women also. This is an example of the generic "he"—the use of the masculine pronoun to refer to both men and women. The pastor didn't say that it was only men, or even mainly men, who are to lead and provide. But why did he mention that this verse was addressed to men when it was written? There is no masculine noun in the Greek text for this verse. Greek has many terms of common gender, and here the word *tis* is used, which means "anyone": man or woman. Since a Greek verb does not require a pronoun, there are no pronouns in this verse or, in fact, in this chapter. There is no need for pronouns at all—it is a simple statement about looking after one's family.

Here is how 1 Tim 5:8 looks word by word from the Greek: "If anyone does not provide for the relatives, and especially for the immediate family, _____ has denied the faith and is worse than an unbeliever." I hope you can see the problem. No pronouns, no "he," no "his," and no "him." But that won't do in English, so the translator must supply English pronouns of some sort or other. In 1 Tim 3, for example, there are sixteen verses in the chapter, and only one pronoun (in the Greek), which is translated as "themselves." That's it. But in English, in a translation that insists on preserving the use of the masculine pronoun, there are ten masculine pronouns, with either "he" or "his" being added into the English text. These pronouns do not exist in the original language, although pronouns are a requirement of the English language.

It is imperative that translators use a translation method that enables readers, including educated readers, to truly understand the Bible in terms that come as close as possible to communicating the meaning of the original. If adding the pronoun "he" prevents readers and preachers from true understanding, as this episode showed, then translators have an obligation

1. 1 Tim 5:8 (NIV 1984)

to revise the translation: Where no gender is indicated in the Greek, there should be an inclusive English pronoun that refers equally to male and female. This level of care with the translation should not be optional—it should be the requirement of any translation that chooses to call itself a faithful or literal translation. Inclusive pronouns are an obligation to the original text and to the English reader.

Some Bibles have now moved in the direction of gender-inclusive language. This can be done in one of two ways: Either the entire passage can be made plural, or the word "anyone" can be used, along with the pronouns "they," "them," or "their." (For example, in everyday speech, one might say, "Would anyone like to ask a question? They can see me after the service.") This careful phrasing is now essential in order to guarantee that most English speakers will understand when a passage refers to both men and women. Many people read "he" in the Bible, assume that this is a reflection of the original inspired text, and proceed to construct their doctrinal thinking from this wording. Gender-inclusive language that best reflects the original text is essential to prevent this from happening.

These gender-inclusive Bibles are called "gender accurate" by those who use them. That is, these translations reflect the actual gender use of the original Greek. Some people also call these Bibles "gender neutral." Wayne Grudem and Vern Poythress, who wrote *The Gender-Neutral Bible Controversy*—a book that critiques Bibles moving in the direction of gender-inclusive language—claim:

> A search using Bible Works indicates that the words "he, him, his" occur 4,200 fewer times in the NRSV than the RSV. However, some of these preserve the singular sense of the verse by using the word "one" (this occurs 495 more times) and "someone, anyone, everyone" (264 more times). If we deduct for these, there are still 3,441 times where "he, him, his" are removed.[2]

It is difficult to tell what this calculation is supposed to mean; on the surface, it simply says that in places where English requires a pronoun, these two translations have supplied different pronouns in 4200 places. In the one case, the translation has supplied masculine pronouns that are not used in Greek; in the other case, the translation does something different—for example, it may supply the singular word "anyone" followed by "they" with a singular sense. The latter usage is known as the "singular they." It is used all the time, and is considered to be acceptable English usage. Alternatively,

---

2. Grudem and Poythress, *Gender-Neutral Bible Controversy*, 133.

the second translation may have shifted the phrase into the plural and used the gender-inclusive "they" to match the gender inclusivity of the Greek.

On a British Columbia ferry, I recently heard this announcement: "We have a set of car keys at the steward's desk. Whoever has lost his keys can come by and pick them up." A minute later, the same person rephrased the announcement: "Whoever has lost their keys can pick them up at the steward's desk." This simple clarification indicated that the keys might not belong to a man after all. The adjustment was intended to improve the listeners' understanding—nobody thought that the keys were the common property of a group of people. In a similar example, I have probably made the following announcement many times as a school teacher: "If a student does not bring in their signed permission form, they cannot go on the field trip." Or, I could have said: "If students do not bring in their signed permission form, they cannot go on the field trip."

Every student knows to bring in an individual permission form. There is no group permission form. Use of the plural does not confuse the issue at all. But imagine the furor if I had said: "If a student does not bring in his signed permission form, he cannot go on the field trip." The girls would want to know why they could not go on the field trip! I think there are many Christian women who want to know why some English Bibles don't invite us on any of the field trips.

In fact, there are several reasons why the Greek may not use a masculine pronoun when an English translation does. The first and most obvious reason is that the Greek simply does not use a pronoun in the same construction. A pronoun isn't necessary in Greek, but is necessary in English. The second reason is that there may be a Greek pronoun, but it might be neuter rather than masculine. For example, in Greek, a child is a *paidion*, which is the diminutive of the word *pais*. *Pais* is a common-gender word that refers to either a boy or a girl; its diminutive, *paidion*, is neuter, neither male nor female, but still referring to a child. When Jesus was a baby, he was a *paidion*, a little child. Here is a line that refers to Jesus: "Herod will seek the young child to destroy him."[3] However, the Greek literally says, "Herod will seek the young child to destroy *it*." Of course, the sex of the child is not at issue here. The word itself is neuter, so the pronoun must be grammatically neuter to match. However, translators are not required to translate the grammatical gender of a pronoun, as this is a feature of language structure

3. Matt 2:13

rather than a feature of meaning. Translators use an English pronoun according to the English rules for pronouns.

Here is another example: "And Jesus called a little child unto him, and set him in the midst of them."[4] We do not know if this child is a boy or a girl. The translators just made the assumption that it was a boy. However, the Greek indicates a neuter gender, so the gender is non-specified; it is simply a little child. Although the word used here is neuter, it can apply to someone who is clearly male (e.g., the baby Jesus), to a girl, or to an indefinite child who stands as an example of all children both male and female. In any case, there is no rule among translators to translate the grammatical gender of the words in Greek. Nobody has suggested that the original Greek neuter pronoun was inspired by God, and that Jesus must therefore be referred to as an "it" when he was a child.

The other person who is referred to in the Greek as neuter is the Holy Spirit. In John 14:16–17, four masculine pronouns are used for the Holy Spirit in most English translations. However, the Greek version contains only two pronouns referring to the Holy Spirit, and both are neuter. In the English translation, the neuter pronouns have been changed to masculine pronouns and two more masculine pronouns have been added:

> And I will ask the Father, and he will give you another advocate to help you and be with you forever—the Spirit of truth. The world cannot accept him, because it neither sees him nor knows him. But you know him, for he lives with you and will be in you.[5]

In Rom 8:26, the Spirit is again represented by a neuter pronoun in Greek and by "himself" in English: "We do not know what we ought to pray for, but the Spirit himself intercedes for us through wordless groans."[6]

In 1 Pet 1:11, although there is no pronoun for the Spirit in the original, predictably, a masculine pronoun is inserted in English: ". . . trying to find out the time and circumstances to which the Spirit of Christ in them was pointing when he predicted the sufferings of the Messiah and the glories that would follow."[7]

It may be difficult to find a suitable English alternative for these verses, and I am not suggesting that anything about these verses needs to

4. Matt 18:2

5. John 14:16–17 (NIV)

6. Rom 8:26 (NIV)

7. 1 Pet 1:11

be changed. However, I was very surprised to notice, when researching the verses for this chapter, that a great many masculine pronouns have been added in the English translation where there are none in Greek; and that where Greek pronouns do exist, other linguistic choices more faithful to the meaning of the original could have been found. The masculine pronoun in Greek does not appear in the Bible with anything close to the frequency with which the masculine pronouns "he," "him," "his," and "himself" appear in traditional English translations.

I cannot think of any good reason why someone would argue to preserve masculine pronouns that are merely a product of previous translations and are not related to the pronoun that is present in the original language. As I pointed out earlier, the use of a singular noun followed by "they" is perfectly understandable in English, and dates back several centuries. It is commonly used by schoolteachers to communicate with their students wherever English is spoken. The "singular they" is a proper way to communicate the indefinite structure of an original that lacks a pronoun or a gender assignment.

Another reason why an English translation might not use a masculine pronoun lies in the fact that many Greek nouns are common-gender nouns that can refer to either a man or a woman. The word *tis*, "someone," is of common gender, as are the nouns *anthropos* (human), *diakonos* (deacon), *pais* (child), and *apostolos* (apostle). If a common-gender noun is used to describe an indefinite person, even if it is preceded by a masculine article, the noun is still intended to represent both males and females in a general statement. Other expressions, such as "believer," fit in this category as well. The masculine article is a feature of Greek grammar, and grammatical gender is not usually translated.

Finally, there are many Greek words that differ only in their grammatical ending and that share the same plural and singular indefinite form; examples include words like *adelphos* (brother) and *adelphe* (sister). The singular masculine form may also be used to represent a generic representative for the purposes of a general instruction. The same is true for the word *aner*, which is normally translated as "man," but which can also be translated as a "person" or "one": "Blessed is the one (*aner*) whose sin the Lord will never count against them."[8]

In the verse above, Rom 4:8, the author (generally agreed to be Paul) is quoting Ps 32. In the Hebrew, the generic word *adam* is used in Ps 32; in

---

8. Rom 4:8

the Greek Septuagint translation, which Paul quotes here, the word *aner* is used. *Aner* usually refers to a man, but it sometimes refers to an individual who may be either male or female. Some translators do not recognize this usage and always translate *aner* as "man," with the accompanying masculine pronouns. But most people believe that this verse has always applied to both men and women.

The same thing happens in the book of James, where most people believe that verses such as the following refer to both men and women: "Blessed is the one who perseveres under trial because, having stood the test, that person will receive the crown of life that the Lord has promised to those who love him."[9]

Especially in the book of James, *aner* is now translated as "person" in some translations. It is difficult to imagine why the author would refer mainly to men, in days when women were martyrs as often as men, and it doesn't make sense that the female readers at the time were intended to think of themselves as being represented by the trials of men.

In summary, then, there are at least four different situations in which the English masculine pronoun has been dropped by gender-inclusive translations: In the first case, there was no pronoun in Greek to be translated. In the second case, a neuter Greek pronoun was present, which had been changed to a masculine pronoun in other English translations. In the third case, although a masculine pronoun was used in the Greek, it referred to a Greek noun of common gender. And in the fourth case, although a masculine Greek pronoun that referred to a grammatically masculine Greek noun was present, that noun was commonly understood in Greek to refer to humans in a generic sense.

Now let's return to the original verse in 1 Tim 5:8. Let's compare the version in the 1984 NIV with the revised NIV published in 2011:

> NIV (1984): If anyone does not provide for his relatives, and especially for his immediate family, he has denied the faith and is worse than an unbeliever.[10]

> NIV (2011): Anyone who does not provide for their relatives, and especially for their own household, has denied the faith and is worse than an unbeliever.[11]

9. Jas 1:12 (NIV)
10. 1 Tim 5:8 (NIV, 1984)
11. 1 Tim 5:8 (NIV, 2011)

The second version is considered to be inaccurate by authors such as Poythress and Grudem, who publicize statistics about the use of "their" instead of "his" in their book critiquing gender-neutral Bibles, titled *The Gender-Neutral Bible Controversy*. This book included five chapters on the masculine pronoun. Here are a few representative statements:

> "He" includes both men and women, but does so using a male example as a pictorial starting point. In a subtle way, this use brings along with it an unequal prominence to men and women. Thus feminism attacks it as "unfair."[12]

Here, Poythress and Grudem argue that readers and listeners will envision a male example when they hear a masculine pronoun. However, they also write:

> And if university students cannot understand generic "he" in an ancient document like the Bible, how then will they understand Thomas Paine, or Abraham Lincoln, or anything written in the history of the world before language police began to dominate our universities in the 1970s?[13]
>
> In sum, native speakers of English have the linguistic ability to understand generic "he." ... no one can abolish this ability to understand and use generic "he." This ability is deep. It belongs to human beings who use language.
>
> Yet some defenders of gender-neutral Bible are apparently convinced that generic "he" will not be understood by Bible readers today.[14]

I am among those who seriously doubt that human beings have the ability to understand the generic "he"; in fact, Poythress and Grudem themselves seem to doubt this ability in the first of these three quotes, and I will soon demonstrate why. These authors then conclude:

> Finally, we must remember that our actual focus is Bible translation. How can we test whether people understand a Bible translation? The most relevant "experiment" of all would be to circulate among Christians, who are the primary people who actually read the Bible and pay attention to the Bible's intended context.[15]

---

12. Grudem and Poythress, *Gender Neutral Bible Controversy*, 145.

13. Grudem and Poythress, *Gender Neutral Bible Controversy*, 179

14. Grudem and Poythress, *Gender Neutral Bible Controversy*, 205

15. Grudem and Poythress, *Gender Neutral Bible Controversy*, 221

This is more or less what I did when I listened to the sermon on 1 Tim 5:8, as described at the start of this chapter. I wondered if this preacher's slip was just an individual case. Surely other preachers understand that just because there is a "he" and "his" in English, it does not mean that there is a masculine form in Greek and that the main provider in 1 Tim 5:8 is a male.

In any case, Poythress and Grudem are members of the Council on Biblical Manhood and Womanhood (CBMW), so I decided to see how many of the men who preach and write for this organization understand that 1 Tim 5:8 generically refers to both men and women. These are some of my findings:

> 1 Timothy 5:8: "But if anyone does not provide for his own, and especially for those of his household, he has denied the faith and is worse than an unbeliever." This is a key text. Men, not women, have the responsibility to provide for their wives and children. (Owen Strachan, president of CBMW)[16]

> Men still have to lead in provision. "[I]f anyone does not provide for his relatives, and especially for members of his household, he has denied the faith and is worse than an unbeliever" Paul wrote in 1 Timothy 5:8. Men bear the responsibility of providing—of knowing where the house payment, the groceries and other provisions are going to come from. (Randy Stinson, former executive director of CBMW)[17]

> As a man, the revelation that I am called by God to lead my family is weighty. In fact, Paul tells Timothy that "if anyone does not provide for his relatives, and especially for members of his household, he has denied the faith and is worse than an unbeliever" (1 Tim. 5:8). (Brandon Smith, associate editor of CBMW)[18]

> Christian men are called to provide for their families. Paul uses some of the strongest language in the New Testament to warn those who do not provide: "But if any man does not provide for his own, and especially for those of his household, he has denied the faith and is worse than an unbeliever" (1 Timothy 5:8). (J. D. Gunter, writer on the CBMW.org site)[19]

16. Strachan, "Biblical Support."
17. Stinson and Dumas, *Guide*, 221.
18. Smith, "4 Lessons."
19. Gunter, "Men as Providers."

What about men who are seminary professors and leaders? Here are quotations from some prominent scholars and leaders:

> We understand that men were made for work, and that a man's responsibility is to care and provide for his wife and family. As the Apostle Paul wrote to Timothy: But if anyone does not provide for his relatives, and especially for members of his household, he has denied the faith and is worse than an unbeliever. [1 Timothy 5:8] Thus, the Christian worldview sees work as a man's assignment. (Al Mohler, president of the Southern Baptist Theological Seminary)[20]

> First Timothy 5:8 says if a man does not provide for his own, that is his own household, he has denied the faith and is worse than an unbeliever. (Daniel Akin, president of Southeastern Baptist Seminary)[21]

> The headship of men in the church and home is rooted everywhere in scripture in protection and provision. This is why the Apostle Paul calls the man who will not provide for his family "worse than an unbeliever" (1 Tim 5:8 ESV). (Russell Moore, head of the Ethics and Religious Liberty Committee)[22]

Mark Driscoll, John MacArthur, Dennis Rainey, and many others share this understanding of 1 Tim 5:8.[xvii] Some women have also accepted this interpretation:

> "But if anyone does not provide for his own, and especially for those of his household, he has denied the faith, and is worse than an unbeliever." (1 Tim 5:8)

> God's Word clearly states that men are to be the providers and the protectors. Women love being provided for and protected. It is the man's responsibility to provide for the family. (Jaye Martin)[23]

Do these men and women realize that there are no masculine pronouns in the original language of this passage, and that "he" is added into the English but is only to be understood in a "generic" sense? Evidently not!

---

20. Mohler, "Men Not at Work."

21. Akin, *Exalting Jesus*, 79.

22. Moore, "Guest Editorial," 4.

23. Martin, "Marks," 17.

The following explanation of this passage was written by Richard Strauss, a respected Bible scholar with a doctorate in theology from the Dallas Theological Seminary:

> Dad must take the lead. But what is involved in properly managing a family? For one thing it means taking the lead in providing physical necessities, such as food, clothing, shelter, and medical care. Paul used masculine pronouns in referring to these kinds of things when he said, "If anyone does not provide for his relatives, and especially for his immediate family, he has denied the faith and is worse than an unbeliever" (1 Tim. 5:8, NIV).[24]

Here, Strauss expresses his conviction that the masculine pronouns in the English text were based on masculine pronouns in the Greek text, and that they explicitly communicated that God intended that a male subject was to be understood by the reader. However, Paul did not use masculine pronouns.

Despite the claims of Grudem and Poythress, it is clear that prominent native speakers of English, including university students, university graduates, doctors of theology, presidents of seminaries, and directors of CBMW both past and present, do not understand the generic "he" in all contexts. In fact, it is worse than that. All of the people quoted above seem to believe that the Greek contains masculine pronouns, and that these are reflected by the English use of the masculine. They do not derive their doctrine from the Greek New Testament, but from a masculinized English translation. All these men and women derive at least part of their belief in male headship from this verse. Not only do they misunderstand the verse; they go so far as to develop a theology and practice from their misunderstanding. They then go on to spread their conviction that man is the provider, based on a false assumption.

Does Grudem think that there are masculine pronouns in the original Greek? Apparently not; he writes:

> Biblical support for the husband having the primary responsibility to provide for his family and the wife having primary responsibility to care for the household and children is found in Genesis 2:15 with 2:18-23; 3:16-17 ... 1 Timothy 5:8 (the Greek text does not specify "any man," but in the historical context that would have been the assumed referent except for unusual situations like a household with no father); ... I believe that a wife's created role as

24. Strauss, "Dad's Many Hats."

a "helper fit for him" (Gen. 2:18) also supports this distinction of roles. I do not think a wife would be fulfilling her role as "helper" if she became the permanent primary breadwinner, for then the husband would be the primary "helper."[25]

Grudem does not discuss the fact that one of the meanings of "helper" in Hebrew and Greek is "sustainer" or "rescuer," which would correspond well with "provider." The expression "helper fit for him" cannot be used by itself to support the notion that women do not provide. Even God's words to Adam about tilling the soil cannot be restricted to men, since women have always worked side by side with men to feed their families. It is also somewhat surprising that the authors resort to "historical context." Context for the passage in 1 Tim 5 is provided in verse 16: "If any believing woman has relatives who are widows, let her care for them."[26]

In his Latin translation of the New Testament, Erasmus used a grammatically feminine pronoun in 1 Tim 5:8. However, Calvin responded in his commentary on this passage:

> Erasmus has translated it, "If any woman do not provide for her own," making it apply exclusively to females. But I prefer to view it as a general statement; for it is customary with Paul, even when he is treating of some particular subject, to deduce arguments from general principles, and, on the other hand, to draw from particular statements a universal doctrine. And certainly it will have greater weight, if it apply both to men and to women.[27]

Erasmus and Calvin were working from the Greek, so they clearly noticed that this verse lacked any masculine markers. Calvin's commentaries are available in English, so it would not be difficult for any preacher to consult this commentary and see that for Erasmus and Calvin, the debate was between the *feminine* gender and a generic application. Nonetheless, the generic pattern of 1 Tim 5:8 seems to be obscure to many. Many Christian leaders do not read a passage in Greek before teaching it, and many of those who call themselves Calvinists do not read Calvin's commentaries, despite the widespread availability of the Greek New Testament and of Calvin's commentary. However, Poythress and Grudem say:

25. Grudem, *Evangelical Feminism*, 44.

26. 1 Tim 5:16

27. Calvin, *Commentaries*, 126.

> . . . it is simply untrue that generic "he" and similar masculine language "restricted or obscured *the meaning of the original text*." And it would be misleading to suggest that such "bias toward the masculine gender" was a problem for English that did not exist in Hebrew and Greek.[28]

In fact, it is clear that the English translation, which supplies so many masculine pronouns that are not present in the Greek text, does in fact create a "bias toward the masculine gender." This bias gives the translators of gender-inclusive Bibles more than adequate justification for attempting to eliminate masculine pronouns in English where there are none in Greek. For the men and women cited above, the presence of a masculine pronoun in English does not communicate a generic sense, but inaccurately signals that a male is the intended subject of the passage. Remember, Poythress and Grudem wrote: "In sum, native speakers of English have the linguistic ability to understand generic 'he.' ... no one can abolish this ability to understand and use generic 'he.' This ability is deep. It belongs to human beings who use language."[29]

But the ability to understand the generic "he" has already been damaged. People decide for themselves, according to the assumptions that they bring to a passage, whether the "he" pronoun is generic or not. For example, if a passage refers to salvation, most people obviously assume that it is a generic reference. However, if the passage refers to teaching, governance, or family leadership, many people assume that "he" refers to a male. This is regardless of the fact that there is no masculine reference in the Greek text. The context itself determines how much readers supply from their own preconceptions. These preconceptions, however, come from a reader's worldview; they do not provide valid contextual information for interpreting the Bible.

It is the responsibility of a Bible translator to render the translation comprehensible to preachers, seminary presidents, university students, and to "human beings who use language," especially those who are native speakers of the language. How is it that Grudem, as the editor of the English Standard Version (ESV), and as an author of the guideline that the generic "he" must be retained, did not field-test his translation—among his fellow members and directors of CBMW, at the very least? Since these people have clearly demonstrated that they do not understand the generic

---

28. Poythress and Grudem, *Gender-Neutral Bible Controversy*, 153.

29. Poythress and Grudem, *Gender-Neutral Bible Controversy*, 145.

"he," it should not be used. This is the reason why we must have Bibles with inclusive language.

One of the major concerns with the role of provider being applied to men only, or even predominantly to men, is that it skews our reading of the Bible and our understanding of many stories in the Bible. Women providers are present in the Hebrew Bible, the Christian scriptures, and the early church, as well as throughout church history. It is not only in our time period that women have contributed in very pragmatic and financial ways to the life of the family, the church, and society in general.[xviii]

In the Hebrew Bible, various women cared for Moses: his mother, his sister, and the princess of Egypt. Rahab[30] and the Shunammite woman[31] provided for others, as did the woman in Prov 31. Throughout Miriam's life, she stood beside her brother, Moses, as a co-leader and advisor along with Aaron. We don't know what specific acts Miriam performed, other than watching over Moses as a baby. However, supporting Moses appears to have become a lifelong habit for her.

As discussed further in chapter 8, Rahab was clearly the head of her household and in a position to represent her family and negotiate their survival during the Israelite invasion. Did her financial position as either innkeeper or prostitute enable her to feed and make decisions for her family? It appears so. The unnamed woman living in Shunem decided to prepare a furnished room for the prophet Elisha. Even though she was married, two reasons suggest why she was able to act as the head of the household: First, she was a wealthy woman; and second, she lived among her own people rather than with her husband's relatives. These circumstances suggest that she had inherited property and wealth from her parents and was able to provide for her husband. There is no negative spiritual evaluation of her ability to act on her own initiative and provide for a prophet.

The woman of Proverbs 31 undertakes all the material work to provide for her family. Her husband sits in the gates of the city as an elder or judge. Although he is not paid for this work, he can undertake it because he is wealthy and supported by his estates and business. However, it is his wife who runs the family businesses and takes charge of the servants. She provides food and shelter, so that he can live the life of a respected and financially independent city councilor. This tradition has survived over the centuries and is still common in certain Jewish communities: The wife

30. See Josh 2.

31. 2 Kgs 4:8

obtains professional training and becomes a teacher or takes on another career that will bring in sufficient income for the household, while the husband studies the Torah full time.

Although many of us would not consider this situation to be ideal, the Hebrew scripture does suggest this pattern, and acting in this way does not run counter to any command of scripture. Nowhere in the Bible does it explicitly say that all men must be the main providers in their marriage—much as some might wish it.

In the Christian scriptures, the Gospels, the Acts, and the Epistles indicate that women provided for men. Joanna, Susanna, and many others provided for Jesus and the disciples out of their own wealth. Paul continues this pattern: He lives with Priscilla and her husband, Aquila, is rescued and cared for by Lydia, and is helped and supported by Phoebe, his patroness. Clearly, these women had control of resources that they used to provide for Paul. One of the patterns that emerges here is that women provided for celibate or widowed male leaders.

In the early church, women (mostly wealthy widows) supported many of the church fathers. We would not have the scholarship and writings of these scholars today if they had not been under the patronage of powerful and wealthy independent women. Origen had his education paid for by a woman; later in his life, female patronage enabled him to continue the life of a scholar, and to acquire the manuscripts and resources he needed for his work.

Jerome's translation of the Bible from Hebrew into Latin in the 4th century became the standard Bible of Western Europe for twelve centuries and more. However, the wealthy young widow Paula provided for Jerome, setting up a convent in Jerusalem with at least fifty women, as well as a hostel for men. In the words of Nancy Hardesty:

> Paula not only paid his living expenses, she also gathered and purchased the expensive manuscripts and supplies needed for his work. Within her convents, she and the other women copied manuscripts by hand in order to facilitate their use and to preserve them.[32]

Olympias was another wealthy widow who provided for Chrysostom in every detail of his life, including basic food and shelter; she also discussed church matters with him when he was a bishop. Melania, another widow,

32. Hardesty, "Paula."

supported Rufinus, who translated the works of Origen into Latin. Some of the best and most prolific church fathers were provided for materially by women and continued intellectual relationships—often lifelong—with the women who supported them. These women themselves were educated in Greek and Hebrew and were well able to discuss theological matters and to have their opinions heard and valued.

Another member of the group of elite women in Rome who studied Greek and Hebrew was Fabiola. She was married to an abusive husband, and negotiated a divorce according to Roman law. Fabiola then married a man she loved and was excommunicated from the church. When he died, Fabiola did penance for her sin of adultery, in living with a second husband while the first one lived, and was received back into the church. She then built a hospital in Rome, the first public hospital in Western Europe, with a nursing home beside it. Fabiola worked with the patients, cared for the worst cases, and later built a pilgrim's hostel. She went to Bethlehem to take up a reflective life with Paula and Jerome, but returned within a year. Her legacy demonstrates that she was a woman of action and compassion; she spent her energy where she saw it was needed, in providing for the poor.

From the time of the Hebrew scriptures to the early church in Rome, women have been providers for men who were prophets, preachers, scholars, and translators. How different would church history be without the provision of these women? Overlooking or diminishing the providing role of women discredits all the women who, throughout history, sacrificed their own wealth and denied themselves not only the comforts but the necessities of life in order to provide for others. Let us celebrate women as the providers they truly are.

Section 3

Gender Terms

CHAPTER 8

Rahab's Sisters

Give me a sure sign that you will spare the lives
of my father and mother, my brothers and sisters.

(JOSH 2:12–13, NIV)

RAHAB'S SISTERS ARE EXPLICITLY mentioned only once in the Bible. In Josh 2, Joshua sends two spies to check out Jericho for the Israelites; they stay at the home of Rahab, a prostitute (or innkeeper, depending on your linguistic leanings) living in the wall of Jericho. Rahab realizes that Jericho is about to be besieged by a stronger force. She asks the two Israelite spies staying overnight in her house if she can be saved, along with her father, mother, brothers, and sisters, and everything belonging to her.

This used to puzzle me—the idea of someone living in a wall—but now I have explored many ancient hill-towns and walked through houses built into constructed rock walls, or even rooms carved into a foundation of solid rock. Rahab's windows must have looked out on the valley below. She was able to let the spies down by a rope, and then communicate with them later, by hanging a scarlet cord out of her window.

While the spies stayed in Rahab's house, she hid them from the soldiers of the king of Jericho. Rahab knew that the Israelites might win this siege, so she saw an opportunity to save her family by bargaining with the spies. She would ensure their safety if they, in turn, would ensure the safety of her whole family. Rahab acted as the representative and protector of her family, since she was in a position to make a deal with the spies. So Rahab asked for a pledge from the spies:

> Now then, please swear to me by the Lord that, as I have dealt kindly with you, you also will deal kindly with my father's house, and give me a sure sign that you will save alive my father and mother, my brothers and sisters, and all who belong to them, and deliver our lives from death.[1]

Rahab asked the spies to save her father, *av*, her mother, *em*, her brothers, *achim*, and sisters, *achayot*. The expression "all who belong to them" could refer to servants, animals, or belongings, since Hebrew does not use the word "who." The men responded:

> Behold, when we come into the land, you shall tie this scarlet cord in the window through which you let us down, and you shall gather into your house your father and mother, your brothers, and all your father's household.[2]

What about the sisters? Are the sisters included in the father's household? Here is the narration of the events after the attack on Jericho:

> So the young men who had been spies went in and brought out Rahab and her father and mother and brothers and all that belonged to her. And they brought all her relatives and put them outside the camp of Israel.[3]

Are Rahab's sisters part of "all her relatives?" The Hebrew word *mishpocha*, which is translated as "all her relatives," refers to the extended family network, rather than to siblings.

What has happened in the language of this narrative? We can probably rule out the notion that the spies refused to save her sisters. But if "sisters" were naturally included in her "father's house" or in the term "brothers," why did Rahab feel the need to mention them in the first place? The expression, "her father's household" is later dropped, so the "sisters" do not seem to be included in that term.

A more likely possibility is that even though Rahab knew that the Hebrew word *achim*, "brothers," included "sisters," she mentioned her sisters specifically, using the word *achayot*, in order to make sure that they would

---

1. Josh 2:12–13
2. Josh 2:18
3. Josh 6:23

94

be included without ambiguity. In this emergency, Rahab wanted to be completely sure everyone was included, so she emphasized the inclusion of her sisters. It is also possible that Rahab was using a typically female manner of speech, in which brothers and sisters are named separately, as *achim* and *achayot,* rather than collectively or inclusively as the men did, as *achim.* In any case, Rahab was told that her *achim* would be saved, as well as "all that belonged to her."

Here, the most likely answer to the disappearance of the word *achayot,* "sisters," is that *achim,* the plural of the Hebrew word for "brother," is ambiguous, and can equally refer to "brothers," or to "brothers and sisters." Rahab used both *achim* and *achayot,* but the spies used only *achim* in their answer; still, the spies were pledging to save exactly the same people Rahab had listed. Although Rahab used two words, *achim* and *achayot,* it does not mean that *achim* by itself cannot be used to refer to both brothers and sisters. In fact, Rahab's story shows that *achim,* the Hebrew word that we might interpret as "brothers only" can also refer to "brothers and sisters."

This pattern of using the masculine plural form of a word to include both men and women exists in some European languages as well. In Spanish, *hermanos* means brothers, but also means brothers and sisters. That is, *hermanos* is the plural of *hermano* (brother) and *hermanas* is the plural of *hermana* (sister); but *hermanos,* the masculine plural, also refers to both sets of people. In Rahab's case, *achim* by itself must have included the same people as the longer expression, *achim* and *achayot.* Surely Rahab would have protested and bartered further if her sisters had not been included in the spies' promise!

Using the masculine plural to refer to a group of mixed gender was a common practice in Greek and Hebrew. *Av,* the plural of "father," could refer to either "fathers" (i.e., ancestors) or "parents" (i.e., the mother and father). *Banim,* the plural of "son" (*ben*), could also refer to all of one's children, both male and female. This usage is an established pattern in both Hebrew and Greek, even though Greek and Hebrew did have other words for children.

This pattern suggests that the Hebrew word *achim* has at least two meanings: "brothers" and "brothers and sisters." This makes the meaning of the term ambiguous, so the reader has to assess from the context whether sisters are included or not. It is usually pretty clear. If only men are mentioned, the word refers to men only, and means "brothers." If both men and women are mentioned, the word probably means "brothers and sisters." *Achim* can also extend to mean the entire tribe, ethnic group, or faith community.

In the Hebrew Bible, the word *achim* usually refers to men only. Women are mentioned when they have an important role to play; otherwise, they are relatively invisible in the text. This practice reflects the patriarchy of an ancient society. In the New Testament, however, the Greek word *adelphoi*, which is the plural of *adelphos* (brother), was used to include both men and women in the church. We know this because the text often includes the names of women in nearby verses—Chloe, Nymphas, Lydia, Prisca, and Lydia are a few of the prominent women named in this way. The Greek word *adelphoi* did not exclude women, but rather included them.

In the Gospel narratives, Jesus alternates between using "brothers and sisters" (*adelphoi* and *adelphai*), and just "brothers" (*adelphoi*). Here are two sermons where Jesus gives similar teaching, but excludes the word *adelphai* (sisters) the second time. Does Jesus intend to exclude women in the second teaching?

> If anyone comes to me and does not hate his own father and mother and wife and children and brothers and sisters [*adelphoi* and *adelphai*], yes, and even his own life, he cannot be my disciple.[4]

> And he said to them, "Truly, I say to you, there is no one who has left house or wife or brothers [*adelphoi*] or parents or children, for the sake of the kingdom of God, who will not receive many times more in this time, and in the age to come eternal life."[5]

It seems unlikely that Jesus has shifted his position on "sisters," and is now deliberately excluding them. It is more likely that he is using the typical linguistic pattern of a masculine plural that includes both masculine and feminine. That is, the word *adelphoi* (brothers) and the phrase *adelphoi* and *adelphai* (brothers and sisters) can have the same meaning. Therefore, given the context, even when using *adelphoi*, Jesus is referring to both brothers and sisters. The question is whether we can support this gender ambiguity in English.

In classical Greek, *adelphoi* has many uses: It refers to "the males in a family," "siblings," "family members," "members of the same ethnic community," or "members of a guild or community."[xix] *Adelphoi* can also refer to a brother and a sister pair. For example, the *theoi adelphoi* are the sibling

---

4. Luke 14:26 (ESV)

5. Luke 18:29 (ESV)

gods, female and male, in the Ptolemaic dynasty: Arsinoë and Ptolemy II, Berenice and Ptolemy III, and (later in that same family line) Cleopatra and Ptolemy XIII. All these pairs are called *adelphoi*, but are clearly "brother and sister," not just "brothers." Electra and Orestes, a brother and sister in a classical Greek play by Euripides, are also called *adelphoi*.[xx]

In the New Testament, the term *adelphoi* is sometimes used to address men only, such as with regard to circumcision; however, it is more often used to address the entire community of Christians. *Adelphoi* is also used in Acts 7:23 to refer to the people of Israel. Referring to Moses, the English Standard Version (ESV) translates: "When he was forty years old, it came into his heart to visit his brothers, the children of Israel." However, the New International Version (NIV) 2011 translates this as: "When Moses was forty years old, he decided to visit his own people, the Israelites." Here, it is clear who the text refers to: Moses' people, the Israelites. The Israelites are not all his "brothers," but they are all his people. In Hebrew, *achim* was used to refer to one's own ethnic people, and "brothers" is still used among some groups today to refer to ethnicity. However, using "brothers" to refer to a group of people is not common in English, other than in very specific contexts.

Given this evidence, all major lexicons (biblical dictionaries) define the plural of *adelphos* as including "brothers and sisters" and "compatriots." The ancient Greek lexicon published by Liddell and Scott in 1869 defined *adelphos* in this way, as do the revisions of that work. Modern copies of Bauer's *Greek-English Lexicon of the New Testament and other Early Christian Literature* (also known as BDAG) do so as well. In fact, BDAG states: "there is no doubt that *adelphoi* = brothers and sisters."[xxi]

Throughout the history of the study and classification of ancient Greek, scholars have always known that one meaning of *adelphoi* was "brothers and sisters." However, this was not an issue for translation, since the word "brethren," a potentially inclusive word, was used in English translations. I was raised in the Plymouth Brethren, and the phrase, "I am Brethren," would rise quickly to my tongue with no sense that I was saying something out of the way in English. I, as a female, was firmly Brethren.

But I was clearly not a brother, nor could I ever become one. Brothers could speak in church, sometimes beginning at the age of sixteen, although they would not be asked to join a "Brothers' Meeting" until they were older. A sister, however, could never speak in church. The "brothers," men only, were invited to Brothers' Meetings, where the business of the assembly was determined. I am confident that no woman in the history of our assembly ever attended a Brothers' Meeting. It would have been unthinkable and truly inconceivable. Women weren't allowed to talk in any meeting of mixed men and women, and we did not attend meetings where business was undertaken. Although "Brethren" was a term of inclusion in our faith community, it was also tied to the silence of women.

However, the word "brethren" did indicate inclusion in terms of identity and social belonging, within a group in which there was (at least theoretically) no hierarchy in the ministry. The general term Brethren included faith communities who had left their state churches, such as Moravian and Mennonite Brethren; it also included the Plymouth Brethren, the Anabaptists, and those of the Pietist movement. At one time, Brethren was a common term for dissenting Christian groups. In these communities, Brethren functioned as a word that included women, while "brothers" was a term of exclusion in every sense of the word. There was no ambiguity to the term "brothers." Women were not included.

As an aside, let me mention that in those days, in our tradition, there were no such things as "Women's Meetings"—perhaps because a Women's Meeting would give women the opportunity to gossip. Although this may sound draconian, in fact, women had plenty of opportunities to "meet," both by themselves and with men. The dining room table was the domain of women, and a lively exchange was always entered into, in which men and women had equal voice. I wonder if many of the things brought up at the Brothers' Meetings were not already discussed and settled at the dining room table. Nevertheless, although we could reside over a dining room table as women, we knew that we were not and never would be "brothers."

Today, those remnants of the Victorian era, with the old-world Brethren and the influence of the dining room table and afternoon tea, have largely gone. The word "brethren" has been erased from all modern Bibles. At first, it was replaced by the bald and exclusionary word "brothers." Women were told that they must now consider themselves included in the word "brothers" in any scripture passage referring to our heavenly destination; but on earth, we are restricted from participating in the role of "brothers." Women must not consider themselves included in scripture passages that apply to the roles of men—teaching, instructing, managing, and so on—even though the word *adelphoi* may be present. Women are only *adelphoi* in certain contexts.

In the last decade of the 20th century, given the limitations of the word "brothers," Bibles began to be published that included the phrase "brothers and sisters." Rather than returning to the blurry ambiguity of the word "brethren," which had once functioned well to describe either "brothers" or an entire group of men and women, this brave new unambiguous term, "brothers and sisters," was put into use. The difficulty is that "brothers" strictly excludes women, and "brothers and sisters" strictly includes women. In abandoning "brethren," English no longer has a dual-function word like the Greek *adelphoi* and the Hebrew *achim*. Bible translators must choose one side or the other of this barbed wire fence. There is no easy answer.

A similar linguistic situation occurs a few times in the Bible. In such cases, the single male term *adelphos* seems to refer to a member of the faith community in a generic sense. The plural of the word for "brother," *adelphoi,* can mean "fellow believers," and the single masculine word, *adelphos,* here refers to a generic fellow believer, whether male or female. In order to avoid any confusion created by implying that women are excluded from certain moral responsibilities, some Bible translations, like the NIV 2011, translate the masculine, *adelphos,* as "brother or sister" in such cases.

Here is some history on this difficult transition: In 1996, an updated revision of the very popular NIV, called the NIV Inclusive, was published in England. It used "brothers and sisters" for *adelphoi,* among many other changes. By late May 1997, a group of twelve North American Christian leaders met with James Dobson of Focus on the Family in Colorado Springs, as described earlier in this book, to agree upon a list of guidelines for gender terms in English Bible translations. This was done in order to address what they saw as the problem of Bibles that used "brothers and sisters"—as well as other female-inclusive words such as "children" and "ancestors"— becoming widely accepted by evangelical churches. This group of leaders wanted publishers and booksellers to adhere to certain standards that restricted the use of inclusive terms such as "brothers and sisters." One of the terms of the Colorado Springs Guidelines read: "'Brother' (*adelphos*) and 'brothers' (*adelphoi*) should not be changed to 'brother(s) and sister(s).'"[6,xxii]

No rationale or references to sources were given, so there is no certainty that lexicons of ancient and early Christian Greek literature were consulted when drafting these guidelines. In fact, in September 1997, this particular guideline was changed as follows: "'Brother' (*adelphos*) should

---

6. Original reading of Guideline B1 from the June 2, 1997 draft

not be changed to 'brother or sister'; however, the plural *adelphoi* can be translated 'brothers and sisters' where the context makes clear that the author is referring to both men and women."[7]

In *The TNIV and the Gender-Neutral Bible Controversy*, Poythress and Grudem later wrote:

> . . . in fact, the major Greek lexicons for over 100 years have said that *adelphoi*, which is the plural of the word *adelphos*, "brother," sometimes means "brothers and sisters" (see BAGD, 1957 and 1979, Liddell-Scott-Jones, 1940 and even 1869).
>
> This material was new evidence to those of us who wrote the May 27 guidelines—we weren't previously aware of this pattern of Greek usage outside the Bible. Once we saw these examples and others like them, we felt we had to make some change in the guidelines.[8]

In this passage, Grudem says that of the twelve Christian leaders who wrote the guidelines, none were aware that *adelphoi* in Greek refers to both "brothers and sisters." Yet anyone with a background in classical or Hellenistic Greek literature would have known this, as would anyone who checked a lexicon. The New Testament is a limited group of writings that makes up a very small part of the wider Hellenistic Greek literature. When studying the New Testament in Greek, it is not possible to know the meaning of Greek words without referring to a lexicon. Greek lexicons have always noted that *adelphoi*, the plural of *adelphos,* can refer to "brothers and sisters." The only other way to get some idea of the meaning of the text is to refer to an English translation.

Nevertheless, the Colorado Springs Guidelines came to influence the translation, publication, and consumption of Bibles for conservative churches. Grudem, who drafted the guidelines, is the author of a popular seminary textbook, *Systematic Theology,* and of *Recovering Biblical Manhood and Womanhood*—a call for male headship and female submission. Here, an author of an influential theology textbook did not look up basic terms in a lexicon before drafting Bible translation guidelines that others were expected to trust as having academic and spiritual authority.

I come from a family where college attendance was presumed on the part of both men and women for several generations. Our great aunt, Elizabeth Hammond, was one of the fortunate young women who were

---

7. CBMW, "Guidelines," B1.

8. Poythress and Grudem, *TNIV*, 425–6.

first allowed to attend McGill University in Montreal in the late 1800s; she graduated with an MA in classics in 1896. Aunt Elizabeth later taught classics at McGill and left to us, her great nieces, a lexicon or two and a couple of Greek New Testaments. She lived with us during the last few years of her life, and I remember writing out an inventory of her belongings in my immature handwriting.

A tradition of studying Greek was passed down in our family: My mother studied Greek, as did several of my older sisters. We started in Grade 10 or 11, at about fourteen years of age, and studied Greek through to the end of university—a total of seven or eight years. My sisters were taught Greek and Latin by the Canadian author Grace Irwin, and I was taught by her friend and colleague, Elizabeth Wilson. Some of us studied mainly Greek and Latin (the classics), but I learned New Testament Greek, Hellenistic Greek, and Hebrew, which I studied at the Near Eastern Studies Department at the University of Toronto, under Al Pietersma. Greek and the biblical languages were a family tradition. However, we all sought our careers elsewhere.

Anyway, this is why we knew, as young teenage girls, that *adelphoi* meant "brothers and sisters" and why we didn't understand how this knowledge was new to adult theologians. However, silence was a pattern for the women in my family, who were taught Greek but kept silent in the church. Although we knew that women could be ordained in the Anglican Church of Canada, and that women were accepted into the seminary program in Toronto as of the mid-1970s, Brethren girls did not aim for seminary training. We had been taught the priesthood of all believers, and we did not anticipate becoming clergy.

In any case, in March 2002, the New Testament portion of Today's New International Version (TNIV) was published by Zondervan Publishers in the United States. This was a revision of the NIV that used the expression "brothers and sisters" for *adelphoi*. The TNIV also used other vocabulary that expressed the inclusive nature of many Greek and Hebrew words. For example, the TNIV used "children of God" in Matt 5:9, where Grudem's guidelines insisted on "sons of God."

Grudem and other members of the CBMW began a campaign against the TNIV. In 2002, over one hundred highly visible conservative Christians signed a public "statement of concern" against the TNIV. This statement said:

> In light of troubling translation inaccuracies—primarily (but not exclusively) in relation to gender language—that introduce distortions of the meanings that were conveyed better by the original NIV, we cannot endorse the TNIV translation as sufficiently accurate to commend to the church.[9]

Most of the signers were members of the CBMW, including Wayne Grudem, Jerry Falwell, James Dobson, and Charles Colson.

Zondervan Publishers went ahead and published the complete TNIV in 2005, while continuing to publish the original NIV 1984, which refers only to "brothers" and "sons." The campaign against the TNIV did not relent, and in 2011, Zondervan stopped publishing the TNIV; instead, Zondervan revised the NIV 1984 in the direction of the TNIV and published it as the NIV 2011, thus replacing both the NIV 1984 and the TNIV. The NIV 2011 was very similar to the TNIV, but was slightly modified in the direction requested by the CBMW. However, the CBMW was not satisfied.

After the publication of the NIV 2011, CBS News reported that Randy Stinson, a member and former chairman of the CBMW, expressed his concern this way: "Evangelicals believe in the verbal plenary inspiration of scripture. We believe every word is inspired by God, not just the broad thought." The news article then goes on to clarify: "So if the original text reads 'brothers'—even if that word in the original language is known to mean 'brothers and sisters' (such as the Hebrew 'achim' or Spanish word 'hermanos')—many evangelicals believe the English translation should read 'brothers.'"[10]

Here, the point is clear. Even if the actual meaning of *adelphoi* is "brothers and sisters," many evangelicals think that the word should be translated as "brothers." The statements of concern that had been made against the TNIV were reiterated by the CBMW and by influential church leaders against the NIV 2011.[11] The NIV 2011 did not cause the CBMW to rescind its statement of concern.

In addition to these statements against the TNIV and the NIV 2011, members of the CBMW decided to create their own version of the Bible, the ESV, which was published by Crossway in 2001. The president and publisher of Crossway Books is Lane Dennis, a member of the CBMW.

---

9. Published by the CBMW on May 27, 2002 and reported by a number of sources; see e.g. http://www.bible-researcher.com/tniv2.html.

10. Stinson, quoted in CBS News, "Gender-Neutral Bible."

11. See e.g. Poythress, "Gender Neutral Issues" and CBMW, "Evaluation."

Some have gone so far as to say that the ESV was created by the CBMW in direct response to the 1997 gender-neutral controversy, and as a result of the Colorado Springs Guidelines, although this is denied by Grudem himself.[xxiii,xxiv] However, this does not seem like an unreasonable assumption to me. The ESV is a revision of the Revised Standard Version (RSV). Although it was never very popular in evangelical circles, the RSV does follow in the tradition of the King James Version (KJV); therefore, it contains language familiar to many church attenders and pastors.

In the ESV, *adelphoi* is translated as "brothers" with a note at the bottom indicating that it can also mean "brothers and sisters." This note satisfies the strict scholarly requirements of acknowledging the original meaning of the Greek; however, it poses a problem in lectern readings, as the reader usually wishes to use the scripture reading to address the entire church. Thus, women are to be taught that they are included in the term "brothers," are equal to men in worth, and have "an equal share in the blessings of salvation."[xxv] When the scripture refers to the "blessings of salvation," women must consider themselves *included* in the word "brothers"; but if the reference is to an activity that some consider restricted to men, such as leading or teaching in the church, women are to consider themselves *excluded* from the term *adelphoi*.[xxvi]

Another Bible, the New Revised Standard Bible (NRSV), which was published in 1989, also follows the KJV but uses "brothers and sisters." Many other evangelical Bibles, such as the New Living Translation (NLT), the New English Translation (NET), the Common English Bible (CEB), and others, use the term "brothers and sisters"; however, these Bibles have not been strong candidates for pew or lectern Bibles.[xxvii]

An additional and unrelated concern that many people perceive is that "and sisters" seems to be adding words to the original text. Should an English translation add words to the original text? Yes! In fact, words are frequently added in a translation, and here is an example. The ESV translates Rom 11:24 as follows:

> For if you were cut from what is by nature a wild olive tree, and grafted, contrary to nature, into a cultivated olive tree, how much more will these, the natural branches, be grafted back into their own olive tree.[12]

---

12. Romans 11:24 (ESV)

A literal translation of the original Greek reads more like this: "For if you were cut from what is by nature a fieldolive, and grafted, contrary to nature, into a fineolive, how much more will these, by nature, be grafted back into the own olive." Of course, the word *elaia* that is used in the Greek can probably be used to mean "olive tree" as well as "olive," but the word "tree" is not present in the Greek. The Greek word for "branches" does not appear in this verse either. This is a typical, non-problematic translation: Words are added to make the meaning clear. The ESV does this, as do most, if not all, translations of the Bible. For example, the ESV adds the word "God" in Rom 12:19, the word "men" in Phil 2:29, and the word "he" in 1 Tim 5:8. These words are not present in the original Greek. If the ESV is able to add words in its translation, why does the statement of concern against the NIV end with the verse, "You shall not add to the word that I command you, nor take from it,"[13] thereby implying that the NIV 2011 is uniquely guilty as a Bible translation?

And what about sisters? Should sisters remain invisible in the text when the context clearly implies their inclusion? Should we continue to read Bibles that use terms that have traditionally been employed to exclude women? Or should we take the risk of including women, as the text clearly does, in spite of the occasional ambiguity? Is it really necessary to maintain strict gender boundaries in epistles that are addressed to the entire faith community?

In both Greek classical literature and the Hebrew narratives, there are stories of sisters and brothers that display loyalty and tenderness to each other. Antigone was shut into a cave to die because she honoured her brother Polyneices in his death, although he was considered a rebel. Electra looked after her brother Orestes. Miriam watched carefully over Moses, and supported and protected him at many crucial points in his life. Rahab protected both her brothers and her sisters. Sisters are often recognized for their loyalty and courage towards their family. Shouldn't brothers offer their Christian sisters this same loyalty, and defend the place of "and sisters" in the English Bible?

---

13. Deut 4:2

CHAPTER 9

Women as Peacemakers

Blessed are the peacemakers

for they will be called children of God.

(MATT 5:9, NIV)

IN THE SECOND BOOK of Samuel, David's general, Joab, hunts down Sheba, the leader of a rebellion against David, and discovers that he has escaped to a town called Abel. Joab decides to besiege the town, and builds a ramp against the city wall in order to invade the town. He does this in direct contravention of the law, which states in Deut 20:10: "When you march up to attack a city, make its people an offer of peace."

Joab is not a peacemaker, and does not offer peace before besieging the town. However, as mentioned earlier in this book, Abel was the home of a wise woman. Although we are not told exactly what role she has in the city, she is clearly in a position to negotiate with Joab. The wise woman of Abel calls out to Joab, and says:

> Long ago they used to say, "Get your answer at Abel," and that settled it. We are the peaceful and faithful in Israel. You are trying to destroy a city that is a mother in Israel. Why do you want to swallow up the Lord's inheritance?[1]

1. 2 Sam 20:18

The city of Abel was known as a place to settle disagreements and make peace. Perhaps it was a city where a wise man or woman traditionally gave judgements. The expression "a city that is a mother in Israel" suggests that it was a city with surrounding towns, or daughter cities, under its protection. The wise woman also refers to the city as an inheritance from the Lord. The matter is settled when the wise woman has the severed head of the rebel Sheba thrown over the city wall. Joab is satisfied, and the city of Abel is saved from invasion.

King David was not a peacemaker. In the Bible, God refers to David's reign as being characterized by bloodshed and violence. However, God promised David a son, Solomon, who would be a man of "rest," and assured David of "peace and quietness" for Israel during Solomon's reign: "He is the one who will build a house for my Name. He will be my son, and I will be his father. And I will establish the throne of his kingdom over Israel forever."[2] Solomon would be a peacemaker; therefore, Solomon will be the one to build a house for God, and God promises to make him his son, and to be his father. According to this passage, God will place Solomon on the throne as his son. This promise shows the value of peacemakers in God's view, and indicates that God will establish a peacemaker as his son and become the father of a peacemaker.

However, Israel was not bereft of peacemakers before the reign of King Solomon; at least three women acted as peacemakers before King Solomon. When Deborah was a judge in Israel, the land had peace for forty years. The next woman to make peace was the wise woman of Abel, who negotiated peace with Joab, as described above. The third woman to negotiate peace was Abigail, the wife of a very wealthy landowner named Nabal. In this particular instance, David offered terms of peace to Nabal's men in return for food for his warriors on a feast day. However, Nabal mocked David and refused him. Fearing an attack and despising her husband, Abigail made a decision and went behind Nabal's back. She personally took supplies to David and negotiated peace with him. In this way, she saved all the hired men belonging to Nabal from being killed by David and his warriors. Nabal died shortly after, and Abigail became David's wife.

These women made tough decisions that involved executing a rebel or acting independently of a husband. What kind of women were they? Deborah called herself a "mother in Israel,"[3] and the wise woman of Abel

2. 1 Chr 22:9
3. Judg 5:7

referred to her city as a "mother in Israel."[4] Clearly, this expression does not refer to the biological mother of someone who is important to the narrative. Rather, a "mother in Israel" appears to have a role in protecting her nation, city, or people. She plays a role that is outside of the home and independent of her husband. This role requires the "mother in Israel" to inform herself, make wise decisions, and act on her decisions in order to maintain peace. Thus, a "mother in Israel" is a peacemaker.

In the Sermon on the Mount, Jesus says: "Blessed are the peacemakers for they will be called children of God."[5] Perhaps Jesus is recalling the Hebrew reference to Solomon in 1 Chr 22:9, as the one who builds God's house and is established as God's son.

According to these passages, those who are peaceful, such as Solomon, will build the house of God to make His name known, and will be called the children of God. The Hebrew Bible also describes how Deborah, the wise woman of Abel, and Abigail negotiated peace or had peace in their day, like Solomon. When blessing the peacemakers, Jesus uses the Greek expression *huioi theou*, or "children of God"—a phrase that refers to both men and women. However, this phrase contains the Greek word *huios*, which is thought by some to mean exclusively "son," along with *theos*, meaning "God."

In the Hebrew Bible, the expression for "children" is *banim*, which is the plural of the Hebrew word *ben* for "son." The word *banim* is commonly used in the biblical expressions "children of Israel" and "children of the living God." For example:

> Yet the Israelites will be like the sand on the seashore, which cannot be measured or counted. In the place where it was said to them, "You are not my people," they will be called "children of the living God."[6]

Here, the phrase "children of the living God" unambiguously refers to the entire nation, including men, women, and children—the people of Israel. When Jesus quotes from the Hebrew Bible, he sometimes uses the Septuagint version—the Greek translation of the Hebrew Bible that had been written two centuries before. In that translation, the "children of Israel" are the *huioi Israel* and the "children of the living God" are the *huioi theou*

---

4. 2 Sam 20:19

5. Matt 5:9 (NIV)

6. Hos 1:9 (NIV)

zontos. These phrases clearly refer to the entire people of Israel. Therefore, it makes sense in every way to translate the Greek *huioi theou* of Matt 5:9 as the "children of God." The "children of Israel" and the "children of God" are two expressions for the people with whom God engages.

However, a small number of Bible translations, including the English Standard Version (ESV) and the Holman Standard Christian Bible (HSCB), now translate the expression in Matt 5:9 as "the sons of God." These translators rigorously follow the pattern of using the English masculine plural for a group of people of mixed gender, in spite of the fact that this is not common usage in the English language. In English, if "sons" are mentioned in a will, then "daughters" are excluded. Masculine plurals in English exclude the feminine.

The 1997 Colorado Springs Gender Translation Guidelines by the Council on Biblical Manhood and Womanhood (CBMW) include a line on the Greek word *huios*: "'Son' (*huios, ben*) should not be changed to 'child,' or 'sons' (*huioi*) to 'children' or 'sons and daughters.' (However, Hebrew *banim* often means 'children.')"[7] This example indicates the opposition that exists to the use of the expression "children of God" when translating the Bible into English. Not only does this document suggest that "sons of God" is the preferred translation, but it also suggests that it is the traditional and only acceptable translation. What was the meaning of Jesus's words in the Sermon on the Mount? Did he intend to communicate the meaning of "sons of God" or that of "children of God"? Imagine that we were in that audience listening to Jesus, perhaps as women with our sons and daughters around us. What would we hear?

There are several possible avenues of investigation to decide on the possible meanings an author may have intended, and to figure out how a phrase or word should be translated. For most literature, the first thing to do is attempt a guess based on the context—that is, who is being spoken to? What is being referred to? The second avenue is to look the phrase or word up in a dictionary or lexicon. The third avenue involves researching previous translations, especially those that lie within one's own creed or tradition. Finally, one might do a wider search of Greek literature to see how else the phrase of word was used.

On the other hand, any Bible translator is usually already very familiar with at least one other version of the Bible. Translators come to the task of translating with a preconceived notion of what most passages say in their

7. CBMW, "Guidelines," B2.

favorite English translation, before they start reading the Bible in Greek or Hebrew. This is completely normal and cannot be avoided. As a result, when investigating a phrase or word, Bible translators usually start with what they are familiar with already—that is, what pops into their mind immediately. Next, they usually turn to lexicons to identify what a word might mean; and finally, they examine the translation tradition.

For the passage in Matt 5:9, only a few Bible versions out of the hundreds of English translations use the phrase "sons of God." The better-known Bibles that use "sons of God" include the Revised English Version (1885), the Darby version (1890), and the Revised Standard Version (RSV, 1973). Some Bibles translated during the mid-1900s, such as the New American Standard (NASB, from 1960 to 1995) and the 1984 New International Version (NIV), also use "sons of God." However, none of the Bibles from the 1800s that used the phrase "sons of God" became popular as pew Bibles; therefore, it was not until the second half of the 1900s, when most churches transitioned to using the RSV, the NASB, or the NIV, that the expression "sons of God" was heard in church.

In striking contrast, the expression "children of God" is found in many early translations, including the Tyndale, Coverdale, Cranmer, Geneva, Bishop's, and King James versions of the English Bible. These are the early English Bible versions (1534–1611) that were used to spread the Gospel during the Protestant Reformation. After that period, the King James Bible remained dominant until the mid-1900s, when a variety of modern language Bibles, including the NASB and the NIV, became available. Therefore, the expression "children of God" was present in English Protestant pew Bibles from roughly the beginning of the 1500s to the mid-1900s, and has common currency in our society and linguistic heritage. The expression "children of God" was spoken and heard in English churches for at least 400 years. Those of us who were raised on the King James Bible have a strong memory of the verse "Blessed are the peacemakers: for they shall be called the children of God."[8]

In addition to these English examples, Luther's German Bible always uses the phrase *Kinder Gottes*, which means "children of God," and Calvin's French Geneva Bible[9] uses *les enfants de Dieu*, which also means "children of God." Going back further, the Wycliffe Bible uses *Goddis children*, and

8. Matt 5:9 (KJV)

9. The French Geneva Bible was first translated by Olivetan and then edited by and attributed to Calvin.

Anglo-Saxon Gospels that date back to the 10th or 11th century also use an equivalent for "the children of God": *godes bearn*. Therefore, the expression "children of God" (or its equivalent) has been used in English Bibles for at least a millennium, and is the most common way to translate the Greek *huioi theou* into English. These were the words that stirred the hearts of thousands, as people responded to the Bible in the Reformation.

Most Bible translators of the Reformation had a great deal to say about their translation philosophy. Of these, the translator who reflected most deeply on his task, and who produced the most linguistically influential Bible, was probably Luther. As a musician as well as a translator, author, poet, and hymn-writer, Luther wrote with such simplicity and rhythm that his Bible translation became a powerful force in establishing the modern German language. Although Luther aimed for consistency with the language style of the Saxon chancellery, it was also his custom to go into town, frequent the markets, and listen to the local village people speaking. He then went back to his retreat in Wartburg Castle and worked on his translation of the New Testament. Luther's translation of the Hebrew Bible, on the other hand, was a collaborative effort that he continued to work on, edit, and revise until his death in 1545. Like his translation of the New Testament, Luther's Old Testament contains meaningful and beautiful language patterns in German. As a French scholar of the Catholic Church wrote about Luther's translation: " . . . The poetic soul finds in this translation evidences of genius and expressions as natural, as beautiful, and melodious as in the original languages."[10]

Luther wrote a great deal about his translation philosophy of paying attention to the meaning of the Greek or Hebrew, and then putting this meaning into the German language of the people of the towns and villages.[xxviii] On one occasion, he explained it like this:

> We do not have to inquire of the literal Latin, how we are to speak German, as these asses [that is, literalists] do. Rather we must inquire about this of the mother in the home, the children on the street, the common man in the marketplace. We must be guided by their language, the way they speak, and do our translating accordingly. That way they will understand it and recognize that we are speaking German to them.[11]

---

10. Audin, quoted in Plass, *This Is Luther*, 338.

11. Luther, *On Translation*.

"Blessed are the peacemakers for they will be called the children of God" is a phrase that has come into the English language to stay. It has become the best known of all the beatitudes contained in the Sermon on the Mount, which is one of the most beloved of all Bible passages.

It is firmly established then, that except for the last few decades, "children of God" was the preferred way to translate *huioi theou* in Bible translations. What about lexicons? The classical Greek lexicon shows that *huios* meant "son"; more generically, in the plural, "people"; and, in the third meaning listed, "child." In some dialects, the Greek word *huios* was replaced by the Greek word *pais*, a word of common gender that can equally refer to a male or female. In addition, the lexicon notes that in Rev 12:5, the word *huios* is qualified by the adjective meaning "male": "She gave birth to a male child, one who is to rule all the nations with a rod of iron, but her child was caught up to God and to his throne…"[12]

When the Bible needs to communicate maleness, it does so unambiguously in both Greek and Hebrew. Abraham was told to circumcise only the "males." Gen 17 specifically refers to the "males" in Abraham's household to avoid confusion. Using *huios* to refer only to men leads to considerable confusion in some passages. Biblically speaking, men marry and women are given in marriage. Thus, the following verse does not make sense if *huios* is used to refer only to sons: "And Jesus said to them, 'The sons [*huios*] of this age marry and are given in marriage.'"[13]

The last question is whether Jesus was referring to men and women equally in the context of his Sermon on the Mount. One must assume that Jesus intended his sermons for both men and women. Jesus regularly interacted with women, both in the crowds and in homes; he had women as personal friends and family; and he taught women the scriptures. Women are mentioned in his family line, and women were assigned the task of announcing his resurrection. When Jesus said, "Blessed are the peacemakers," he was surely referring to both men and women.

Bible translators sometimes offer another reason to promote the phrase "sons of God." They argue that sons had a special place in the laws of ancient Israel, Greece, and Rome, and that women inherit all the benefits of being a "son" when they receive salvation in Christ. However, it is also true that the CBMW, who advocate for the translation "sons of God," do not accord women the same rights as men. An article on the CBMW

12. Rev 12:5

13. Luke 20:34 (ESV)

website claims that in heaven, women will exist in eternal submission to male headship: "There is every reason to believe, then, that male headship will continue as the divine order for male-female relationships."[14]

Apparently, those who advocate for the translation "sons of God" believe that women will, in fact, never inherit the full rights of a son. This kind of confusion complicates our understanding of our position in God's family; a return to the accepted pattern of "children of God" throughout the Bible, as used in the Reformation, would enable readers to better understand that women are not excluded from God's kingdom in any way, and are not given a position of lower rank than men.

Joab did not offer peace terms when he should have, and Nabal did not accept peace terms when they were offered. In each case, it was women who restored peace through decisive action. A peacemaker is not necessarily someone who avoids conflict; rather, it is someone who *resolves* conflict. The main role of a peacemaker today is played by police officers, whether in local or national police forces, or in international armed forces. The term "peacemaker" is also used for those who advocate for peace in their community or nation, outside of the armed forces.

A banner high on the wall of the main police station in Vancouver, Canada, declares in letters approximately two feet high: "Blessed are the peacemakers for they will be called the children of God." The Vancouver Police Department has a proactive approach to enrolling women as officers, and 27% of its force is now female. Many might question the effectiveness of female police officers. However, one study reports:

> Both female and male patrol officers responded to similar kinds of calls for service and encountered the same number of dangerous, angry, upset, drunk, or violent citizens. Although both groups obtained similar results when handling angry or violent citizens, the study noted that women patrol officers tended to be more effective than their male counterparts in avoiding violence and defusing potentially violent situations.[15]

In fact, women have been found to be effective in a policing role, and have been found to use less excessive force than male officers. The Vancouver Police Department has not cut back on hiring women, and no one has

---

14. Walton, "Relationships and Roles," 15.

15. Quotation from an article in *Police Foundation* that is no longer available: http://www.policefoundation.org/content/policewomen-patrol, accessed 2009.

suggested that this police department is less effective because of its relatively high proportion of women.

Women can be peacemakers in many different ways, as can men. Both sexes can work together on peacemaking missions. Both can benefit from recognition in the familiar text, "Blessed are the peacemakers, for they will be called the children of God." To replace the word "children" with "sons" may imply that women rank as men in God's kingdom; but this then brings up the question of whether men rank above women in God's kingdom. However, as peacemakers, women were able to speak to men as equals in the Hebrew narratives. Although the warriors and kings in these stories were male, women participated by negotiating with men. God created women with the same ability for peacemaking as men. Although women in the Hebrew Bible are not reluctant to use force when it is called for, they may have made peace with less excessive force than the men. For example, the wise woman of Abel spoke wisely to all the people in her city, and decided that the rebel Sheba would die so that the city could be saved. In the harsh culture of the ancient world, women were still able to play the role of peacemakers.

CHAPTER 10

Fully Adam

For dust you are

And to dust you shall return.

(GEN 3:19, NIV)

THE BIBLICAL NAME *ADAM* is a puzzling word—sometimes used in the Bible as a proper name, sometimes as a plural containing two different sexes, and sometimes as a mass noun referring to a group of people that may be male, female, or mixed. What does *Adam* actually mean? Names in the Bible often have a particular meaning, or are related to another word or place name by word play. This connection can derive from a similarity in either the meaning or the sound of the word. The name Adam is related to the Hebrew word for ground or soil—*adamah*—and is thus associated with the idea of something that is "earthy" or "made of the earth." This implies that the main feature of Adam is that he is mortal and made of matter, in contrast to God, who is immortal. The first chapter of the Bible divides beings into the immortal and the mortal, as well as into human creatures and other creatures.

In ancient society, this was the major classification of beings. To call someone *adam* in Hebrew means that they are mortal; it also means that they are human—that is, they are not animals. *Adam*, whether male and female, is made in the image of God: humans are different from animals. In Hebrew, there is no plural of the word *adam*, so the plural of the word for "person," *anashim*, acts as its plural. Otherwise, the word *adam* is used to refer to the human race. Although the biblical narrative also refers to an individual who was named Adam, the Hebrew noun *adam* does not mean that the person is necessarily male, as we shall see later. The word *adam* refers to a class of beings that includes male and female.

In the second chapter of Genesis, the first woman is made out of Adam, and is therefore made of the same matter as he is. Adam is made from the ground, and the woman is made of the same substance.[1] She shares a common mortality with Adam. A woman dies in the same way that a man dies; there is no difference. Both are *adam*, of the soil, and both return to the soil. This is the nature of mortality: belonging to the physical and material world, which consists of growth and decay.

The biblical use of the word *adam* makes sense if we understand at once that *adam* means a human being—a being made of soil, whether male or female. According to the biblical narrative, the first human was male. However, he shared the nature of his being with the first woman. In the narrative, Adam the man is the source of the woman, just as the ground is the source of Adam. As a result, both man and woman return to the soil out of which they have been formed—dust to dust.

> By the sweat of your face
> you shall eat bread
> until you return to the ground,
> for out of it you were taken;
> you are dust,
> and to dust you shall return[2]

Although women differ from men in that they bear children within their own body, this does not save women from mortality; they become dust along with men. However, it is important to note that men and women share a common participation in immortality by bearing children together, since men and women have an equal share in reproduction. Both men and women invest in their offspring, and both experience sorrow at the losses involved in bearing and raising children.[3] So the main implication of the word *adam* is of mortality and on the common human fate of working

1. See Gen 2:21–23.
2. Gen 3:18 (NRSV)
3. See Rashi, *Complete Tanach*.

hard, aging, and dying. Different Hebrew words, *ish* and *ishshah*, are used when the narrative talks about men and women as male and female.

In most English Bibles, however, the Hebrew word *adam*, when it is not used as a proper noun for the name of the person Adam, is translated as "man." This translation detracts from the original focus of the word, which emphasizes the common mortal nature of both men and women. It doesn't reflect the connotation of the Hebrew word, which refers to human beings, nor does it reveal the connection of the word to soil. The reader is constantly distracted by the notion that Adam is male, in contrast to the woman, Eve, the female. But, in fact, the woman will die in same manner as the man, and this is the point of the word *adam*: It means "of the earth" or "mortal," and indicates that both males and females share a common fate. The word *adam* emphasizes the similarity or commonality in the nature of men and women, not the differences between them.

For example, men and women had common and shared work. In early agricultural societies, before the domestication of large animals and the technological advances of the plough, people dug the soil with wooden implements. Both archeological evidence and current global practice demonstrates that this kind of agriculture—hoe agriculture—was the work of both men and women equally. In fact, some books suggest that women began gardening while men were hunting and foraging.[4] So in every sense, working the soil belongs both to woman and to man. The struggle to produce food from the land is a shared struggle. The soil is the origin and destination of human beings, and is worked by both men and women for the purpose of food production. This is the focus of the Hebrew word *adam*, meaning earthy.

Understanding the meaning of *adam* leads to a different understanding of Gen 3:16–19:

> To the woman he said,
> "I will greatly increase your pangs in childbearing;
> in pain you shall bring forth children,
> yet your desire shall be for your husband,
> and he shall rule over you."
> And to the man he said,
> "Because you have listened to the voice of your wife,
> and have eaten of the tree about which I commanded you,

4. McKay et al., *A History*, 19, 24.

'You shall not eat of it,' cursed is the ground because of you;

in toil you shall eat of it all the days of your life;

Thorns and thistles it shall bring forth for you;

and you shall eat the plants of the field.

By the sweat of your face

you shall eat bread until you return to the ground,

for out of it you were taken;

you are dust,

and to dust you shall return."

We can read this passage and understand it as a commentary on life at that time, but not as a rule for different gender roles. Men also reproduce and women also return to dust. This is a common goal and end.

Modern Jewish translators have seriously engaged with the translation of the word *adam* into English. The task of recent Jewish translators of the biblical text into English has become one of attempting to reveal as many features of the Hebrew language as possible in the translation. This includes finding unique translations for each word if possible, as well as revealing word play, related words, alliteration, repetition, parallelism, and rhythm.

Jewish translators of the Bible into English had to look for a way to differentiate the original Hebrew word *adam*, "a human," from the usual Hebrew word for "a man," which is *ish*. They also wanted to connect *adam* to the word *adamah*, or soil, in order to communicate to the reader the word play and connotation of the word *adam*. Jewish translators wanted to create in English a similar effect to the one created by the original Hebrew text.

One American translator, Everett Fox,[5] translated *adam* as "earthling," from the word "earth." His translation involved crafting English words and phrases in order to display as much as possible of the original Hebrew meaning and word play. However, Fox's translation also uprooted the normal English word order in order to imitate the original Hebrew word order. The result was illuminating and lent transparency to the Hebrew text, although it is somewhat awkward to read in English. Nevertheless, this translation remains a favorite of those who wish to view the Hebrew phrasing in the English language.

---

5. Fox, *Schocken Bible*.

Robert Alter,[6] another modern Jewish-American scholar, recently translated the Five Books of Moses—that is, the Torah—and other selections from the Hebrew Bible into English. Alter is primarily an English literary critic and theorist, but he was well educated in the Hebrew language from childhood, and is a recognized Hebrew scholar. The difference between his translation and that of Fox's may lie in this explanation by Alter:

> To do translation, you have to have an intimate relationship with each of the two languages, the language of the source and the language into which you're translating, and you have to have a kind of love affair with both of them.[7]

For Alter, it is important to become intimately familiar with the sounds, rhythms, meanings, and relationships within both the Hebrew and the English languages. He set out to write a beautiful English text that revealed as much of the Hebrew as possible. Alter did not want to err on the side of excessive strangeness, nor on the side of unnecessarily idiomatic English. He wanted to produce a translation that sounded smooth and rhythmic in English, but also revealed more of the underlying Hebrew than is typical of traditional English translations. Here is Alter's translation of Gen 2:6–7:

> And there was no human to till the soil, and the wetness would well from the earth to water all the surface of the soil, then the LORD God fashioned the human, humus from the soil, and blew into his nostrils the breath of life, and the human became a living creature.[8]

Here, Alter not only replicated the word play of *adam* from *adamah* in "human" and "humus," but also created a translation with alliteration by using "wetness," "well," and "water," as well as "surface of the soil." Using "human" for *adam* at this stage provides a smooth transition to using "man" later when the Hebrew uses *ish*, referring to Adam as a "husband" in contrast to Eve, a "wife." For Alter, the English word "human" is the best counterpart of the Hebrew word *adam*.

The only other English translations that I have noticed using "human" in this passage are the Common English Bible (CEB, 2011) and The Voice (2012). Although The Voice is a less literal translation, the recently translated CEB is a literal and close translation of the Hebrew into modern

---

6. Alter, *Five Books*.

7. Robert Alter, interviewed in Mindell, *Jewish Ledger*.

8. Alter, *Five Books*, 21.

English, and is perfectly suitable for liturgical use. Other popular evangelical Bibles such as the New International Version (NIV, 2011), the English Standard Version (ESV), the Living Bible, and even the New Revised Standard Version (NRSV) translate the word *adam* in Gen 2:7 into "man"—the male human being—thus depriving us of the connotations of earthiness and mortality, and distancing the reader from the reality that humans, both men and women, work the soil.

However, throughout the Hebrew Bible, the word *adam* is used in many contexts that support its use to mean a human being, whether male or female. In some contexts, *adam* is actually translated as "human being." For example, the word *adam* is used in the following verse: "One who kills an animal shall make restitution for it; but one who kills a human being shall be put to death."[9] In the next citation, the Hebrew word *adam* is not directly translated, but is simply reduced to "someone": "This is the law when someone dies in a tent: everyone who comes into the tent and everyone who is in the tent shall be unclean seven days."[10]

Some claim that in all these verses, the word *adam* applies to man, a male human being, and that the male human represents the human race. Wayne Grudem of the Council on Biblical Manhood and Womanhood (CBMW) writes:

> God gave the human race a name that, like the English word *man*, can either mean a male human being or can refer to the human race in general. ... Nor did he give the human race a name such as "humanity," which would have no male connotations and no connection with the man in distinction from the woman.[11]

For Grudem, the English word "man" must be used to translate the Hebrew *adam* to communicate the connection with the man as distinct from the woman, regardless of whether this connotation exists in Hebrew or not. Therefore, in the Colorado Springs Guidelines, the line referring to *adam* says: "'Man' should ordinarily be used to designate the human race, for example in Gen 1:26–27; 5:2; Ezek 29:11; and John 2:25."[12]

However, in some biblical contexts, it is evident that the word *adam* has no male connotations. Thus, the ESV Bible edited by Grudem does not translate *adam* as "man" in all contexts. In passages that are used to

9. Lev 24:21 (ESV)

10. Num 19:24 (ESV)

11. Grudem, *Biblical Foundations*, 30.

12. CBMW, "Guidelines," A3.

demonstrate the leadership of the male, the ESV translates *adam* as "man," but in laws relating to hygiene, *adam* is translated as a "human being." Laws regarding the life of a human being, uncleanness, and the treatment of a dead body obviously refer to human beings as physical and living (or dead) entities. Male priority is not in view, so these passages do not need the word "man." This is a decision that was made by an editor.

A passage in Gen 17 refers to circumcision; here, the Hebrew word *anashim* is used. Although this is a different Hebrew word than *adam*, *anashim* is used as the plural for *adam*. The most common translations of this chapter say: "every male among the men [*anashim*] of Abraham's house." But doesn't this really mean "any male among the people or humans of Abraham's house"? If the word *anashim*, acting as the plural of *adam*, already clearly designated only men, then why would this word need to be qualified by the Hebrew word for male? Rather, because *anashim* does not unambiguously designate only males, it needs to be qualified by the adjective meaning "male" (*zakar*).

In fact, a passage in the Bible uses the word *adam*, a human, and the expression *nephesh adam*, a "human being," to refer exclusively to females, with no males involved at all. In Num 31, all prisoners of war are killed except for women and female children who have never "known" a man (*ish*) by lying with him. The spoils of war are thus composed only of virgin females and animals. These females are referred to as both *adam* and *nephesh adam*, meaning that they are human beings, in contrast to the animals. The use of *adam* does not refer to the descent of these women and girls from a male; rather, it designates them as different from the animals. That is, the word *adam* has no male connotation in this passage. Therefore, the evidence indicates that *adam* and *nephesh adam* can mean a generic person, a human being of either sex, or it can refer either to a group of men or women. It is not a word that carries male connotations.

In most contexts, *adam* defines something as human rather than animal, or human rather than divine. The English equivalent is "human being" or "person," and the race of human beings is normally called the "human race." Therefore, one would expect that when Gen 5:2 refers to the human race, it would use these words. In spite of the Colorado Springs Guidelines, many modern Bibles today do use the word "human" in some form or another to designate the human race in Gen 5:2. The NRSV, Common English Bible (CEB), New Living Translation (NLT), and New English Translation (NET) use "humanity" or "humankind." For example: "Male and female he created them, and he blessed them and named them 'Humankind' [adam] when they were created."[13]

However, the ESV and the Holman Christian Standard Bible (HCSB), which abide by the Guidelines for Translation of Gender-Related Language in Scripture, use "Man" and "man," respectively, and the NIV (2011) uses "mankind," which similarly concedes a male connotation for the human race as a whole: "Male and female he created them, and he blessed them and named them Man (adam) when they were created."[14]

It is a goal of these translations to keep the connotation of maleness in view. The ESV is perhaps the translation that best demonstrates how a version of the Bible can give prominence to males over females. In the ESV Bible, vocabulary must be used that attributes the human race to the male. Bruce Ware of the Southern Baptist Theological Seminary explains the reasoning:

> In Gen. 5:2, we read that God created man in the likeness of God, as male and female, and "when they were created he called *them 'man.'*" It appears that God intends the identity of *both* to contain an element of priority given to the male, since God chooses as their *common* name a name that is purposely *masculine* (i.e., a name that can be used also of the man alone, as distinct altogether from the woman, but never of the woman alone, as distinct altogether from the man). As God has so chosen to create man as male and female, by God's design her identity as female is inextricably tied to and rooted in the prior identity of the male.[15]

Despite Ware's argument, Num 31 (discussed above) shows that *adam* can refer to women alone, as distinct to man. In Num 31, only the virgin females were allowed to live; these women were referred to as the *adam*, that is, the humans, who had never slept with an *ish*, that is, a man. In the same way, the word *anashim* in Gen 17, which in this chapter refers to men only, requires the adjective for "male" to specify "male human beings." In many ways, translating *adam* as "man" creates confusion, because there are four different words in Hebrew that can possibly be translated as "man." The meaning of the Hebrew would be clearer if translators more consistently translated *adam* as "human," "humankind," or "person," and used "man" when only males were specifically being referred to in Hebrew.

13. Gen 5:2 (NRSV)

14. Gen 5:2 (ESV)

15. Ware, "Male and Female," 19.

CHAPTER 11

Anthropos

... what you have heard from me through many witnesses entrust to faithful people who will be able to teach others as well.

(2 TIM 2:2, NRSV)

AS THE PREVIOUS CHAPTER discussed, the Hebrew word *adam* is not simply used to refer to a person of either sex, but is rather used for the specific purpose of attributing the quality of being human to a particular and known male or female. The close equivalent of *adam* in Greek, *anthropos*, is used in the same way. In ancient narratives, which often told tales of gods and mortals, it was fairly common for the structure of the language in the narrative to distinguish whether the person being referred to was human or divine. Rather than being used in cases where the gender of the person was in question, the word *anthropos* was used to identify someone as human. In translating *anthropos* into English, it is especially helpful to use the word "human," which brings into focus the real issue of classifying the individual as mortal or immortal, regardless of gender. That is, in Greek literature, *anthropos* can refer to either a man or a woman, in contrast with the gods. Therefore, the word "human" communicates the message of the original language more accurately than "man."

A humorous story from an ancient Greek political campaign illustrates this point. In this story, the dictator Pisistratus was returning from exile. As he rode into Athens in a chariot, he wanted to demonstrate that he had the support of the goddess Athena herself:

> There was in the Paeanian deme, a woman called Phya, three fingers short of six feet, four inches in height, and otherwise, too, well-formed. This woman they equipped in full armor and put in a chariot, giving her all the paraphernalia to make the most impressive spectacle, and so drove into the city; heralds ran before them, and when they came into town proclaimed as they were instructed: "Athenians, give a hearty welcome to Pisistratus, whom Athena herself honors above all men and is bringing back to her own acropolis." So the heralds went about proclaiming this; and immediately the report spread in the demes that Athena was bringing Pisistratus back, and the townsfolk, believing that the woman was the goddess herself, worshipped this human creature [*anthropos*] and welcomed Pisistratus.[1,xxix]

Here, *anthropos* shows that the woman was a "human creature." The translation makes it clear that the word *anthropos* was communicating that she was not a goddess, but a mere human being. It does not designate her as male.

I once asked a Bible translator why the expression "man of God" in Tim 6:11, which is "*anthropos* of God" in the Greek, was not translated as "person of God." In Latin, this phrase is written *homo Dei*, not *vir Dei*, meaning "human of God" rather than "man of God." However, in English, this phrase is always written as "man of God." Why? Because, I was told, all uses of this expression in the Hebrew part of the Bible used the phrase *ish Elohim*, and referred to men. I will discuss *ish*, the Hebrew word commonly used for "a man," in a later chapter. However, I have it on the word of several Jewish men, both scholars and speakers of modern Hebrew, that *ish* has always had a generic use which includes women. I will return to this later.

In fact, Greek speakers are quite comfortable with the expression "*anthropos* of God" being used for a woman. A woman in the 4th century named Melania was called an *anthropos* of God.[2,xxx] In this case, a feminine article was used. As a result, this passage has sometimes been translated as "Melania, the female man of God."[3] Is Melania really a man of God, or is she a person of God? Aren't men also, as the accompanying Latin translation *homo* indicates, human beings of God? Anyway, the use of *anthropos* of God to describe a woman is quite normal in Greek, even though it is not found in the Bible. Since the Bible is a very small part of the ancient Greek

1. Herodotus, *Histories*, 1:60.
2. Palladius, *Lausiac History*, IX.
3. Borresen and Vogt, *Women's Studies*, 256.

literature available to us, it is always worth checking to see how an expression like this is used in other contemporary pieces of literature.

The reason why it is possible to use the word *anthropos* for a woman in Greek is because the word *anthropos* is not a masculine word at all, but a word of common gender. Many Greek words are words of common gender; examples include *theos, iatros, ippos, diakonos,* and *apostolos,* which respectively mean "divine being," "doctor," "horse," "deacon," and "apostle." These words have no semantic content that indicates gender, although they can be preceded by either a masculine or a feminine definite article (the equivalent of "the" in English), depending on the gender of the item or person they refer to. In fact, there are many places in classical Greek literature where *anthropos* is used to refer to a woman.[xxxi] Sometimes the *anthropos* in these cases is translated simply as "the woman"; at other times, it is clear that the word *anthropos* is indicating that the woman in question is a human and not divine, and the word is translated as "human" accordingly.

However, the Colorado Springs Guidelines[xxxii] state: "The singular *anthropos* should ordinarily be translated 'man' when it refers to a male human being."[4] Although this sounds logical enough, it also means that the word *anthropos* cannot be translated as "human" when it refers to a man. It follows, then, that there is no way in English to communicate the meaning of the Greek—that the focus of a passage using *anthropos* is that this particular male person, whom we know is male, is also a human being. Therefore, according to this translation guideline, Christ can never be called a "human" or a "human being," but only a "man." His maleness comes before his humanity, and his humanity cannot be described in so many words.

Here are three contrasting versions of 1 Tim 2:5:

> For there is one God, and there is one mediator between God and men, the man Christ Jesus (ESV)

> For there is one God and one mediator between God and mankind, the man Christ Jesus (NIV)

> There is one God and one mediator between God and humanity, the human Christ Jesus (CEB)

The first example, from the English Standard Version (ESV), is of dubious accuracy, since the preface to the ESV[5] says: "the words 'man' and 'men' are retained where a male meaning component is part of the original Greek or

4. CBMW, "Guidelines," A5.

5. Preface to *English Standard Version.*

Hebrew." Has Christ then come as a man in order to be a mediator between God and "men"—that is, as a mediator for males only? If "men" are males, and Christ is a "man," then did Christ come as a man in order to relate to men exclusively? According to English usage of the word "men," that is what the ESV says.

The second version is quite clear, if somewhat outdated. The human race has historically been called "mankind," and the meaning of this word is still clear to us. However, it lacks the emphasis on Jesus being human. In Greek, the word *anthropos* means "human" and is different from the word for a man. In this passage in the original Greek, the words used are *anthropos* and its plural, both of which apply to both women and men—in contrast to the expression "men" in English, which can never designate "women."

In the third example above, no question of gender arises. Christ came to be the mediator between God and humanity, and he became human in order to do so. The message is clear and does not require an explanation or footnotes. When gender does become an issue, later in the same chapter,[6] a completely different vocabulary is used in Greek. At that point, the Greek shifts to using the word *aner* for men, and *gune* for women. There is no semantic link back to the word *anthropos*, which is used in the passage above. It is now easier to see that 1 Tim 2 first describes the common access that both men and women have to God, and then moves on to give gender-specific instructions.

There are many other places in the New Testament where "person" or "human" is the best translation for *anthropos*, but many translations still use "man." One example is Matt 12:12:

> Of how much more value is a man than a sheep! (ESV)

> How much more valuable is a person than a sheep! (NIV)

> How much more valuable is a human being than a sheep! (NRSV)

Which Bible would we want to give to someone who is unfamiliar with biblical language? A few readers may remember that in the King James Version (KJV), a "man" may refer to any human being, whether male or female. However, the preface of the ESV explicitly says that when the English word "man" or "men" is used, the Greek has a male-meaning component. So the reader cannot avoid the question of whether Jesus really intended to talk

6. See 1 Tim 2:8–15.

just about men, or whether his teaching was about both men and women. Did Jesus place equal value on women, or did he simply think that women weren't worth mentioning?

Here is another example. Eph 4:8 has been translated in two different ways:

> he gave gifts to people (CEB)

> he gave gifts to men (ESV)

The gifts mentioned here refer to the ability to be apostles, evangelists, pastors, and teachers.[7] The translators of the ESV hesitated to translate the plural of *anthropos* as "people"; instead, they used "men," in spite of the fact that the original Greek does not actually indicate that these gifts were restricted to males. That is, the translators themselves made the decision that the English text ought to clarify that these gifts were given to males only. However, in order to acknowledge the actual meaning of *anthropos*, a footnote explains that the word can refer to both men and women. In this way, the ESV demonstrates that the preferred translation is "men," even though another possible translation is "people" or "both men and women." The ESV notes provide no analysis or explanation as to why "men" has been preferred.

Earlier in the letter to the Eph 3:5, a translation decision was made by the ESV editors to introduce the male-only expression "sons of men" instead of "children of man" when referring to both men and women. The author of the epistle writes:

> When you read this, you can perceive my insight into the mystery of Christ, which was not made known to the sons of men in other generations as it has now been revealed to his holy apostles and prophets by the Spirit.[8]

This term in both Hebrew and Greek has historically been translated as "the children of men" or "children of man" in the KJV and other translations, thus including both genders; it is now translated simply as "humans."[9] The writers of the New Testament would have known from the Septuagint that this Greek expression did not refer to men only, but was usually used to re-

---

7. See Eph 4:11.

8. Eph 3:5 (ESV)

9. See Ps 53:2, where the ESV translates this same expression as "children of man," implying all humans.

fer to all of humanity. There were women among the prophets and apostles, so why suggest male exclusivity in this verse? A counter example in Mark 3:28 uses the identical Greek expression as is found in Eph 3:5: "Truly, I say to you, all sins will be forgiven the children of man, and whatever blasphemies they utter."[10]

Why is the same Greek expression translated as "sons of men" in some places in the ESV, and translated in other places as "children of man?" The fact that the ESV vacillates between "sons of men" and "children of man" is odd, since the Greek remains the same in every case. Clearly, a decision was made to translate a Greek expression that normally includes both men and women as "men only" when the context includes apostles, prophets, teachers, and pastors. However, when it comes to the forgiveness of God, then the exact same term was translated as "children of man," which includes women. In the ESV, the English text seems to be carefully managed so that certain offices and roles in the church appear to be restricted to men only.

Once again, in 2 Pet 1:21, the ESV translates the Greek word *anthropos*, which refers to all human beings, as "man" and "men" when it relates to prophecy: "For no prophecy was ever produced by the will of man, but men spoke from God as they were carried along by the Holy Spirit."[11]

Are the translators of the ESV Bible trying to minimize the fact that prophecy was also given to women in both the Old and New Testaments? Are they trying to make prophecy by women appear less worthy of mention? Did only men speak from God, or did women also speak from God? The list of female prophets in the Bible includes Miriam, Sarah, Deborah, Hannah, Huldah, Anna, Mary, Elizabeth, Prisca, and the daughters of Philip. How much more accurate and true to the text it would be if the word *anthropos* was translated as it is in the following versions:

> For prophecy never had its origin in the human will, but prophets, though human, spoke from God as they were carried along by the Holy Spirit.[12]

> . . . because no prophecy ever came by human will, but men and women moved by the Holy Spirit spoke from God[13]

10. Mark 3:28 (ESV)

11. 2 Pet 1:21 (ESV)

12. 2 Pet 1:21 (NIV)

13. 2 Pet 1:21 (NRSV)

These Bibles more accurately and literally translate the words in the original language. Women did prophecy, and the text should not be subtly reshaped to suggest that they did not. The NRSV is by far a more accurate reflection of the Greek original text than the ESV.

One Bible verse in particular, related to this discussion, has taken up residence in my mind, and haunts me from time to time. When I let it enter my consciousness, I am overwhelmed with a sense of betrayal and abandonment, as if some voice says to me, "The Bible is not for you." It is a verse that was used frequently by many Christian groups a few years ago to inspire small group Bible study and to encourage everyone to evangelize and disciple others. It was used by Inter Varsity Christian Fellowship (IVCF), a group that is active in Canada both on university campuses and in Pioneer Camps for children. Two of the early outstanding national IVCF leaders were Stacy Woods and Cathie Nicholl; the latter was a camp counsellor and mentor for my mother when she attended Ontario Pioneer Camp in the 1930s. The IVCF was propelled forward by the four-step process outlined in 2 Tim 2:2:

> . . . and what you have heard from me through many witnesses entrust to faithful people who will be able to teach others as well. (NRSV)

> . . . and what you have heard from me in the presence of many witnesses entrust to faithful men who will be able to teach others also. (ESV)

There is, of course, a footnote in the ESV as follows: "The Greek word *anthropoi* can refer to both men and women, depending on the context." However, the main text uses the word "men" which, as the preface affirms, refers to males. Reading this verse in the ESV was a jolt for me personally, since a verse that I had memorized and lived by was now altered in meaning, if not in form. I felt disoriented by this new translation in the ESV, which implied that this instruction was for men only. If the ESV was used as the pew Bible in the church I attended, how would I feel when this verse was taught for men only? Wouldn't this challenge and contradict the reality of my earlier Christian experience? What about all those other verses where the word "men" is used for the Greek plural of *anthropos*? Are women not teachers and evangelists? In the New Testament, some women functioned as house church leaders and even apostles. For me, 2 Tim 2:2 has been a lifelong guide. I felt alienated by the male leadership implied by this translation, since the translation had overturned the understanding that most Christian organizations had taught in the 1970s and 80s. There was a turning away from including women in the normal transmission of Christian beliefs. The ESV translation encouraged new restrictions on women.

What about the context of this verse? Could it possibly exclude women? This epistle is addressed directly to Timothy from Paul. In it, we learn that Timothy "from childhood" was "acquainted with the sacred writings, which are able to make you wise for salvation through faith in Christ Jesus." So Timothy, as a child, was taught the scripture, which is:

> inspired by God and is useful for teaching, for showing mistakes, for correcting, and for training character, so that the person who belongs to God can be equipped to do everything that is good.[14]

In the first chapter of 2 Timothy, Paul explicitly states that the faithful people who taught Timothy the Bible were his mother Eunice and his grandmother Lois. This suggests that it was women who taught Timothy the very scriptures that are useful for both salvation and training. At the end of the book, Paul sends greetings to several people, including Claudia and Priscilla. It is hard to see why Paul would exclude women from his instructions in 2 Tim 2:2, since women are both receivers and teachers of God's word in this epistle. Throughout the scriptures, women heard God's word and transmitted it. Were Paul's teachings so different, so exceptional, that only men could transmit them? Was this a new mandate, introduced by the apostle? Or is it a mandate that has been newly interpreted by the ESV?

As it happens, Wayne Grudem, general editor of the ESV, and Lane Dennis, the head of Crossway Publishers (the publisher of the ESV) are both members of the Council on Biblical Manhood and Womanhood (CBMW), of which Grudem is also a founder. The charter document of the CBMW is the Danvers Statement, which specifies: "In the church, redemption in Christ gives men and women an equal share in the blessings of salvation; nevertheless, some governing and teaching roles within the church are restricted to men."[15]

The ESV has been translated in such a way that this statement is now reinforced by many verses in the New Testament. It appears in the ESV, because of the way the translators have chosen to translate certain verses,

---

14. 2 Tim 3:16–17

15. CBMW, *Danvers Statement*.

that God gave the gifts of prophecy, teaching, pastoring, and apostleship only to men. Yet individual women in the scriptures are named as prophets, teachers, leaders, and apostles. Many women were entrusted with God's word and transmitted it, including Sarah, Samson's mother, Hannah, Huldah, Mary Magdalene, Eunice, Lois, Phoebe, and Chloe.

In addition to these women of the Bible, many women throughout history heard the word of God and transmitted it to others. In the book *Recovering Biblical Manhood and Womanhood*,[16] edited by Wayne Grudem and John Piper, this rich history of women is addressed in chapter 15, "Women in the History of the Church," written by William Weinrich. Some of the early female biblical scholars mentioned in that chapter are Marcella, Paula, Melania, Eudoxia, Olympias, and Macrina. The list goes on and on. Hilda of Whitby was the abbess of a double monastery (a monastery for both men and women) in Whitby, Northumbria, England, in the 7th century. She was described as a skilled administrator and teacher. Five members of her monastery became bishops, and kings and church leaders sought out her advice. Hilda studied the scriptures and passed on her knowledge. Hildegarde of Bingen, Theresa of Avila, and Catherine of Siena—the latter two now recognized as doctors of the church—represent a later period in the history of the church. Near the end of the chapter, the author mentions Evelyn Underhill, who "was the first woman invited to give a series of theological lectures at Oxford University."[17] Many other women are honoured in that chapter as well.

Weinrich acknowledges that these women studied the Bible, taught, spoke in mixed company, had administrative authority over double monasteries, and conversed with men in authority in the church. One of the few things these women could not do was excommunicate. Weinrich writes:

> By selected example we have illustrated the broad and respected contributions that Christian women have made to the church throughout its history. These contributions have been intellectual, diaconal, and evangelical, and have carried with them spiritual power and recognized authority.[18]

However, Weinrich maintains that despite these contributions, women have not traditionally served at the altar, nor have they been allowed to teach in the assembly when men are present. He does say that women

16. Grudem and Piper, *Recovering Biblical Manhood*.

17. Weinrich, "Women," 270.

18. Weinrich, "Women," 273.

taught and had authority in convents and abbeys, in correspondence and debates. In fact, women have displayed all the spiritual gifts mentioned in the Epistles. Women, as deacons, pastored other women, and led convents of men and women. The fact that women have traditionally been unable to use these gifts in the assembly in front of men is no reason to translate every occurrence of the Greek word *anthropos* that relates to gifts and teaching as "men" in the English Bible. God's equal gifting of women and their exercise of these gifts should be the measuring stick, not the presence of men to witness the exercise of these gifts.

In the more recent past, missionaries and the Bible Women of China and India were teachers who heard the word of God and passed it on to those who would also teach others. Women have evangelized, taught, and pastored over the last two centuries. The first woman ordained as an Anglican priest came from China. Already a deacon, Li Tim Oi (also known as Florence Li) was ordained a priest in 1944. At the end of the war, not wishing to be the focus of controversy, she resigned her license, although she did not surrender her ordination. When women were next ordained as Anglican priests, in Hong Kong in 1971, Li Tim Oi was present and was officially recognized by the diocese as an Anglican priest. At that time, my sister was teaching Greek to seminary students in Hong Kong; she was fortunate enough to be present at this inaugural ordination of women in the Church of England. Not long ago, I stood in St. Martin in the Fields, a church in the heart of London, looking at the plaque that commemorates the ministry of Li Tim Oi.

Li Tim Oi spent the last years of her life in Toronto, where women were first ordained in the Anglican Church in 1976. The ordination of women in the Anglican Church primarily stemmed from a recognition of the work that women were already doing, rather than coming from a demand for women to enter a new sphere. As a student in Toronto in 1976, I knew the first female students in the class just after mine who entered seminary with the expectation that they would be ordained.

In Israel, throughout the 20th century, there was a necessary consolidation of biblical scholarship. European Jews had focused more on the Talmud (the rabbinical commentaries) than on the biblical canon itself. In Israel, interest in the Torah (the Five Books of Moses) played a central role in validating the state of Israel and its relationship to the land. It also acted as a foundation for ethnic cohesiveness, not only for the state of Israel, but also for Jewish communities around the world. However, for many Jewish immigrants, the emphasis had been on the Talmud, the traditions and commentary of the rabbis over the centuries.

A young and determined woman was key in changing this emphasis. Nehama Leibowitz[19] was born in 1905, and grew up in a studious Orthodox Jewish home in Latvia. German, Hebrew, and Yiddish were all languages of literacy for both Nehama and her brother, who were taught by their mother and private tutors. Many Jewish homes promoted Hebrew literacy for the boys and Yiddish literacy for the girls, resulting in few university options for the girls. However, with her background in both Yiddish and Hebrew literacy, Nehama went to university in Germany and completed her PhD at the university in Marburg in 1930, writing a dissertation on early Jewish Bible translations. She also studied in Berlin. Throughout her life, Nehama projected the attitude that women should not challenge men or cross the boundaries into the world of male obligations under the Jewish law. However, she also promoted and acted on the notion that women could take on the same ethic of lifelong study, biblical scholarship, and public teaching as the men.

Nehama Leibowitz emigrated to Israel and began a distinguished career as an instructor of biblical exegesis, drawing on the very best Eastern European rabbinical training, German higher criticism, and a reading of the text based on her experience living in the land of the Bible itself. She herself had traveled from Eastern Europe, the rabbinical periphery of Judaism, then studied in Germany, and finally found a home in the land of Israel. She had been immersed in the three different worlds of exegesis.[20] Nehama developed a close, literal style that, although it rejected modern higher criticism, displayed an awareness of the latest scholarship. In addition to her outstanding scholarship, her major accomplishment was that she established a system of teaching the Bible by correspondence to adults throughout Israel and the international Jewish community. Nehama became a professor at Tel Aviv University and Hebrew University, and eventually taught exegesis through a radio program commenting on the Torah.

Nehama received the Israel Prize for her work in 1956. In *The Making of the Modern Jewish Bible*, Levenson opens his chapter on Leibowitz as follows: "Nehama Leibowitz (1905–1997) was the most influential teacher of Torah in the twentieth century."[21]

19. See Abramowitz, *Tales of Nehama*, 282.

20. Levenson, *Making*.

21. Levenson, *Making*, 133.

Closer to home, in 2000, the Vancouver Sun[22] named Bernice Gerard as the "most influential religious figure in British Columbia in the 20th century." Bernice Gerard started out as a neglected foster child in an abusive household in the interior of British Columbia. She became a Christian during an evangelical crusade and went on to train as a teacher. Gerard then traveled nationally and internationally as a preacher and evangelist, helping to found 200 churches throughout Canada, the USA and Europe. She eventually settled down in Vancouver as the pastor of Fraserview Assembly, and become a city counselor. Many years ago, I used to watch her TV broadcasts; listening to her firm, deep voice filled with compassion and warmth became a haven for me during the long, dark, melancholy winter evenings in a small town in the Purcell Mountains of British Columbia. For me, she stood out as model: a conservative but enlightened TV evangelist who was respected in the wider community.

Looking back on my first encounter with the ESV, I now realize the futility of trying to reconcile its translation with my own understanding of the Bible. The larger community celebrates women as teachers of the Bible. Women have earned the respect of nations. However, the ESV translation asks me to reject a biblical stamp of approval on the ministry of many women, who were honored as uniquely outstanding among both male and female biblical scholars. I now have a copy of Today's New International Version (TNIV), an inclusive Bible that translates *adam* as "human beings" and *anthropos* in the plural as "people." This Bible is no longer published, in part because over a hundred church leaders signed a statement saying that it was not trustworthy. But I still have my copy.

---

22. Todd, "Vancouver Sun Archives," A1 and Todd, "British Columbia's 25."

CHAPTER 12

Every One Among You

And they came, both men and women, as many as were willing hearted, and brought bracelets, and earrings, and rings, and tablets, all jewels of gold: and every man that offered, offered an offering of gold unto the Lord.

(EXOD 35:22, KJV)

WHEN WE WERE YOUNG children, our parents took us out on weeknights to the reading meeting and the prayer meeting, and to special services given by itinerant preachers. One time, there was a series of three weeknight meetings called "The Tabernacle Talks." These talks presented the spiritual significance of the design of the original tent of assembly set up by the Israelites in the wilderness. The preacher had built a model of this tabernacle and its courtyard that covered a tabletop. We children were allowed to gather around afterwards and learn about the laver of brass made with the mirrors of women and about the staves and sockets and hooks. There were also the curtains of purple and scarlet and blue, the goat hair, and the fine twined linen. Then there was the fascination of ram skins and badger skins. I was just tall enough to see what was on the table without standing on tippy toes.

The next evening, I brought an offering with me. I had found a tiny plastic figure of a woman, more appropriate in my mind than a male figure since she was wearing a dress, and I had fashioned some kind of tiny white robe to make her look like a priest. The figure was about the right scale, and the preacher carefully placed her in the courtyard of the temple. Of course, I have no idea whether this little figure made the grade and was displayed in the next town that the "Tabernacle Talks" traveled to. No matter—I was happy.

In the chapters about the tabernacle, the story makes it obvious that when "every man" was to bring an offering to the tabernacle, it really meant "men and women": "every wise hearted man, in whose heart the Lord had put wisdom, even every one whose heart stirred him up to come unto the work to do it".[1]

As the story develops, women donate earrings, bracelets, and looking glasses. Women dye and spin goat's hair into blue and scarlet and purple, and offer it to the tabernacle. And women serve at the entrance to the tabernacle. The hearts of women, not just men, are stirred up to serve the Lord.

When it says "man" or "every man" in these passages, it includes women. People who donated to the tabernacle gave individual gifts of some material or product. In this case, gold and precious metals were donated; later, women gave textiles—a valuable commodity in that society, and a gift that was commonly presented to kings. The word used here for the individual, which is translated as "man" and "everyone," is the Hebrew word *ish*. This word is often considered to mean simply a "man"—that is, a male. However, in this passage about donating to the tabernacle, the word *ish* is used in combination with the word *kol,* "every," and *kol ish* refers to "everyone," both men and women. In the English translation, when it says "every man" it really means "everyone"—both men and women. So the King James Bible (1611), which sometimes tends towards a word-for-word translation, rather confusingly says "both men and women" and then "every man," with these two expressions referring to the same people.

> And they came, both men and women, . . .
> and every man [*kol ish*] that offered,
> offered an offering of gold unto the Lord[2]

In the broadest sense, *ish* is "a member of the particular group in question who is involved in the event described."[3] It may also be any person, male or female, who represents a group and has agency—that is, someone who is able to act as a participant in the event. Therefore, *ish* is regularly used

1. Exod 35:21 (KJV)

2. Exod 35:22 (KJV)

3. E.g., see Stein, "The Noun *ish,*" 1–24.

for males only, such as for a husband or a warrior, since there are frequent events in the Bible in which men are the main actors. Yet often enough, as in the story of building the tabernacle, *ish* also included women when the context demanded it.

The tabernacle was built with the contributions of the members of the community, and women—who owned jewelry and controlled the production of textiles, one of the most important commodities at the time—were an integral part of building the tabernacle. In this case, the expression *kol ish*, "every man," meant every capable adult member of the people of Israel, male or female; thus, this phrase is sometimes best translated as "everyone." Here is a verse about the tabernacle in the very popular Geneva Bible (1560), where "everyone" is used instead of "every man" to translate *kol ish*:

> Both men and women, as many as were free hearted, came *and* brought taches and earrings, and rings, and bracelets, all *were* jewels of gold: and every one [*kol ish*] that offered an offering of gold unto the Lord:[4]

In Num 21:9, the word *ish* refers to every member of the children of Israel who might be bitten by a snake—that is, to every member of the group: "So Moses made a bronze serpent and set it on a pole. And if a serpent bit anyone [*kol ish*], he would look at the bronze serpent and live."[5] In Ezek 9:6, the Hebrew expression *kol ish* is used again, this time with a negative, and is translated as "no one": "Kill old men outright, young men and maidens, little children and women, but touch no one [*kol ish*] on whom is the mark." Clearly, the command to "touch no one" includes anyone at all that has a mark on their forehead, so once again members of a particular group, whether man or woman, adult or child, are all referred to by the word *ish*. Surely not only the men are saved by a mark on the forehead.

In this next passage, the people who are referred to as *ish* are all female. However, sons and daughters are mentioned later. The verse says: "They took captive the women who were in it, from the youngest to the oldest, but they did not kill anyone [*lo ish*]. They simply carried them off and went on their way."[6]

Some people suggest that the core meaning of *ish* is that of an adult male human being, and that this word occasionally, by extension, refers

4. Exod 35:22, Geneva Bible, 1560
5. Num 21:9 (ESV)
6. 1 Sam 30:2 (NET Bible)

to women. They suggest that *adam* means all human beings, but that *ish* means male human beings, and that it would not be logical to have two words that mean human being in general. The idea is that there is always a sense of maleness in the meaning of the word *ish,* but that males can represent females. Therefore, *ish* can still be used for mixed groups of men and women.

This seems to be the reasoning behind drafting the gender guidelines, since A4 of the Colorado Springs Guidelines states: "Hebrew *ish* should ordinarily be translated 'man' and 'men'".[7]

On the other hand, if *ish* has the particular meaning of "each member of a group," it does have a meaning that is distinct from *adam,* although it is still a meaning that does not necessarily indicate maleness. In fact, curiously, the word *ish* does not even have to indicate humanness:

> Moreover, each stand had four bronze wheels and axles of bronze, and at the four corners were supports for a basin. The supports were cast with wreaths at the side of each [*ish*].[8]

In other places, the word *ish* refers to each tribe or group of people: "So no inheritance shall be transferred from one tribe to another, for each [*ish*] of the tribes of the people of Israel shall hold on to its own inheritance."[9]

If *ish* has the overall sense of "a member of a group, male or female, animate or inanimate, that is relevant to the event,"[10] then *ish* has a single meaning that works in all contexts. When the context demands that only males are relevant, then *ish* refers only to males. However, maleness is a narrowing of the overall sense, which is "each individual person or thing." Maleness is not the overall sense of the word, which pertains to all contexts.

The examples cited above indicate that the Hebrew word *ish* cannot always, and maybe not even ordinarily, be translated as "men." If *ish* were translated as "men," then salvation by gazing on the brass serpent, or by having a mark on one's head, would save men only, and women and children would be left to die. The dictionary meanings for *ish* range from "man, male, and husband," to "human being, person, servant, mankind, champion, great man, whosoever, and each."

7. CBMW, "Guidelines," A4.
8. 1 Kgs 7:30
9. Num 36:9
10. See Stein, "The Noun *ish,*" 1–24.

Biblical expressions with *ish* include "servant of God," "a Hebrew," "a Galilean," and "an Israelite"; these expressions imply a representative or an inhabitant of a city or region. These examples provide a wide range of ways to translate *ish* according to the context. Why should translators be restricted to using the English word "man," thus implying that maleness is significant in contributing to the tabernacle or being saved from death by snakebite?

It is true that *ish* is sometimes contrasted with woman, *ishah*, and can refer to men, warriors, and husbands; however, at other times, *ish* simply means all the inhabitants or everyone in the group, whether man, woman, or child. The context usually makes the meaning of *ish* obvious. There are also at least twenty times in the Bible where *ish* refers to non-human entities and inanimate objects. In those cases, *ish* simply means "each one." If *ish* is always translated into "every man" in English, it cannot refer to each and every thing, or each person in a group that is mentioned; it only means every man—that is, every male. Therefore, it would be best not to translate *ish* as "man" and "men" unless it is clear from some other information in the passage that *ish* refers only to a man or to men. Some passages in the Bible do not provide this information.

In modern Hebrew, the range of meaning for the word *ish* remains. Sometimes the word *ish* means "man" or "husband," or refers to an all-male group. At other times, *ish* really does mean "person." In a song written in the middle of the last century, both the title and the first line use the word *ish* to refer to "every person": *Le kol ish yesh shem* [Every person has a name].[11] This phrase, "Every person has a name," and this song have become commonly used at Holocaust memorials. Here, *ish* does not mean "every man"; rather, it means every individual, every human being—everyone has a name. This context also seems to imply that the group being referred to is the human race: Every member of the human race has a name. The word *ish* emphasizes the individuality and humanity of every person—man, woman, and child. In this case, it also specifically refers to those who died in the Holocaust and were buried in unmarked mass graves. In Hebrew, the word *ish* is routinely used for the notion of "each," "everyone," and "one another."

Therefore, even though it may be more common to see the word *ish* used to refer to men only, it is still relatively common for this word to refer to "any person." This kind of ambiguity does not cause a problem for native speakers of the language, who use such words in context. For us,

---

11. Mishkovsky, *Le kol ish.*

the readers of an ancient text, although the context sometimes shows that women are included, at other times we can only speculate and leave it at that. We cannot presume that the word *ish* excludes women unless the context makes it obvious, and we cannot automatically omit women from the various passages where the word *ish* is used. We cannot omit women from the Holocaust memorials. We cannot claim that it is enough to name "men" since men represent women. A disaster on the scale of the Holocaust means that the fertility of women and the survivability of young children are key to the preservation of the next generation. Such a disaster is about Rachel weeping for her children, because they are no more. The word *ish* used in this context does not only include men; it includes women and children, as each individual is equally valuable and each is equally worthy of full representation and remembrance.

The use of *ish* to refer to a member of a group explains why a familiar verse has been changed in modern translations. Ps 1 used to start, "Blessed is the man,"[12] but now it is more common to read, "Blessed is the one."[13] This change is not an attempt to minimize the role of the righteous man; rather, it is a recognition of the fact that the word *ish* can often mean "each person" or "an individual as a member of a group." Surely, before God, the righteous woman is also blessed. There is no reason to exclude women from generic examples of the faithful believer in the Bible.

The closest English example of a word that is used like the word *ish*, albeit not a complete parallel, is the word "fellow." This word refers to a man or a boy; however, it also means an "associate" or "colleague." The word "fellowship" has no implication of maleness, even though one of the meanings of "fellow" includes maleness. In English, we know from the context when a person is a "fellow" in the sense of being male, or when a person is a "fellow" in the sense of a colleague, member, or peer. In fact, the origin of the word "fellow" had no association with masculinity at all, but simply meant "partner." Fellowship implies a warm association, or a relationship of affection and reciprocity; here is a word that is commonly used to refer to males, but that does not carry masculinity as a core meaning.

David E. Stein, the editor of the *Contemporary Torah*, makes a similar point about *ish*—that this word doesn't primarily mean male, but conveys maleness only in certain contexts. He writes:

12. Ps 1:1 (ESV)

13. Ps 1:1 (NIV)

The Bible treats 'ish primarily as a term of affiliation, conveying social gender only in certain constructions; this understanding is superior to the conventional view that its primary sense is "adult male." Hence rendering 'ish in English as "man" distorts the biblical text more than is usually recognized.[14]

Stein continues:

The key to understanding 'ish is to see it as a term of association more than of gender. In my view, the primary sense of our noun in biblical Hebrew is "an affiliate" or "an associate," comprising the English concepts "a member of the group in question," "exemplar," and "representative."[15]

Stein cites several dictionary entries, many of which do present "a man, male" as the primary meaning of ish; however, the 1993 Concise Dictionary of Classical Hebrew also has "man, person, often without contextual emphasis on gender" as the first meaning.[16]

It is possible, then, that the first meaning of ish is not "male" but rather "an individual as a member of a group who has agency regarding whatever activity or event is occurring." Given the frequent context of land allocation, census-taking for war readiness, and the pervasiveness of warfare in ancient Hebrew society, this meaning of ish would still often refer to a male. As a result, the word ish became used for a man, leader, representative, or warrior. However, ish did not lose its generic sense of an individual human being as a representative member of a certain community or of the human race. Therefore, even though ish often referred to men, in other contexts it could still refer to mixed groups of men and women, to groups of all women, or to an indefinite member of a group. A woman could be an ish in some contexts of that society, but not in others.

Although the term ish refers to a generic member of society in many passages, the word also has a counterpart: the word ishah, which refers specifically to women. However, the ishah, that is, the women, were still included in many occurrences of the single word ish. In the plural, the word ish was often a gender-inclusive word that referred to a group of men and women. As mentioned earlier, there is no plural for the Hebrew word

14. Stein, "What Does It Mean."
15. Stein, "Part 1: Initial Case," 1.
16. Clines, Concise Dictionary.

adam, the generic word for "humankind." The plural of *ish*, *anashim*, was used as the plural for both *adam* and *ish*.

On the one hand, a known and identified man and woman are referred to as *ish* and *ishah*; on the other hand, when *ish* is used to describe an indefinite person, such as a representative member of a group in a law or a proverb, the word generally refers to a generic member of society. Maleness does not appear to be a consistent part of the meaning of *ish*. As part of a common biblical expression, "one to another," *ish* appears to include men and women. This expression is first used to describe people building the tower of Babel: "they said to one [*ish*] another, 'Come, let us make bricks, and burn them thoroughly.'"[17] Here, the complete expression in Hebrew is *ish al re'ehu*, meaning "each one to the neighbor," or "every person to the one next to them"; the use of this phrase does not indicate that only men were making bricks. Brick-making was a task usually assigned to both male and female workers.

The same phrase occurs later in the Bible:

> Therefore the Jews of the villages, who live in the rural towns, hold the fourteenth day of the month of Adar as a day for gladness and feasting, as a holiday, and as a day on which they send gifts of food to one another [*ish al re'ehu*].[18]

Purim is a celebration of Esther's actions to protect the Jewish community in Persia. It is a festive occasion that is still widely practiced in some Jewish communities. Men, women, and children give parcels of food or sweets to their friends and neighbors. Purim is a time to recognize neighbors, even those you may not know well. Giving baskets of food, candies, or flowers on Purim fulfills two goals for Jews who continue this custom: It is a way to give to those in need in a gracious manner; and it is an important means of fostering community membership, strengthening bonds between neighbors, and building bonds between those of the same ethnic or religious group. This practice reinforces group cohesion, as members recognize each other in a way that has no doctrinal measuring stick, but focuses on sharing food. Children are involved in Purim so that they will grow up with the habit of recognizing and respecting other members of the community. The word *ish*, used to describe the beginning of Purim in the book of Esther,

---

17. Gen 11:3 (ESV)
18. Esth 9:19

refers specifically to a member of the community, and not to "people" in general.

Thus, from the way *ish* is used, it appears to have a generic meaning; it can refer to both men and women. It only refers to men in circumstances where it is clear that only men are involved. In contrast, the word "male" (*zakar*) is routinely used in text relating to circumcision, or when choosing a specifically male animal for a sacrifice. The word "male" exists in Hebrew, and is used in conjunction with the word *ish* whenever it is crucial to specify the male gender.

It is not possible to make Hebrew categories for human beings align with the expectations of English readers. Just as the word *adam* established that a person was neither a god nor an animal, so the word *ish* established that a person was a member of the group who was relevant to the event. An *ish* was any member, and an *ishah* was a female *ish*, a female member. Although these two words are not etymologically related,[19] they function robustly to refer to an adult male and adult female. Also, although the word *ish* and its plural *anashim* are used for a mixed group, there is no implication that these words refer to men only and that, by extension, men may represent women. No, the use of *ish* and *anashim* simply indicates that the masculine form is used to refer to groups of mixed gender. This is a linguistic artifact of a patriarchal society and not a theological statement.

Therefore, referring to a group of women as *kol ish* ("every person") does not indicate the primacy of the male; rather, it brings attention to the primary sense of the word *ish*: a group member, an insider, or a relevant individual. *Ish* is sometimes used to refer to the scales of a crocodile, shapes on the temple basins, or cuts of meat for sacrifice. It is also used for households, tribes, names, and faces; in these contexts, *ish* means "side by side" (more literally, "side by each") or lined up. Thus, *ish* brings a focus on each and every one; its emphasis is on the person or object that is a part of a whole.

In many of the Bible verses that refer to people, the intent to include women as well as men can hardly be missed. However, this intent may be invisible in an English translation. The fact that one Bible version translates *ish* as a "person" or "anyone" rather than "a man" slightly more often than another Bible is not a sign of a liberal trend; rather, it is a recognition that in the current English language, the word "man" refers to a male, and not to a human being in general, as it did at the time of the King James Version

---

19. Although they are so similar, the two words come from different roots.

(KJV). In fact, the focus intended by *ish* is on every member of the group, or "every one among you."

However, in spite of the occurrences of the word *ish* that refer to group membership for men, women, and children, the Colorado Springs Guidelines say: "Hebrew '*ish* should ordinarily be translated 'man' and 'men'".[20]

What does "ordinarily" mean? How do translators know what an ordinary occurrence of *ish* is, and what is otherwise? Do translators have the freedom to say that every member of the community may be saved by looking at the brass snake? Can they indicate that all Jews, not just male adults, are to give parcels of food to each other? Is anyone with a mark on their forehead preserved from the massacre, or only men? In other words, do these guidelines allow translators to translate in such a way that a reader may understand what group membership actually meant, and how the survival and participation of women and children were included?

Some Bibles, such as the ESV and the HCSB, follow the Colorado Springs Guidelines, and in these translations, the inclusion of women in community activities is often veiled or hidden. Other Bible translations are affected by these guidelines in more subtle ways, as the translators attempt to compromise and use male language in many places where the original languages do not necessarily use male-specific terms. Given a modern translation, it is very difficult to know whether the word "man" in English is a translation of a specifically male term, or a translation of a term that would have been understood by the audience of that time as including all members of the community.

Another important part of the meaning of *ish* is that of being an associate, a partner, or a peer. This is not inherently hierarchical; that is, an *ish* may be a representative or an ambassador, but is more commonly an affiliate member of a group who has a reciprocal relation with others in the group.

Not long ago, I was sitting in a restaurant discussing the meaning of *ish* with a friend. Incredibly, Gil's mother had escaped from Auschwitz as a girl, and his father had survived his service in the Russian army, which was also unusual. Gil was born to this young Jewish couple in a displaced persons camp somewhere in Germany; from there, the family came to New York City. Gil grew up in New York, gained a PhD in English literature, and made *aliya*—that is, immigrated to Israel in order to return to the land. In Israel, Gil got married and taught English literature at Hebrew University.

20. CBMW, "Guidelines," A4.

His wife eventually wanted to come to New York, so Gil left Israel and returned to New York. He and his wife felt a sense of relief on arriving in the United States; during a stroll through New York's lower east side, they remarked on the lack of nervous tension, and the difference between life here and life in Israel, where there was always a risk of bombs and violence. Ironically, this occurred on the eve of 9/11, when the twin towers came down.

Some years have gone by, and Gil still lives in New York, although his wife passed away due to a sudden illness. Sitting in the restaurant, talking of Gil's future, the question came up: If Gil were to remarry, would he deliberately choose to marry a Jewish woman? Or, as Gil put it, would he marry a woman who was strong and powerful in personality, as Jewish women are? We failed to come up with solid advice for him, so I changed the subject. I brought up my book, and this chapter on *ish*, which is also the Hebrew word for "husband." Gil responded:

> The word for husband in Israel used to be *baal*. A woman would call her husband *baali, my baal*. But that sounds too much like "master" or "lord"—women don't want to use that anymore. Now they call their husband *ishi*, "my man." This matches *ishti*, "my woman." So the Hebrew language is changing.

I knew that both *baal* and *ish* were used in the Hebrew Bible for "husband," but I had never thought much about the differences between the two. Saying *ishi* and *ishti* is not unlike calling someone your spouse or partner, using matching male and female terms. In fact, the equality that these terms imply is supported by a biblical passage: "And in that day, declares the Lord, you will call me 'My Ish,' and no longer will you call me 'My Baal.'"[21]

A different verse has caused considerable confusion to translators who were uncertain how to express the meaning of *ish* in English: "And Adam knew Eve his wife; and she conceived, and bore Cain, and said, I have gotten a man [*ish*] from the Lord."[22]

Did Eve really intend to say "man?" The Good News Bible (GNB) says "son," and the HCSB uses "a male child." However, the *Contemporary Torah* edited by Stein, says: "I have created a person with the help of YHWH." In Genesis, the woman was taken out of the first human being; now, she has created a new human being—a person who belongs in their human family.

---

21. Hos 2:16
22. Gen 4:1

The child is not simply a human or a male human; this baby is someone who belongs. That first human child was a member of a family, precious and beloved. This child was Cain. Even though Cain murdered his own brother, God still loved him in a special way, by putting a mark on his forehead to signify that God had decided Cain should be protected and not killed in revenge. Although Cain was exiled from his family, God gave him a sign that he was still a concern of God.

The word *ish* refers to being in relation with someone else, or with a member of a community. This is not a matter of being Hebrew, in particular; rather, it is a recognition that every human being belongs to a family and to a people. It is about being an insider of the group, whatever group that is. We all want to be insiders—to be in relation to others, and to know who we are in relation to the group.

Although men were often the main representatives in certain situations, whether a census, war, or land ownership, women could also fulfill certain of these functions. A widow or heiress could own land and slaves, trade goods, and have a reputation for being related to the right people. This may not have occurred often, but it did sometimes occur. Women were as much a part of many of the laws as the men were, for better or worse.

David Stein's *Contemporary Torah*, which translates *ish* according to its meaning in context, is subtitled *A Gender-Sensitive Adaption of the JPS Translation*. Some may flinch at the term "gender-sensitive"; however, this simply means that the translator has taken into account the fact that certain words in the original do not convey information regarding gender, even though the English language assigns gender to them. For example, in Greek, *anthropos* is grammatically a word of common gender. There is no gender assigned to this word. One could say that it is gender neutral, although it is not a word in the neuter gender, but is equally either masculine or feminine. There are many Greek words of common gender, although these have been understood as masculine in the translation processes of some Bibles.

Furthermore, some words become gender inclusive in the plural. This is just the way the language works. The normal dictionary meaning of *adelphos*, in the plural, is "brothers and sisters." This has not been modified to include women; it is the normal usage of the word.

In addition, all beings, whether animate or inanimate, must be represented by pronouns at some point in order to construct unambiguous sentences. But the pronoun system of every language varies, and this system is part of the grammatical pattern of the language. A rather humorous case of gender confusion in pronoun usage occurs in the original story of Beauty and the Beast. In French, Belle is feminine, and la Bête, the Beast, is also a feminine word. So in French, "elle," that is the Beast, wishes to sleep with "elle," that is Belle. Of course, this is a heterosexual relationship: The beast is a male, but the pronoun is not.

A gender-sensitive translation is one that first studies the way gender was represented in the world of the language in question, and then attempts to use the English language in a way that replicates this. For example, we would refer to the Beast as "he" even though the French uses a feminine pronoun. In a gender-sensitive translation, the word *ish* would be translated to indicate that women and children were also saved by looking at the snake, can also exchange gifts of food, and can also produce trade goods— they are full members of their nation and people. Although women and children exist in relation to their family, they also exist in relation to their tribe and to the people outside the immediate household. They exist for others, not only in relation to the male who is the head of the house.

A friend of mine has an adult autistic daughter. This young woman longs to feel that she is a part of things and that she has friends that she is connected to. Her conversation sounds quite sophisticated, but is often limited to discussing options for having tea: which teahouse, what brand of tea, when will you pick me up, and so forth. At the church I attended, she poured tea after the service. Belonging, having a role, and being accepted are crucial for her. She is completely and utterly aware of when she doesn't fit in. More than anything else in the world, this young woman longs for a community where she belongs, where she is a community member. She wants to give to the tabernacle too, and she wants her offering to be accepted. Being accepted is essential to everyone among us—our hearts ache to belong.

CHAPTER 13

Many Manly Deeds

The blessed Judith, . . . exposed herself to peril and went forth for love of her country and of her people which were beleaguered; and the Lord delivered Holophernes into the hand of a woman.

(CLEMENT, *EPISTLE TO THE CORINTHIANS*, 55:4)

I READ NANCY DREW and the Hardy Boys when I was younger; however, the great stories that moved my imagination came from the Greek tragedies. Antigone, Elektra, Polyxena, and Iphigenia were strong and beautiful Greek princesses who suffered at the whim of the fates. The first Greek girl I met in literature, however, was Nausicaa, a teenage princess playing ball on the beach while the household slaves did the laundry. Odysseus washed up on the shore naked, and Nausicaa gave him some of the laundry to wear; he was able to get help from her parents, who, on discovering who Odysseus was, offered him their daughter in marriage. However, he was much too old for her, and already married, with adult children of his own. Nausicaa pined after Odysseus for a while, but that was all. On the other hand, Nausicaa is important in her own right, as she is the first person to be recorded in literature as playing with a ball. She is a young woman caught between childhood and adulthood—a typical teenager.

The other young women who interested me had a tragic fate: Iphigenia's father sacrificed her on an altar to the gods before setting out to do battle with Troy, and she went courageously to her death; and Polyxena and Alcestis were noble Greek women who died with great courage and dignity for the good of their family or out of recognition that their death was inevitable. As Aristotle wrote:

> Hence it is manifest that all the persons mentioned have a moral virtue of their own, the temperance of a woman and that of a man are not the same, nor their courage and justice, as Socrates thought, but the one is the courage of command, and the other that of subordination . . .[1]

In Aristotle's opinion, although women have courage [*andreia*], it is the courage of subordinating oneself to the greater good and submitting to be sacrificed in war or for some other end. Unfortunately, many of these stories portray women who were sacrificed by the men in their family rather than being protected.

Antigone broke the trend of submissive women. She defied her uncle, Creon, who was the ruler of the state, in order to bury her brother, a rebel and traitor against the uncle. Antigone argued that it was a moral necessity set down by the gods that she honor her brother, in spite of the command of her uncle. Creon felt strongly, according to his beliefs, that if Antigone resisted him, then she was a man, and he was no longer a man. He ordered her death, saying: "while I live, no woman will rule me." Creon lived by Aristotle's interpretation of the world: "rule or be ruled."

Antigone did not repent, and was shut up in a cave to die. She hanged herself rather than wait for the end. Her fiancé, Creon's son, persuaded his father that she should be rescued, but he came too late and found Antigone dead. He committed suicide, and then his mother did the same—Creon ended his life alone. Although Aristotle claims that it is woman's nature and her courage to submit, Antigone shows that a woman also has the courage to resist.

The story of Antigone is so powerful and unique that in 1942, Jean Anouilh rewrote the play in French; it was performed in Paris in 1944. The Germans permitted the performance of Antigone as a classical drama, while the French understood that Antigone represented resistance to an immoral authority. Antigone became a symbol for the French Resistance, with the theme that it is better to die than to submit to wrongful authority.

In ancient drama and fictionalized history, a woman often represents a weaker nation or ethnic group that is enslaved by an empire. Her resistance

---

1. Aristotle, *Politics*, 1260a:20.

is understood to represent the righteous action of those who defy an improper government, and who often die out of loyalty to a higher moral code or because of their faithfulness to the one God. In Antigone's case, she acted out of deliberate defiance to the male who was not only the ruler of the state but also the head of her family. Creon was Antigone's patriarch, but she flouted his authority in order to do the right thing.

In ancient Greek literature, such a woman is often labeled as *andreia* or "courageous." The word *andreia* is derived from the Greek word *aner*, which is usually understood to mean "man." The verb related to *aner* is *andrizomai*. Some Bible translators insist on translating every occurrence of *aner* as "man," and assume that *andrizomai* urges men to "act like men." However, women were often described as *andreia* in the literature of that time. What if women are also included in biblical groups that are addressed as *andres* (the plural of *aner*)? What if *aner* can refer to an indefinite person, whether male or female? Then surely there would be some reason to translate *aner* or *andres* as "person" or "people." If women are included in the Greek noun *aner*, then the English translation ought to use a noun that includes women. *Andreia* would be translated as "courageous," and *andrizomai* would be translated as "be courageous." Since women can be courageous, one would not want to translate *andrizomai* as "be men of courage," or "be manly"; rather, it would become "be courageous." Let's get back to how the ancient Greeks used these words.

In the quotation from Aristotle above, it doesn't make sense to say that it is the "manliness" of a woman to submit; rather, it is the "courage" of women to submit. And indeed, "courage" is how *andreia* is traditionally translated into English in the classical Greek texts. Since women are described as *andreia* as often as men are, and in similar circumstances, *andreia* is usually thought to be better interpreted as "courage" rather than "manliness."

Aristotle had a theory about the nature of women: that women have the deliberative function—that is, they can think—but that they lack authority or sovereignty—that is, they cannot make decisions or rule. According to Aristotle, women are under the protection of the male who rules them. Women do not have the same *andreia* as men. However, the Greek plays demonstrate that the submission of a woman in no way protects her. In the stories, an ancient Greek princess or queen is often a pawn of war; she may be traded, enslaved, or sacrificed on altars. Polyxena, a princess of Troy, was sacrificed on the grave of Achilles, who was the greatest of the Greek warriors. Before the war, Achilles might have married Iphigenia; however, she had been sacrificed to the gods by her father, who was pleading for success in battle. It was not safe to be a Greek princess and worthy of marriage to a great warrior. On the other hand, Alcestis was a woman who voluntarily died in the place of her husband because she considered him to be more essential to the survival of her children.

When placed in a difficult situation, Elektra and her sister chose to take action. After their father sacrificed Iphigenia and left for Troy, their mother took a lover. On their father's return from Troy, their mother killed their father for having sacrificed their older sister Iphigenia, and then married her lover. This new husband then proved to be a danger to the remaining children, especially to Elektra's twin brother Orestes, the new heir. Orestes escaped, leaving his sisters uncertain of whether he was alive or dead. Elektra suggested to her younger sister that they should take action and kill their mother and her new husband, which the gods decreed to be morally correct. Even though their mother had had just cause to kill her husband, she was not committed to the value of carrying on the family line.

Elektra declared to her sister that if the two of them killed their mother, they would be spoken of throughout Greece for accomplishing this deed. People would say:

> Behold these two sisters, my friends! They saved their father's house, and at a time when their foes were firmly established, they took their lives in their hands and administered bloodshed! Worthy of love is this pair, worthy of reverence from all. At festivals, and wherever the citizenry is assembled, let these two be honored by all men for their manly courage [*andreia*].[2]

In this case, the translator chose to translate *andreia* as "manly courage" rather than simply "courage," perhaps in order to suggest that the girls were aware that they were taking an action that belonged to their brother. However, before the sisters kill their mother, Orestes returns and does the deed himself. At first tormented, Orestes is ultimately pronounced innocent by the gods, and Elektra and her sister are proven right in having supported their brother and shared in his intent.

Some women in Greek drama behave according to the nature of women as Aristotle defined it, but many do not. They take on courageous actions, or "manly deeds." It is difficult to tell in translation, since the word *andreia* is sometimes translated as "manly" and sometimes as simply "courageous."

2. Sophocles, *Electra*, 975–80.

In the Septuagint (the 2nd century BCE Greek translation of the Hebrew Bible), the word *andreia* is used for women in two memorable verses:

> An excellent [*andreia*] wife who can find?
> She is far more precious than jewels.[3]

> An excellent [*andreia*] wife is the crown of her husband,
> but she who brings shame is like rottenness in his bones.[4]

It is impossible to translate *andreia* in these instances as "manly." Who would want a "manly" wife, and how could a "manly wife" be "the crown of her husband"? Clearly, another interpretation of *andreia* is needed—one that has nothing to do with maleness or manliness. Here, *andreia* seems to suggest nobility or, as the English translator chose, "excellence." To me, the most interesting thing in Prov 12 is the contrast between "excellence" (*andreia*) and "shame." This contrast gives *andreia* a moral quality that must pertain equally to men and women, and prevents a woman from bringing shame to her husband. Courage itself is a moral virtue for all humans; it is not just a masculine trait. According to Aristotle, courage is the highest of all moral virtues. Thus, a better translation of the verse in Prov 12 might be "A courageous wife is the crown of her husband."

Translations of the Septuagint vary somewhat in their wording of Prov 31:10. The first translator of the Septuagint, whose work was published in 1808, was an American named Charles Thompson; he discreetly used "virtuous" for this verse, as does the King James Bible. The translation by Sir Lancelot Charles Lee Brenton (1844) does the same. Neither refer to courage here. However, it can be argued that in the past, the word "virtuous" did convey a sense of courage. Nevertheless, I have never noticed the adjective "virtuous" being used for a man in an English translation of the Bible. Joshua was not told to be "virtuous" before setting out to invade Canaan—he was told to be "courageous." The New English Translation of the Septuagint (2007) properly translates *andreia* as "courageous."

Although the Septuagint is in Greek, it is a translation from the original Hebrew. The story of Ruth and Boaz may therefore provide some insight here, since it uses the same Hebrew word as the one used in Proverbs. The Hebrew word *chayil* (power) is used to describe both Ruth and the wife in Prov 12 and 31. In chapter 2 of the book of Ruth, Boaz is described as a

3. Prov 31:10
4. Prov 12:4

powerful man (*dunatos*). In chapter 3, Boaz tells Ruth: "You are a woman of power" (*dunameos*). There are various interpretations for why *dunameos* was used to describe Ruth. One interpretation is that the book of Ruth establishes the lineage of King David, her great grandson, and thus presents David as a powerful king from a powerful family. However, this phrasing also echoes a lesson that is evident in the narratives of the Hebrew patriarchs and matriarchs: A powerful husband ought to have a powerful wife. In some sense, the wife of a powerful man should have nobility, courage, and strength that are equal to those of her husband. For example, the wife might often need to represent the husband's business interests (see chapter 1).

Another recounting of women who perform *andreia* ("manly" or "courageous") deeds can add to our understanding of the term. In the first epistle of Clement of Rome, written in the 1st century CE, Clement describes the love and courage that the great leader Moses had towards his people; he then describes Esther and Judith as also performing "manly" deeds:

> Many women being strengthened through the grace of God have performed many manly [*andreia*] deeds.
>
> The blessed Judith, when the city was beleaguered, asked of the elders that she might be suffered to go forth into the camp of the aliens. So she exposed herself to peril and went forth for love of her country and of her people which were beleaguered; and the Lord delivered Holophernes into the hand of a woman.
>
> To no less peril did Esther also, who was perfect in faith, expose herself, that she might deliver the twelve tribes of Israel, when they were on the point to perish. For through her fasting and her humiliation she entreated the all seeing Master, the God of the ages; and He, seeing the humility of her soul, delivered the people for whose sake she encountered the peril.[5]

Although Clement attributes the accomplishments of these women to their faith and to God's intervention, this does not differentiate them from male heroes in Hebrew narratives. In literature and art, Esther is often represented as matching Joseph: Both were foreigners in a strange land and in a vulnerable position, and both ultimately became the saviors of the Jewish nation. Judith hacked off the head of the Assyrian General Holofernes, making her a worthy female counterpart to David, who beheaded Goliath.

---

5. Clement, *Epistle to the Corinthians*, 55:3–6.

It is still tempting to view these stories as gendered. After all, both Esther and Judith used their beauty as a means of seduction. However, it is worth remembering that Joseph and David were also marked by exceptional beauty. Thus, the attribution of beauty, vulnerability, strength, and courage do not seem to be gendered in these narratives. In some places in ancient literature, men and women are portrayed as "ruler" and "ruled," respectively, as in Aristotle; however, in other places, the narratives contradict this and present men and women as sharing God-given characteristics that belong equally to both sexes.

Therefore, it appears that the core sense of the word *andreia* does not necessarily entail manliness, or having the physical attributes of a male human being; rather, this word refers to being strong and courageous. Yet the word *andreia* certainly derives from the word *aner*, which is generally interpreted as "a man." But which attributes of a man does *andreia* portray? And, even more to the point, is "maleness" the core meaning of *aner*, from which *andreia* derives? In some ways, yes, it is, as we can see from Creon's speech. But in other contexts, different meanings come to light. There are thousands of occurrences of the word *aner* in the Bible and in ancient literature. As we will see, some of these occurrences significantly depart from the meaning of "a male human being" and are in fact gender inclusive—that is, they refer to both men and women.

Some conservative Christian scholars have argued that the main difference between *aner* and *anthropos* is one of gender; they argue because *anthropos* means "human beings in general," *aner* must therefore mean "a male human being." Poythress writes:

> After all, another Greek word *anthropos* is available that can be used in referring to situations involving both sexes. It is linguistically improbable that we would find *aner* moving toward near synonymy with *anthropos*, leaving Greek with no obvious, convenient term to use when one wants to specify that one is talking about male human beings.[6]

First, it is obvious that many languages have more than one word that can be used to refer to human beings. For example, in English, we have *human*, *person*, and *individual* in the singular, and *humans*, *people*, *individuals*, and *persons* in the plural; also, in Hebrew, four distinct words are translated as "man" in English. Second, Poythress is missing something here: The difference between an *anthropos* and an *aner* is a matter of class and quality

6. Poythress and Grudem, *Gender-Neutral Bible Controversy,* 321–33.

rather than one of gender. *Anthropos* was the usual way to address a slave or person of low status. It also refers to general human qualities. Although *anthropos* sometimes simply means a human being, it also has the connotation of being nothing more than a lowly and mortal human being. For example, when commenting on a losing battle, Herodotus[7] writes, "They made it evident to every man, and to the king himself not least of all, that human beings [*anthropos*] are many but men [*aner*] are few."[8] Clearly, everyone fighting in the battle was male; however, some of these males were behaving as poor-quality and untrained *anthropos* rather than men of warrior quality.

Many passages in Greek literature use the words *anthropos* and *aner* in contrasting ways that have nothing to do with gender. Gender, male or female, is a narrow lens through which to view how the ancient Greeks classified human beings. The men in the passage above were not being compared to women; they were being compared to men of a lower class or quality. Of course, women could also fight with courage, as is shown elsewhere. For example, Thucydides[9] writes: "And the women also manfully assisted them, throwing tiles from the houses and enduring the tumult even beyond the condition of their sex."[10]

To be or to act as an *aner* in war was not contrasted with the behavior of women in war; rather, it was contrasted with the behavior of slaves or cowards. Women were not honoured for being weak, but for being strong and "manly." Thucydides was caught between Aristotle's view of women—that submission is their courage—and a contrary view that was shared by other Greek philosophers. Yes, women have weaknesses and are not as strong as men; however, making a show of manly strength is nonetheless the glory of women. Thucydides also writes:

> And, if I am to speak of womanly virtues to those of you who will henceforth be widows, let me sum them up in one short admonition: To a woman not to show more weakness than is natural to her sex is a great glory.[11]

---

7. Herodotus was a Greek historian around 484–425 BCE.

8. Herodotus, *Histories*, 7:210.

9. Thucydides was an Athenian historian in 460–400 BCE.

10. Thucydides, *Peloponnesian War*, 3:74.

11. Thucydides, *Peloponnesian War*, 2:45.

Although an *aner* was sometimes contrasted with a woman, as in Creon's speech, an *aner* was more often contrasted with an *anthropos* or with the gods, the *theoi*. It is worth emphasizing here that the word *theos* is a Greek word of common gender. Athena is a god, a *theos,* as is Aphrodite. In some poetic literature, the word *theia* is also used for a goddess, but this does not mean that a female god is not a *theos*. So contrasting *andres* and *theoi,* gods and humans, does not relate to gender. The contrast here is not between male gods and male human beings, but between gods and humans in general. The Iliad[12] states that Zeus is the father of gods and men, of *theoi* and *andres*; this means that Zeus is the father of gods (both male and female) and of humans (both male and female). This is a gender-inclusive use of *andres,* the plural of *aner.*

The contrast between gods and humans is more poignantly illustrated by the dilemma of Thetis, a goddess, who was married to Peleus, a mortal. She mourns:

> Hephaestus, is there now any goddess, of all those that are in Olympus, that hath endured so many grievous woes in her heart as are the sorrows that Zeus, son of Cronos, hath given me beyond all others? Of all the daughters of the sea he subdued me alone to a mortal [*aner*], even to Peleus, son of Aeacus, and I endured the bed of a mortal albeit sore against my will. And lo, he lieth [435] in his halls fordone with grievous old age, but now other griefs are mine. A son he gave me to bear and to rear, pre-eminent among warriors, and he shot up like a sapling; then when I had reared him as a tree in a rich orchard plot, I sent him forth in the beaked ships to Ilios to war with the Trojans; but never again shall I welcome him back to his home, to the house of Peleus.[13]

Here, Thetis is grieving that as a goddess, she has given birth to a famous warrior, Achilles, who will die in battle. Achilles is a mortal like his father. The word *aner* here describes the condition of being human and mortal, whether experiencing death through aging, as her husband has, or by death in battle, which her son will suffer. Achilles then honors his mother with this eulogy:

> You alone of all the gods saved Zeus the Darkener of the Skies from an inglorious fate, when some of the other Olympians—Hera,

---

12. An ancient Greek epic poem, usually attributed to Homer.
13. Homer, *The Iliad,* 18:428.

Poseidon, and Pallas Athene—had plotted to throw him into chains . . . You, goddess, went and saved him from that indignity.[14]

The word *aner* is also contrasted with a child. To be an *aner* is to be an adult. In Greek, an *aner* is a different stage of life than a child. *Pais* is the word for child; it is used for a girl in Luke 8:54 and for a boy in Luke 9:42. Contrasting an *aner* with a *pais* is not necessarily a gendered meaning. When contrasted with a woman, or a wife, the *aner* is clearly a man. In war, the *aner* is a man. But sometimes the *aner* is an adult, whether a mortal or an example of a generic human being. In Lucian's *Anacharsis*[15] on the physical training of athletes, the word *andrizomai* ("to be a man") is translated as "when their frames begin to set," and refers to physical maturity.

Some of these usages of *aner* are gender inclusive, as I will demonstrate. First, the *aner* is a citizen or a person of the citizen class. Next, the *aner* is an individual, or an indefinite person, who represents all humans in proverbs and idioms. Third, the *aner* is a member of a nation or city. All of these types of people include females.

Plato had a very different view of humanity than Aristotle. He idealized the human being, and wrote about what human beings could be, or should be, if they were trained according to their nature. Plato wrote about a utopian state in which women received the same training as men in music, philosophy, athletics, and war. Certainly, women would likely only be fit to be auxiliaries in war; however, this was a necessary role that women could fill. If a woman had the inclination to be a musician or a medical doctor, then why train her in anything else? She must be trained according to her nature. I should add here that Plato was not exactly a feminist. On the one hand, Plato believed that women were weaker than men, although in what sense he did not specify. On the other hand, he considered that women should be guardians or rulers of the state alongside men. Plato may have simply meant that women are *physically* weaker than men, which is usually true. However, it is also possible that Plato may have meant that women were weaker overall—although that is another discussion altogether. In any case, our focus here is on how Plato used language, particularly the word *aner*.

In Plato's ideal state, women were full citizens, or *aner*, alongside men. Plato writes:

14. Homer, *The Iliad,* 18:428.
15. Lucian, *Anacharsis,* 195.

The sum and substance of our agreement was simply this: that whatsoever be the way in which a member of our community—be he of the male or female sex, young or old—may become a good citizen [*aner*], possessed of the excellence of soul which belongs to man [*anthropos*].[16]

It is not possible to interpret *aner* as a male human being in this passage. Thus, an *aner* does not contrast in any gendered way with the word *anthropos*. The *aner* is a person of the citizen class, male or female, whereas an *anthropos* is a human being with all that that entails. Poythress' suggestion, then, that *aner* must be a male human being, in contrast to *anthropos* as a generic human being, does not stand up to the evidence—how Plato, a major authority, uses these words in his writings. Although *aner* and *anthropos* do have different meanings, gender is not predominate among them. Instead, the difference is one of citizenship and adulthood, and the courage and responsibilities pertaining to that class. Herodotus 5:63 also uses the word *aner* to mean "citizen"; in this case, Herodotus is referring to a man. Thus, *aner* and *anthropos* have meanings that do not relate to gender.

Because *aner* can refer to a generic human being, it can sometimes be used as a synonym for *anthropos* in designating a representative and indefinite human being or individual. Over the years, from the 1800s until the present, *aner* has been translated by classical scholars into a variety of terms: "citizen," "mortal," "person," "everyone," "they," and "individual." Here are a few examples:

Why, surely it would be wrong of me not to obey a good and wise person [*aner*].[17]

Slave or free, every one [*pas aner*] is glad to gaze upon the light.[18]

Every individual [*aner*], because of his greed for silver and gold, is willing to toil at every art and device, noble or ignoble, if he is likely to get rich by it.[19]

In many instances, classical scholars have not translated *aner* as "man." This pattern started in the 1800s and is not related to a feminist agenda in any way. In sayings about the nature of humankind, the word *aner* represents

16. Plato, *Laws*, 6:770d.
17. Plato, *Hipparchus*, 228b.
18. Euripides, *Orestes*, 1523.
19. Plato, *Laws*, 8.831d.

a generic human being. Women are no different from men in any of the examples given above. In other situations, as shown earlier, it is impossible to translate *aner* as "man" because the word explicitly includes both males and females.

Finally, the plural of *aner* is used in a gender-inclusive way when addressing or referring to a group of citizens of a certain country or people in assembly. In the plural, *aner* becomes *andres*, and this term is very commonly used when addressing a group. The most recorded and referred-to example is *Andres Athenoi*, which means "citizens of Athens." The plural *andres* has also been translated as "people" or "friends." But how can we be certain that the expression *andres* includes females? It is very difficult to tell from the context—some scholars say that of course women are included, while others disagree. Fortunately, we don't have to guess. In at least one clear instance, females are explicitly included in the formal address *andres*. Needless to say, this single authoritative counterexample disproves Grudem's claim that the word is always used to mean males only, and proves that the word can include women.

Lucian of Samosata was a satirist and comedian in the second century CE; we can reasonably assume that he obeyed the rules of the Greek language and wrote in a way that was comprehensible and grammatically faithful to the Greek language. Lucian wrote a play called *Zeus, the Tragedian*. Although this play is a satire that questions the very existence of the Greek gods, in it, Zeus addresses the assembly of the gods, which includes Hera, Athena, Aphrodite, Apollo, Poseidon, and Hermes.

In helping Zeus address the assembly of gods, Hermes attempts to get things started. He calls out, using both *theoi* for both male and female, and then he switches to the feminine *theainai* for the female gods. First Hermes says:

> any female gods [*theoi*], or any male[20]

And later he adds,

> Listen to me, all gods [*theoi*] and all goddesses [*theainai*][21]

When Zeus eventually addresses the assembly, he says:

> *O Andres Theoi*[22]

20. Lucian, *Zeus, the Tragedian*, 6.
21. Lucian, *Zeus, the Tragedian*, 14.
22. Lucian, *Zeus, the Tragedian*, 15.

Here, Zeus may be saying, "oh you mortal gods," or he may mean "citizens of heaven." In any case, he is imitating the normal way of addressing an Athenian assembly. How likely is it that Hera, Athena, and Aphrodite are being addressed as "men" or even as "gentlemen"? Could they be called "men and gods?" As noted earlier, the word for god, *theos*, was not a gendered term and referred equally to male and female gods, even though the word *thea* clearly meant "goddess."

The clearest cases where *aner* or *andres* are used to refer to generic human beings, or a group of mixed men and women, appear in literature that is satirical or utopian. Does this invalidate these occurrences as evidence? A quick test is all that is needed. No matter what genre the passage is, does it make sense in English to say "a man, either female or male?" Does it make sense to address a group of mixed men and women, including one's wife, as "men" or "gentlemen?" It is doubtful that this kind of phrasing was ever possible. Furthermore, unlike the English use of "men" in the time of the King James Bible, the word "men" today always refers to male human beings. Aside from Bible translations that contain dated language or idioms, the word "men" no longer refers to a group of mixed gender. Women today do not consider themselves included if there is a request that all "men" stand up. And we certainly cannot accept that a man can be either "female or male."

Therefore, it is clear that *aner* and its plural, *andres*, can sometimes be translated as "person," "people," "citizen," "mortal," "fellow," "everyone," "they," "any individual," or another such term that refers to generic human beings.

The New Testament contains two different patterns where *aner* demands a generic translation. The first occurs when the apostles address a crowd. Here are a few examples with contrasting translations. In Acts 1:11, regarding Jesus' ascension into heaven:

> *Andres Galilaioi* (original Greek)
>
> Men of Galilee (ESV)
>
> Galileans (CEB)

In Acts 2:22, at Pentecost:

> *Andres Israelitai* (original Greek)
>
> Men of Israel (ESV)

Fellow Israelites (NIV)

In Acts 3:12, when Peter addresses the people:

Andres Israelitai (original Greek)

Men of Israel (ESV)

You Israelites (CEB)

In Acts 19:35, when Paul addresses a crowd at Ephesus:

Andres Ephesioi (original Greek)

Men of Ephesus (ESV)

People of Ephesus (NIV)

Either there was a mysterious absence of women from all of these momentous occasions and major sermons in the book of Acts, or else *andres* does, in fact, include women, and is an acceptable and normal way to address groups of men and women. For example, the woman Damaris is present in Acts 17, when Paul addresses the assembly on the Areopagus, saying:

Andres Athenoi (original Greek)

Men of Athens (ESV)

People of Athens (NIV, CEB)

What then about the singular *aner*—can it be used to mean a generic human being, not necessarily a man? Here are some biblical uses of *aner* that imply that this word refers to a representative of the human race. In Rom 4:8:

Blessed is the man [*aner*] (ESV)

Blessed is the one [*aner*] (NIV)

In Eph 4:13:

Until we all reach ... mature manhood (ESV)

Until we all ... become mature adults (CEB)

The Liddell-Scott-Jones Lexicon[23] makes it clear that *aner* is a "man" in contrast to (a) a woman, (b) the gods, and (c) a youth. In this entry, both (b) and (c) refer to a generic person. In older dictionaries, it was normal to use the term "man as opposed to gods" to define a human being. This

23. Liddell and Scott, *A Greek-English Lexicon.*

archaic use of the word "man" did not refer to a male. As noted earlier, other common-gender terms in Greek included "gods" and "child." Thus, it would be normal for Greek to have a term to refer to adults and citizens and that could include both men and women, when necessary. The fact that this word was also used for a husband would not confuse a native speaker.

Based on the evidence of Greek literature, scholars have been translating the word *aner* into "person," "citizen," "mortal," "friend," "everyone," "people," "they," and so on for hundreds of years. Unfortunately, when *andres* appears as a plural word in the New Testament, it is not always clear whether it refers only to male persons or to persons in general. Although this presents a difficulty in translation, however, the answer should not be decided by a mandate that lies outside of the translation task.

Grudem and over one hundred Christian leaders signed this statement against the TNIV, based in part on the argument that this translation did not translate words such as *aner* into the purely masculine word "men."[24] Does this mean that the great canon of Greek literature should also be plundered? Should any texts that translate *aner* and *andres* as other than as "man" or "men" be removed from schools, libraries, and bookstores? Should we get rid of Homer and Plato, and give Aristotle more exposure than he already has? Nevertheless, Grudem was able to generate enough distrust of the TNIV for it to be taken off the market. A compromising revision of the NIV was published in 2011. In fact, some Bible scholars at that time did check to see whether *aner* could include women, but it was not enough. Grudem is cited as saying: "Thousands upon thousands of examples of it [*aner*] are found in Greek from the 8th century BC (Homer) onward. If any meaning 'person' existed, scholars would have found many clear examples years ago."[25]

My concern is that most people listening to Grudem and Stinson do not read classical Greek, and are therefore unaware that it is possible that Grudem and Stinson do not read classical Greek either. Grudem and Stinson show no awareness that *aner* means person, citizen, mortal, friend, everyone, and so on. They show no awareness that *aner* is sometimes used to translate the Hebrew word *adam*, or that the Greek word *anthropos* is often used to translate the Hebrew word *ish*. The Septuagint, which was translated from Hebrew to Greek in the 2nd century BC, does not align

---

24. Note that although the statement of concern does not specifically refer to the Greek word *aner*, the Colorado Springs Guidelines include this criterion.

25. Grudem, quoted in "Better Bibles Blog."

with the translation guidelines drafted by Grudem. Nevertheless, Jesus himself cites the Septuagint in the Gospels. Jesus' own example contradicts the guidelines of Grudem and the CBMW.

I would now like to return to the verb *andrizomai*, which comes from *aner*. This word was mentioned earlier in the context of physical maturity. Often, being a "man" refers to being an adult; however, it also refers to courage. In Josh 1:9, the NET Bible (2009) translates *andrizomai* as "be strong and manly." However, in the Latin Vulgate, this phrase is translated as "*confortare, et esto robustus*," which the Douay-Rheims Bible (1609) phrases as "take courage." These early translations were clearly not based on a pro-feminist choice; that was simply considered to be the usual way to translate *andrizomai*. In the 4th century, this phrase was interpreted as having less to do with being a man, than with showing particular qualities of a responsible and courageous adult. Considering that the adjective *andreia* is associated with the verb *andrizomai*, we must recall that the wife in Proverbs is required to be *andreia*, and that Elektra, Esther, Judith, and many other women throughout Greek literature were referred to as *andreia*, or performed *andreia* deeds. Surely *andrizomai* means "to be manly" in the sense that the Proverbs 31 wife was "manly," and in the way that Esther and Judith were "manly." Rather than saying "to be manly," however, we would normally say "to be courageous." In fact, "to be courageous" is the usual translation for *andrizomai* in classical texts. In Plato's *Theaetetus*, the related word *andrizo* is translated as follows:

> And never say that you are unable to do so;
> for if God wills and gives you courage [*andrizo*], you will be able.[26]

Of course, I could accept a translation that implied that it was natural and expected for Christian women to act like men. However, practice teaches us that this is not to be understood. At the *Act Like Men* conferences,[27] it is made explicit that acting like a man is to *not* act like a woman, even a Christian woman. Therefore, the passage in 1 Cor 16:13 is not viewed by some as a part of the Bible addressed to women. In some Bibles, this verse says:

> Be watchful, stand firm in the faith,
> act like men, be strong. (ESV)

And in others, it says:

---

26. Plato, *Theaetetus*, 151d.
27. See https://www.actlikemen.com.

Be on your guard; stand firm in the faith;
be courageous; be strong. (NIV)

If women were explicitly taught that Christian women are to act like men, and will be treated as men, and can function like men, then all would be well. But it is not so. In fact, another translation makes it clear that, according to that translator, the author of this epistle is not talking to women at all. In the *Mounce Reverse Interlinear Greek-English New Testament*, I was surprised to read Mounce's interpretation of this verse:

Stay on guard, continue to stand firm in the faith,
Be men of courage, grow in strength.[28]

This is one of the least literal translations that I have seen, and I have not seen this translation anywhere else.

This chapter has been a long discussion, filled with examples, to demonstrate the richness of the literature that the Colorado Springs Guidelines ignore. One story that may be unfamiliar to readers is that of Judith, who was briefly mentioned earlier. The book of Judith is in the Deuterocanon, sometimes called the Apocrypha or the intertestamental books. It is unknown whether the original was written in Greek or Hebrew, as only a Greek copy survives. Along with about a dozen other books, this book was written in the tradition of the Hebrew scriptures, albeit after the 4th century BCE. However, these books were included in the Septuagint, and were therefore part of the scriptures of the early Christian Church, the Roman Church, and the Greek Orthodox Church. These books were included in Luther's Bible and in the King James Bible. However, Protestants were ultimately unwilling to accept as canonical any books that were written before the New Testament, but that were not a part of the Hebrew canon.

Judith was a pious but beautiful widow in a city that was being threatened by the Assyrian general Holofernes. Not believing that her city could resist such a siege, Judith set out to seduce Holofernes and cut off his head.

Many people consider that the story of Judith and Holofernes is not historic, but is more in the genre of heroic national fiction. However, recent evidence has emerged along with an idea that this story may really be about Salome Alexandra, the reigning queen of Judea in the first century BCE. She is still honoured by the Jewish people as a wise and powerful queen,

---

28. Mounce and Mounce, *Mounce Reverse-Interlinear New Testament*, 1 Cor 16:13.

who by diplomacy secured safety for her nation from a threatening hostile force.

I have been thinking of another courageous woman, who was a member of the French Resistance in Limoges, France. Annie Vallotton was the daughter of a Swiss protestant pastor, and became an artist. In 1966, she became the illustrator of the Good News Bible (GNB), which was published by the American Bible Society and translated into many languages worldwide. The popular cover had the appearance of newsprint. Vallotton is now said to be the most published artist of all time. Living out her life in Lausanne, Switzerland, Vallotton died in December 2013 at the age of 98. I was fortunate to be able to watch her draw when she came to the Institut Emmaus, located a few miles from Lausanne, where I studied in 1976–77. Anyone who has heard of the French Resistance will realize that Annie (along with her sister Gritou) was a very courageous woman.

Section 4

Gender of the Divine

CHAPTER 14

L'Éternel

God also said to Moses, "Say this to the people of Israel, 'The LORD, the God of your fathers, the God of Abraham, the God of Isaac, and the God of Jacob, has sent me to you': this is my name for ever, and thus I am to be remembered throughout all generations.

(EXOD 3:15, RSV)

WHEN I WAS IN my early teens, my parents took my younger sister and me on a trip to Switzerland to visit the place where our grandfather grew up. His family had been Darbyite Christians, a Brethren group that separated from the Reformed Church and met without ministers. Originally from Ireland, John Darby preached and founded assemblies in the Jura area of Switzerland along the French-Swiss border and close to Italy. In the late 1800s, Darby translated the Bible into French, German, and English.

Our mother read D'Aubigné's *History of the Reformation of the 16th Century*[1] to us, to prepare us for this trip. I remember being taken to see the Wall of the Reformation in Geneva, which was composed of an imposing quartet of statues thirty feet high depicting Calvin, Knox, Beze, and Farel. Although I did not realize it at the time, I now think that one of the most influential scholars of the Reformation, Calvin's older cousin Pierre Robert Olivétan, should probably have been included also.[xxxiii]

---

1. This book was written in Geneva in the early 1800s.

In the first few decades of the 16th century, Strasbourg, Germany, and then Geneva became the refuges of protestant Christians from all over France and England. Olivétan was born in in 1506 in Picardy, Northern France. He studied law in France, and then came to Strasbourg, where he studied Greek and Hebrew for three years with Martin Bucer. Starting in 1531, Olivétan worked in Neuchatel and Geneva as a teacher of children. A few years later, his younger cousin Jean Calvin followed in his tracks, first studying in Basel, and then ending up in Geneva.

Members of the dissenting Waldensian church, which arose in the 12th century in France and spread to the Piedmont valley of Northern Italy, wanted to dialogue with the Geneva reformers and join forces with them. Along with other Genevans, Farel attended the synod of Chanforan in the Piedmont valley. One of the major concerns of this synod was the production of a French translation of the Bible from the original languages, rather than from the Latin Vulgate. The Italian Waldensians agreed to a French Bible that would serve as a common text for all French-speaking Protestants, and financed the project.

Farel was convinced that only Olivétan was capable of accomplishing this task, considering his studies with Bucer and the scholars in Strasbourg. At first, Olivétan resisted, denying his own competence. However, Olivétan did have a wonderful personal library that included Greek and Hebrew lexicons, Christian and rabbinical commentaries, Pagnini's Latin translation of the Hebrew Bible, and Erasmus' Latin translation of the New Testament. Olivétan also had a copy of LeFevre's translation into French from the Latin Vulgate. Olivétan took his library, parted with a young woman in Geneva that he had been starting a relationship with, and retreated into an alpine valley in Piedmont for two years.

When Olivétan returned, with his translation completed, it was published in Neuchatel. His cousin, Jean Calvin, who had recently arrived in Geneva, wrote the preface. It is often thought that Calvin helped with the translation. Although this may be true in a sense, Calvin's help came after the translation was completed, not before. The text was slowly revised over the next few decades under Calvin's guidance, and was published in 1560 as the French Geneva Bible, which was attributed to Jean Calvin. This translation served as the predominant and unifying Bible of the French Reformation and the French-speaking Protestant community, until Louis Segond's translation was published in the late 19th century. The French Geneva Bible also served as a base for the popular English Geneva Bible.

Olivétan completed his translation quickly in under two years, where-as Pagninus had worked on his Hebrew-to-Latin translation for twenty-five years. However, Pagninus was trying to produce an entirely new translation from the Hebrew, while Olivétan, Coverdale, and Luther—the authors of the three most influential complete vernacular Bibles into French, English, and German—all had the benefit of using Pagninus' literal Latin translation of the Hebrew along with several lexicons that were published after Pagninus had completed his work. For their work on the New Testament, Olivétan, Coverdale, and Luther also had Erasmus' Latin translation. In addition, they had access to earlier vernacular Bibles translated from the Latin Vulgate.

Like Pagninus, Olivétan was a philologist first and a theologian second. Olivétan's translation did not allegorize or try to read meanings that were revealed in the New Testament back into the Hebrew Bible. This was partly due to the influence of rabbinical commentaries that gave additional insight into Jerome's 4th century Latin translation, and partly to their commitment to linguistic literalism and historical accuracy.

Olivétan's translation has two very significant features. First, it was not dedicated to or authorized by any civic or church authority; rather, it was offered as a gift to the poor believers of the Waldensian church. Olivétan called himself "the humble translator" and offered his translation from one believer to other believers. He did not claim any authority for his translation. Second, Olivétan's translation introduced a new way of rendering the name of God. Instead of translating YHWH (the name of God) as LORD, Jehovah, or Yahweh, Olivétan used "*L'Éternel*," a word that interprets the meaning of YHWH in a way that does not compare God to a male human being.

YHWH is represented in the Hebrew Bible by four consonants, and is often called the tetragrammaton (meaning "four letters"). In commentaries, this name is often written as either "Jehovah" or "Yahweh." However, traditional English Bibles translate the name YHWH as LORD, using all capitals. In the original Hebrew liturgy, the name YHWH was never pronounced aloud; instead, Jews said "*adonai*," meaning "my Lord." This tradition found its way into subsequent Greek, Latin, and English translations.

However, this tradition makes it a bit confusing for readers of an English translation who wish to know what the original Hebrew text said, since God is addressed in the Hebrew Bible as both YHWH and *adonai*. To avoid confusion, the King James Version (KJV) uses "LORD" for YHWH and "Lord" for *adonai*.

In Jewish copies of the Septuagint (the Greek translation of the Hebrew Bible from the 3rd century BCE), Jewish translators did not translate the name YHWH. Instead, they wrote YHWH in Hebrew letters, within an otherwise Greek text. Jewish readers then read YHWH out loud in Greek as *Kurios*, the Greek word for "lord." Non-Jewish readers of this text often misread or misunderstood the Hebrew letters; in fact, copies of the Septuagint from the 3rd century BCE onwards, especially those of the early church, translated YHWH directly into Greek as *Kurios*. However, this translation of YHWH was based on the traditional vocal reading by Jews, and is not a translation of the text itself.

In Latin translations, including Jerome's and Pagninus' translations, YHWH is translated as *Dominus*, the Latin word for "lord." Again, the words *Kurios, Dominus,* and LORD are not a text-based translation of YHWH, but rather a tradition-based rendering of the original text.

In 1535, Olivétan broke new ground with his translation of YHWH into *L'Éternel*, the Eternal One, and his translation has endured to the present day. Although Olivétan did some revision of his Bible over the next couple of years, he died of unknown causes in Italy in 1538, leaving half of his books to the woman in Geneva that he might have married, and half to Calvin. Calvin sold most of these books except for one rabbinical commentary.[2]

French Protestant and Jewish Bibles all translate YHWH as *L'Éternel*. Exod 3: 14–15 provides one example:

> *Dieu dit encore à Moïse:*
> [God said again to Moses]
> *Tu parleras ainsi aux enfants d'Israël:*
> [You will say this to the children of Israel]
> *L'Eternel, le Dieu de vos pères,*
> [The Eternal One, the God of your fathers,]
> *le Dieu d'Abraham, le Dieu d'Isaac et le Dieu de Jacob,*
> [the God of Abraham, the God of Isaac and the God of Jacob]
> *m'envoie vers vous. Voilà mon nom pour l'éternité,*
> [Sends me to you. This is my name for eternity]
> *voilà mon nom de génération en génération.*[3]
> [My name for generation to generation]

2. Gilmon, *John Calvin*, 145.
3. *La Sainte Bible*

In line 3 of this verse, the translator translates YHWH *Elohim* as "*L'Éternel, le Dieu.*" Traditional English translations use the phrase "LORD God," as found in the King James Bible and its many descendants. However, unlike "LORD," *L'Éternel* ("the Eternal One") is not anthropomorphic: it does not compare God to a human character or role, or endow God with human attributes.

The Bible gives us many rich images for God, including father, shepherd, judge, the one who gives birth,[4] warrior, and lord of hosts. However, *L'Éternel*, the Eternal One, is a name that distances itself from other human-sounding names. It allows us to enter a dialogue about the transcendent and non-gendered God without using a word that is semantically masculine or feminine in content. This God is beyond our material reality, and is the one who existed before the material world was created and who will exist after it ends.

On the other hand, the names "God" and "Lord" in English are both semantically gendered and bring a masculine metaphorical image to mind, because each exists in contrast to a feminine partner: "Goddess" and "Lady." It is not possible to "ungender" these words in English without twisting the language.

In Hebrew, the word for God is *Elohim*; although this word is grammatically gendered—that is, a masculine pronoun is used for *Elohim*—it is not semantically gendered. In fact, the female goddess Ashtoreth is also called *Elohim* in the Hebrew Bible.[5]

Like *Elohim*, YHWH, which is translated as LORD, has masculine grammatical gender in Hebrew. However, because it has no feminine partner, it appears to be semantically ungendered. YHWH can be interpreted as "the One who exists eternally, beyond material constraints." Thus, in Hebrew, *Elohim* and YHWH can be considered as semantically non-gendered. Calling God "the Eternal One" allows English speakers to talk about God in a way that is not semantically gendered. It allows us to engage in dialogue about God's transcendence, and the way in which God is apart from and distinct from creation. Ultimately, referring to God in this way often leads to a discussion of God's immanence—that is, how God is present with creation and with human beings.

As a further note regarding the grammatical gender of the words *Elohim* and YHWH, it is important to know that grammatical gender is a

4. Isa 66:9

5. 1 Kgs 11:5 and 33

feature of the language, rather than of context. For example, a mother eagle is a grammatically masculine word, and the soul of a man, like the soul of a woman, is a grammatically feminine word.

Although *L'Éternel* became the standard way to refer to the LORD in French, this did not transfer over into English Bibles. In English, it was more common to use the phrase "Everlasting God." However, "everlasting" does not replace the term "LORD," nor does it evoke the image of eternity past and eternity to come.

Calvin was not the one who came up with the name "*L'Éternel*," and he often used "Jehovah" in his commentaries when refer to YHWH. However, Gilmon[6] states that Calvin did revise some of his commentaries, replacing LORD or Jehovah with *L'Éternel*, and that Calvin supported the use of *L'Éternel* in Bible translation. Here is Calvin's justification for this term:

> I am who I am. The verb in the Hebrew is in the future tense, "I will be what I will be;" but it is of the same force as the present, except that it designates the perpetual duration of time. This is very plain, that God attributes to himself alone divine glory, because he is self-existent and therefore eternal; and thus gives being and existence to every creature. Nor does he predicate of himself anything common, or shared by others; but he claims for himself eternity as peculiar to God alone, in order that he may be honored according to his dignity.[7]

The next translator to introduce the concept of *L'Éternel* into a translation was Moses Mendelssohn, a Jewish German philosopher of the 18th century and the grandfather of the famous musicians Fanny and Felix Mendelssohn. Mendelssohn remained an Orthodox Jew throughout his life. In his later years, he produced the first Jewish translation of the Bible into German. He translated YHWH as "*der Ewige*," or "the Eternal One," and from that time on, most Jewish German translations followed the same pattern.

Mendelssohn based his choice on the *Letter of Baruch*, an early apocryphal writing; on the Aramaic translation of the Hebrew Bible, the *Targhum Onkelos*; and on the writings of Rabbi Saadya in the 9th century and of Maimonides, a 12th century Jewish philosopher. In the early 20th century, Franz Rosenzweig, who translated the Hebrew Bible with Martin Buber, commended Mendelssohn for parting from the term "LORD," or

6. Gilmon, *John Calvin*, 145.

7. Calvin, *Commentaries*, Exod 3:14.

"*HERR*" in German. However, he also questioned Mendelssohn for following "Calvin's lead" in choosing "*der Ewige*."[8] Rosenzweig himself translated God's name as "*ICH BIN DA*," meaning "I am there, that is, with you."

Was Rosenzweig accurate in suggesting that Mendelssohn was following Calvin's lead? Calvin first got the term "*L'Éternel*" from his cousin, Olivétan. Although Calvin wrote the preface to Olivétan's Bible, this was done after the translation was complete. Calvin was not in Geneva when Olivétan received the assignment for this translation. At that time, Calvin was 25 years old, and was just starting to become vocal in the Reformation movement.

In fact, we can come full circle to ask: How might Olivétan have derived the name *L'Éternel* from the original Hebrew literature that he was exposed to? Olivétan had access to a wide variety of translations in addition to Christian and rabbinical commentaries. Although it is doubtful that Olivétan could have become a skilled Hebrew scholar in his three years in Strasbourg, he was still able to benefit extensively from the scholarly works that he took with him into his retreat in the Alps. Olivétan benefited from the first wave of Christian Hebraism, which was led by Pagninus.

The *Adon Olam* is a popular prayer in the Hebrew liturgy that dates back to the 12th century, if not earlier. Although the first line is usually translated as "Lord of the Universe," a look at the biblical language reveals that "Lord of Eternity" is a better translation. Reform Judaism now uses translations with phrases such as this:

> You are our Eternal God,
> who reigned before any being had been created;
> when all was done according to Your will,
> then You were called Ruler.[9]

This prayer was part of the Siddhur, which was printed in Italy in the late 15th century; thus, it would have been available to Olivétan. Rather than describing Mendelssohn as following Calvin's lead, it makes more sense to think of Olivétan gaining insight from the Hebrew literature in his personal library—the same literature that Mendelssohn was familiar with.

At least two English translations use "the Eternal One." The first is James Moffat's 1924 translation, and the other is The Voice (2012). Here is Exod 3:15 in The Voice:

---

8. See Batnitzky, *Idolatry and Representation*.
9. הלפת וכשמ: *A Reform Siddur*, 361–2.

> This is what you are to tell Israel's people: "The Eternal, the God of your fathers, the God of Abraham, the God of Isaac, and the God of Jacob is the One who has sent me to you." This is My name forevermore, and this is the name by which all future generations shall remember Me.

Unfortunately, The Voice has been attacked for changing the name of God and "watering down" the Bible. I wonder if the same people would accuse Calvin of doing the same thing. Although The Voice has an excellent preface explaining its use of the term "Eternal," it does not mention the connection this term has to Calvin, the French Reformation, or Italian and Jewish Bibles.

There are several good reasons to inform ourselves about this other name for addressing God. Calling God "the Eternal One" may not be the ultimate solution to the problem of how feminist theologians, or anyone wanting to explore an ungendered way of addressing God, can do so. But it is an example of one way to research the attributes of God without trying to create new terms or to remove or ignore the gender implications of the other names and metaphors for God. The Eternal One is a non-anthropomorphic, ungendered term that we can use to address or refer to God.

The name "the Eternal One" can also move us away from contrasting the *attributes* of God in a gendered way; for example, some theologians have labeled righteousness and compassion as masculine and feminine, respectively. This name can open up opportunities to explore new and non-gendered attributes of God, in a dialogue about God's transcendence— the fact that God exists apart from creation and outside of the material world—and God's immanence—the fact that God is present with humans. Although some people may associate transcendence with the masculine and immanence with the feminine, we need only think of how the transcendent God gave birth to the universe, and how the immanent God is a warrior, to see these attributes as non-gendered. The Eternal One gives us common language to discuss the attributes of God without having to impose a necessarily masculine or feminine metaphor. The real issue here is how an eternal God is present and active in history. We can use this name to enter new philosophical domains.

In addition, using the name "Eternal One" provides us with language that is associated with Calvinism, the French and Swiss Protestant traditions, and the Jewish literary tradition. It can connect some of us to our religious roots, and remind us of our heritage. I will always remember my Swiss grandfather reading Bible verses aloud from the French daily

scripture calendar that hung on the kitchen wall, and intoning the word
"*L'Éternel.*"

Finally, the realization that other traditions—or our own tradition in
another language—have a name for God that we may have been unaware of
can open up space for us psychologically. New ideas and thoughts and new
linguistic terms—or rather, old ideas and terms that we are unfamiliar with
and that are not used by our immediate community—should not automatically be treated as heretical or inimical to our faith; they are just something
that we are not familiar with. How great it is to learn something new about
the history of the Bible, and about the scriptures that have shaped our culture for so many years! How wonderful it is to be able to focus on thinking
more freely about certain aspects of God, without tangling ourselves in the
question of gender!

CHAPTER 15

Mother God

As newborn babes, desire the pure milk of the word, that you may grow thereby

(1 PET 2:2, NKJV)

THE ISSUE OF THE Mother God is one of the most contentious issues regarding gender in the Bible. What do the original languages tell us about the gender of God? Can we legitimately call God our mother? Many people criticize the trend of looking for the female side of God as being a consequence of feminism. But what if an ancient Christian tradition, derived from the Gospels, pointed to the presence of a mother in the trinity? Would this change how we feel about addressing God as our mother?

I want to step back a bit here and say that, for me, God is not anthropomorphic. I do not view God as being human in this way at all. In my view, God is beyond male and female and is also beyond masculine and feminine. However, human language and human experience have resulted in God being addressed by masculine names, whereas the imagery used for God evokes both male and female characteristics. So, on the one hand, I resist thinking of God as having either sex or gender, but on the other hand, I still want to consider the influence that the original biblical languages have had on the ways that we address God.

If we examine pronouns—that is, "he," "she," or "it"—and verb agreement, then the answer to how God is referred to in the Bible is fairly simple. God is referred to as "he" in Greek and Hebrew; Jesus is referred to as "he" when he is an adult, and as the neuter "it" as a child. In the Hebrew, ninety percent of the references to the Holy Spirit use a feminine verb, and in the Greek, the neuter reference "it" is used.

However, an ancient literature exists in a language that is very close to Palestinian Aramaic, which is the language that Jesus spoke. This literature is written in Syrian Aramaic and is written with its own writing system, the Syriac alphabet. The language is called Syriac, and the body of writing is called Syriac literature. Early copies of the Gospels were translated into this language, and these refer to the Holy Spirit as "she." Religious literature in this language frequently refers to the Holy Spirit as "mother." This is not surprising, since Aramaic is a language that is related to biblical Hebrew. We would expect the Holy Spirit to be feminine in both Hebrew and Aramaic—or Syriac.

However, once again, the perceived gender of the word changed over time. In later Syriac manuscripts, written in the 5th and 6th centuries after Christ, the Syriac word for "spirit" was assigned a grammatically masculine gender when it occurred in the phrase "Holy Spirit." Therefore, by the 5th century in the established church, the Holy Spirit was neuter in Greek, and masculine in Latin and Syriac. Although the word for "spirit" was definitely feminine in Hebrew, only traces of the feminine spirit remained in the later church.[xxxiv]

Evidence that the early Syriac Gospels had a grammatically feminine spirit became available in the 19th century, when two manuscripts of the early or "Old Syriac" Gospels were discovered. The first manuscript was fragmentary; it was found among some Syriac manuscripts that were acquired by the British Museum in the 1840s. William Cureton recognized the manuscript as the text of the Gospels, but due to its fragmentary nature, it remained unpublished.

In the late 1800s, two unusual Scottish women were instrumental in bringing another, more complete, copy of the Old Syriac Gospels to the attention of British scholars. At the age of 23, Agnes Lewis and her twin sister Margaret Gibson were left a fortune by their father. These women were familiar with the biblical languages, and traveled throughout Europe and the Middle East learning to communicate in the native language of each country they visited. They learned languages expressly so that they could undertake the planning for their voyages themselves, and not be dependent on travel guides for more than pragmatic assistance.

In particular, Agnes learned to speak modern Greek and became familiar with the Greek Orthodox tradition. When she heard that there were previously unknown manuscripts in the Syriac language stored in Saint Catherine's Monastery in the Sinai desert, Agnes immediately began to study ancient Syriac. Although other scholars at the time doubted that the two sisters would gain access to this remote Greek Orthodox monastery, Agnes and Margaret set out from England. They took photographic equipment with them, and finished the trip across the Sinai desert on camels.

Due to her ability to communicate in Greek and thanks to her familiarity with the Orthodox tradition, Agnes became friends with the librarian of the monastery. She was thus able to gain access to Syriac manuscripts that had not been in use for many centuries. One of these manuscripts was a narrative of female martyrs dating from the 7th or 8th century. However, beneath this writing and in the margins, another text was visible. The vellum (i.e., the fine calfskin parchment that the pages were made of) had been scraped clean of its original writing and reused. Over the centuries, the original text had darkened again and had become partly legible.

Agnes noticed that this original layer of writing might be a text of the Gospels in Syriac. However, it was not the version that was commonly in use in the Syriac Church; rather, it appeared to come from a couple of centuries earlier. The sisters photographed most of the pages of this manuscript, and developed the film back in Cambridge, England. To this day, the manuscript itself remains in Saint Catherine's Monastery.

The photographs of the manuscript were only partially legible, so Agnes and Margaret put together an excursion to go back to Saint Catherine's. The excursion included three scholars of Syriac, whose task was to transcribe the text line by line. This text was finally translated and published in 1904 by Frances Crawford Burkitt, a member of the expedition, who was originally working on the fragmented Curetonian (named after William Cureton) Syriac manuscript. The Sinai manuscript from Saint Catherine's was more complete than the fragmented version, so it facilitated the final publication of the Old Syriac Gospels with comparative notes.

Agnes Lewis went on to travel and discover more unknown manuscripts; with her sister, she published a series of books on Syriac and other ancient manuscripts. Two other manuscripts found by Agnes were the Hebrew original of the Greek book of Ecclesiasticus, also known as *Ben Sirach*, a book of the Deuterocanon (or Apocrypha); and the manuscript called the *Rescriptus Climacus*, which includes in its original layer pages of biblical text in Palestinian Aramaic. This manuscript is currently being worked on, and will be displayed in the Green Collection of the Bible Museum, which opened in Washington in 2017.

Although these two women were granted doctoral degrees by European universities, they were never awarded such an honor by Cambridge, the city in which they lived and worked, as it did not grant degrees to women at that time. Agnes and Margaret did not work from within an institution; enabled by their personal wealth and their belief that God had a mission for each individual, they fulfilled their calling to uncover and expand our knowledge of early biblical manuscripts. Fortunately, these women were not in the least influenced by the notion that men were supposedly called to lead and women to follow. They were able to make a unique and worthy contribution to our knowledge of the ancient biblical texts with their dedication and persistence in scholarship.

In 1904, Burkitt published his translation of the two Old Syriac Gospels with comparative notes. It is in this book that we can read about the feminine spirit. Burkitt remarks several times on how the Holy Spirit is feminine in both of the Old Syriac manuscripts, in contrast to the later Syriac Gospels, which have been used since the 6th century in the Syriac Church. At some point in time, between the translation of the Gospels into early Syriac and their translation into the Syriac now held by the Syriac Church as its standard text, the gender of the Holy Spirit was changed by scribes and translators from feminine to masculine.

Burkitt picked out John 14:26 especially, and noted that in the early Syriac, this verse should be understood as saying: "The Spirit, the Paraclete, . . . She will teach you."[1] Burkitt further remarked that the feminine gender of the Holy Spirit was not a purely grammatical matter, but was also theological; he cites an ancient writer, Aphrates, who commented: "that the Father and Mother whom a man leaves when he marries a wife are God and the Holy Spirit."[2]

In the same way, the Syriac word for "the Word" In John 1 was feminine: "The word became a body and She sojourned among us."[3] Later, this word became masculine in the standard Syriac Gospels.

[Editor's Note: Suzanne's text ends here, although the chapter is incomplete. Rather than finishing the chapter using another person's words, we have chosen to leave Suzanne's words to stand on their own.]

1. John 14:26
2. Aphraates 354, in Burkitt, *Evangelion Da-Mepharreshe*, 44.
3. John 1:14 [translation unavailable]

Fully Adam

Lying on the soft duff
A sprinkle of snow on the moss
Salal cushions the twigs
And hard earth.
Splayed towards the sky
Surrounded by firs
Watching trunks tower in parallel lines
Narrowing to a meeting point
Just beyond my view – infinity
Crowns spray like black fireworks
Thrown against the winter lemon sky

Wandering those paths in August
Leaning underneath the lacy branches
Of high huckleberry
Tart red berries tiny to the hands
Are collected in the pail
And musky salal berries
Stain the fingers
With their dark bitter fruit
Cast along with sharp
Mouth puckering Oregon grape
Whose lemon yellow sprigs
Herald late winter.
Wilderness berry jam
Brings the woods inside.

But often I think of lying
On the warm dirt path
With duff scuffed away to humus
And cedar roots exposed
Fungus in the air
Overwhelmed by the smell
Of pungent needles, sage and saxifrage.
I want to lie spread eagle down
And drink in the scent of earth

All are Eve open to the sky
And harvesting the woods
But she is fully Adam facing down to dirt
Embracing that return.

ENDNOTES

Chapter 1

i Note that the Hebrew word *gibbor* can be translated as "strong, mighty, or men," while the word *eshet* can be translated as "woman, wife, or female." The word *chayil* can be translated as "power, strength, or army." (Translations taken from Strong, *Strong's Exhaustive Concordance*.)

ii Translated by Jerome between 382 and 405 CE.

Chapter 2

iii See

. . . in the heart of every man is a desperate desire for a battle to fight, an adventure to live, and a beauty to rescue. (Eldredge, *Wild at Heart*, p. 9)

and

We think you'll find that every woman in her heart of hearts longs for three things: to be romanced, to play an irreplaceable role in a great adventure, and to unveil beauty. (Eldredge and Eldredge, *Captivating Revised*, p. 8)

iv The Hebrew word *yafeh* can be translated as "fair, beautiful," the word *toar* can be translated as "outline, form," and the word *mareh* can be translated as "sight, appearance, vision." (Translations taken from Strong, *Strong's Exhaustive Concordance*.)

v See

And women in the city said, 'The wife of al-'Azeez is seeking to seduce her slave boy; he has impassioned her with love. Indeed, we see her [to be] in clear error.'

So when she heard of their scheming, she sent for them and prepared for them a banquet and gave each one of them a knife and said [to Joseph], 'Come out before them.' And when they saw him, they greatly admired him and cut their hands and said, 'Perfect is Allah! This is not a man; this is none but a noble angel.'

She said, 'That is the one about whom you blamed me. And I certainly sought to seduce him, but he firmly refused; and if he will not do what I order him, he will surely be imprisoned and will be of those debased.' (Qur'an, Surat Yusuf 12:30–32, quote taken from *qur'an.com*)

vi In Ps 42, the King James Bible translated this passage "As the hart panteth after the water brooks, so panteth my soul after thee, O God," using "hart," a male deer, for the Hebrew word *ayil*. This was done because the Latin translation by Jerome from the 4th century used *cervus*, a male deer. In the 16th century, Pagninus translated this passage, as part of what was considered by Jewish scholars to be the best Latin translation of the Hebrew. Pagninus understood *ayil* to be a female deer, *cerva*, in a poetic parallel construction with the Hebrew word for soul, which is feminine, since the two verbs were in the feminine form. Thus, Pagninus' translation of Ps 42:1 is as follows:

Quemadmodum cerva desiderat ad torrentes aquarum,

[As the doe desires torrents of water,]

Ita anima mea desiderat ad te deus.

[So my soul desires you, my God.]

The New English Translation (NET) Bible also uses "doe," indicating the parallel of the female deer with the feminine soul.

vii See

By his sheer youth, he has been excluded from consideration, as a kind of male Cinderella left to his domestic chores instead of being invited to the party. But the tending of flocks will have a symbolic implication for the future leader of Israel, and, in the Goliath story, it will also prove to have provided him with skills useful in combat...David's good looks will play a crucial role in the magnetic effect he is to have on women and men. (Alter, *David Story*, p. 87)

viii See

The *birya* [the food Tamar makes] is not simply a food, and making it is not simply an act of cooking; it is the preparation of a medicinal concoction. Perhaps, we could speculate, the princesses of the realm were instructed in the creation of healing foods. (Frymer-Kensky, *Reading the Women*, 158)

ix See

Esther's story also reminds one of Joseph in Egypt. Their beauty is described with almost the same words (Est. 2:7; Gen. 39.6) and both are endangered because of their beauty. Esther is caught by the king's agents and brought into the king's harem. Joseph is molested by Potiphar's wife and thrown into prison. Imprisoned in the king's harem, Esther experiences signs of favour and grace just like Joseph in his captivity (Est. 2; 9.15/Gen. 39.4; Est. 2:17/Gen. 39.21). Finally, Esther is raised to become the queen of Persia. She, too, becomes the second to the king in a foreign country as did Joseph in Egypt. And just as Joseph uses his position to save his people from a famine, Esther as queen of Persia succeeds in saving her people from impending persecution. (Brenner, *Feminist Companion*, 240)

x   The Hebrew word *tovat* can be translated as "beautiful"; see Endnote iv for translations of the other words. (Translations taken from Strong, *Strong's Exhaustive Concordance*.)

Chapter 4

xi   Maggie Anton, author of the historical fiction trilogy, *Rashi's Daughters,* has taken up this question in a recent blog post, entitled "Rashi's 'feminist' commentary on Gen.3."

xii   For more information on this topic, see Hunt, "Defenders of Women," read about the Zenana Missions established in the 1850s, or see Hacker, *Indomitable Lady Doctors.*

xiii The inscription, as reported by Levine, *Ancient Synagogue*, 508, reads:
Tation, the daughter of Straton, son of Emphedon, built out of her own [money] the synagogue building and the colonnade of the courtyard, and gave them to the Jews. The community of Jews has honored Tation, daughter of Straton, son of Emphedon, with a gold crown and a front seat [in the synagogue].

xiv Also see the 1937 translation by Charles Williams, which reads "for she has given protection to many, including myself," and the 1963 translation by William Beck, which reads "she has become a protector of many, including me."

xv See https://www.newswire.ca/news-releases/vancouver-foundation-ubc-and-united-church-of-canada-receive-one-of-the-largest-personal-bequests-in-bc-history-512452111.html for an article about a large donation to the Vancouver Foundation from Judith Jardine.

Chapter 6

xvi *Sperma* is a technical biblical term for "offspring/descendant(s)," and this is by far the most common usage of the word. In my view, this is the best foundation for understanding Heb 11:11. Many translations that are not dependent on English tradition have taken this exegetical route, including the revised Luther Bible:
> *Durch den Glauben empfing auch Sara, die unfruchtbar war, Kraft, Nachkommen hervorzubringen trotz ihres Alters*, [bring forth descendants]

and Münster:
> *Durch Glauben empfing auch selbst (die) unfruchtbare Sarra Kraft zur Grundlegung von Nachkommenschaft* [lay the foundation for posterity]

I could cite many other non-English versions, such as the Svenska 1917 translation into Swedish:
> *Genom tron fick jämväl Sara, fastän överårig, kraft att bliva stammoder för en avkomma, i det hon höll den för trovärdig, som hade givit löftet*
> [through faith even Sara, even though too old, received power to become founding-mother for a descendant]

A Norwegian translation reads:
> *Ved tro fikk også Sara kraft til å bli mor for en ætt, og det til tross for sin høye alder*
> [by faith Sara, too, received power to become mother for a group of descendants, and that in spite of her old age]

(The latter two quotations are thanks to Larsen, "Biblio Greek.")

xvii See e.g., Rainey, "What Robs Men."

xviii Also see Poythress and Grudem, *Gender-Neutral Bible Controversy*, 123:
The issue is whether a Bible translation systematically excludes male components of meaning that are there in the original text. If it does, the translation is "gender-neutral," and we argue in this book that such a translation does not

properly translate some of the details in the Word of God. Generic "he" is also part of the issue, because in many cases one cannot eliminate it without altering meanings.

Chapter 8

xix See Liddell and Scott, *A Greek-English Lexicon.*

xx Euripides, "Electra." In this text, Orestes and Elektra were called *duoin adelphoin*, a "brother and sister pair," which was an early dual form of the masculine plural reserved for only two people.

xxi Liddell and Scott, *A Greek-English Lexicon* and Bauer, *A Greek-English Lexicon.*

xxii In *The TNIV and the Gender Neutral Bible Controversy*, 425–426, Poythress and Grudem write, "Examination of further lexicological data (as indicated in chapter 12) showed that this guideline was too narrow."

xxiii See http://baylyblog.com/blog/2007/10/denying-origin-english-standard-version-and-bible-marketing for an interesting discussion on the possible relation between the ESV and the gender-neutral controversy of 1997.

xxiv See CBMW, *Danvers Statement.* This statement was prepared by several evangelical leaders at a CBMW meeting in Danvers, Massachusetts, in December, 1987. It was first published in final form by the CBMW in Wheaton, Illinois in November, 1988. Wayne Grudem also helped to draft the Danvers Statement. For example, part 6 of the Affirmations in the Danvers Statement reads as follows:
> 6.1 In the family, husbands should forsake harsh or selfish leadership and grow in love and care for their wives; wives should forsake resistance to their husbands' authority and grow in willing, joyful submission to their husbands' leadership (Eph 5:21-33; Col 3:18-19; Tit 2:3-5; 1 Pet 3:1-7).
> 6.2 In the church, redemption in Christ gives men and women an equal share in the blessings of salvation; nevertheless, some governing and teaching roles within the church are restricted to men (Gal 3:28; 1 Cor 11:2-16; 1 Tim 2:11-15).

xxv See CBMW, *Danvers Statement.*

xxvi Note that in 1 Cor 14:26, which reads: "What then, brothers? When you come together, each one has a hymn, a lesson, a revelation, a tongue, or an interpretation. Let all things be done for building up," the ESV does not include the usual footnote that "brothers" can mean "brothers and sisters."

xxvii In 2007, our church, St. John's, asked for input from the congregation on acquiring new Bibles. Other Anglican Churches were using the NRSV. It soon became evident that the leaders of our church would opt for the ESV, since Dr. Jim Packer, the chief editor of the ESV, was a member of our congregation. I presented to the minister my concerns about the fact that Packer was the editor of another Bible while signing a statement in 2002 against the translators of the TNIV. The translators of the NIV were also well-known members of our local community, and sometimes preached in our church. I felt that there should not be such contention in our church community. I then had to let the minister know that unless Packer withdrew his signature from the statement, I would have to leave the church, as I felt that there was not sufficient evidence to declare a Bible "inaccurate" which translated Greek and Hebrew words according to the meaning of these words. Packer did not remove his signature, although I am not sure that anyone ever directly asked him to. I did ask him about the statement, but he said that he "agreed with the substance if not with the precise manner of expression." The matter did not go further and I left that church.

xxviii For an article on Luther's translation practices, see Wendland, "Martin Luther," 16–36.

Chapter 11

xxix Although Pisistratus was a dictator, he championed the poorer levels of Athens society and was responsible for various public services for their benefit, including building an aqueduct for drinking water. His reign was prosperous, and was commonly referred to in ancient times as a "golden age."

xxx See
> In the mountain of Nitria there was an ascetic named Or, to whose great virtue the whole brotherhood bore witness, and especially Melania, that woman of God, who came to the mountain before me. (Palladius, *Lausiac History*, IX)

xxxi For example:
> Cratinus once had a dispute over a farm with the brother-in-law of Callimachus. A personal encounter ensued. Having concealed a female slave (*anthropos*), they accused Cratinus of having crushed her head, and asserting that she had died as a result of the wound, they brought suit against him in the court of the Palladium on the charge of murder. (Isocrates, "Against Callimachus," 52–54)

or
> What country, stranger, do you claim as your fatherland? And what woman (*anthropos*), of mortals on earth, bore you from her aged womb? Do not befoul your story with most hateful lies, but tell me of your birth. (Pindar, *Pythian Odes*, IV:72)

xxxii According to Grudem, Adam, not Eve, had a special role in representing the human race:
> It is unmistakable, then, that Adam had a leadership role in representing the entire human race, a leadership role that Eve did not have. Nor was it true that Adam and Eve *together* represented the human race. It was *Adam alone* who

represented the human race, because he had a particular leadership role that God had given him, a role that Eve did not share.

We are not saying here that the word *ādām* in the Hebrew Bible always refers to a male human being, for sometimes it has a broader sense and means something like "person." But here in the early chapters of Genesis the connection with the man in distinction from the woman is a very clear pattern. God gave the human race a name that, like the English word *man*, can either mean a male human being or can refer to the human race in general. (Grudem, *Biblical Foundations*, 26–27)

On page 30 of the same book, Grudem argues:

If the name *man* in English (as in Hebrew) did not suggest male leadership or headship in the human race, there would be no objection to using the word *man* to refer to the human race generally today. But it is precisely the hint of male leadership in the word that has led some people to object to this use of the word *man* and to attempt to substitute other terms instead. (Grudem, *Biblical Foundations*, 30)

Of course, this must be measured against certain facts and traditions: The Hebrew used *adam* instead of *ish*, the Greek used *anthropos* instead of *aner*, the Latin used *homo* instead of *vir*, and the German used *Mensch* instead of *Mann*. Is it any wonder that modern Jewish Bibles use "human" instead of "man," given the legacy of interpretation over the generations and across many languages? In all the languages mentioned above, a human being was distinguished from a man. Only in English, in spite of the fact that we now have the vocabulary available, do the Colorado Springs Guidelines attempt to limit the use of vocabulary for humans and humanity, and restrict Bibles to the use of "man."

Chapter 14

xxxiii   We then traveled up through the Canton de Vaud, north of Geneva, and along the French border to the village of Le Brassus, to see where our great grandparents were born and raised and where they attended a little Christian assembly. We also climbed the Dent de Vaulion, on whose slopes our grandparents had gotten engaged.

We continued up to Neuchatel, and came back down from the Jura range into Lausanne, driving along the shores of Lake Geneva, through Montreux, visiting the Chateau de Chillon. A decade later, I came to live a few miles up the mountain from Montreux. But at that time, our destination was L'Abri, the alpine chalets of Edith and Francis Schaeffer, missionaries to the younger generation of the 1960s hosteling in Europe.

Chapter 15

xxxiv   In Bible translation, not only the early Greek and Hebrew manuscripts are significant. In fact, there are only small portions of the Greek text available from before the 4th century CE. Complete Greek manuscripts, such as the Codex Sinaiticus and the Codex Vaticanus, which include the Greek translation of the Hebrew, the gospels, and epistles and are bound as books, date from after the early church councils determining Christian doctrine.

Bibliography

Abramowitz, Leah. *Tales of Nehama: Impressions of the Life and Teaching of Nehama Leibowitz*. Jerusalem: Gefen, 2003.

Akin, Daniel. *Exalting Jesus in Song of Songs*. Nashville, TN: B&H Academic, 2015.

Alter, Robert. *The David Story*. New York: W. W. Norton & Company, 2000.

———. *The Five Books of Moses: A Translation with Commentary*. New York: W.W. Norton, 2008.

Anton, Maggie. "Hebrew Text on *Rashi's Daughters*." http://rashisdaughters.com/blog/archives/2009_11.shtml.

———. *Rashi's Daughters, Book 1: Joheved*. New York: Plume, 2007.

Aristotle. *Politics*.

Batnitzky, Leora. *Idolatry and Representation: The Philosophy of Franz Rosenzweig Reconsidered*. Princeton, NJ: Princeton University Press, 2009.

Bauer, Walter. *A Greek-English Lexicon of the New Testament and Other Early Christian Literature* (3rd edition), edited by Fredrick W. Danker. Chicago: University of Chicago Press, 1957, 1979, 2000.

Beck, William. *Translation of the New Testament*. St. Louis, MO: The Lutheran Church-Missouri Synod's Concordia,1963.

Berlin, Adele. *Poetics and Interpretation of Biblical Narrative*. Warsaw, IN: Eisenbrauns, 1994.

"Better Bibles Blog," EnglishBibles.blogspot.ca. http://englishbibles.blogspot.ca/2007/04/aner-and-grudem.html?m=0.

Borresen, Kari Elisabeth, and Kari Vogt. *Women's Studies of the Christian and Islamic Traditions*. New York: Springer, 1993.

Brenner, Athalya, ed. *A Feminist Companion to Ruth and Esther*. Sheffield, UK: Sheffield Academic, 1999.

Brill, E. J. *The Hebrew and Aramaic Lexicon of the Old Testament*. Boston, MA: Brill, 1996.

Burk, Denny. "A Christian Vision for Gender Non-Conforming Boys." *Denny Burke*. http://www.dennyburk.com/a-christian-vision-for-gender-non-conforming-boys/.

Burkitt, Francis Crawford, ed. *Evangelion Da-Mepharreshe Vol. 2*. Cambridge, UK: Cambridge University Press, 1904.

Bushnell, Katharine C. *God's Word to Women*. CreateSpace Independent Publishing Platform, 2016. http://www.godswordtowomen.org/brief%20sketch.htm.

Calvin, Jean. *Commentaries on the Four Last Books of Moses*. c. 1555.

Calvin, John. *Calvin's Complete Commentary, Volume 1: Genesis to Joshua*. Harrington, DE: Delmarva, 2013.

———. *Commentaries on the Epistles to Timothy, Titus and Philemon*. Edinburgh, Scotland: The Calvin Translation Society, 1856.

CBMW. *Danvers Statement*. Wheaton, Illinois: Council on Biblical Manhood and Womanhood, 1988.

———. "An Evaluation of Gender Language in the 2011 Edition of the NIV Bible," Council on Biblical Manhood and Womanhood at CBMW.org. https://cbmw.org/ uncategorized/an-evaluation-of-gender-language-in-the-2011-edition-of-the-niv-bible/.

———. "Guidelines for Translation of Gender-Related Language in Scripture [a.k.a. 'Colorado Springs Guidelines']." *Journal of Biblical Manhood and Womanhood* 2 no. 3 (1997) 6. https://cbmw.org/journal/.

———. "Satisfied and Complementarian?" Council on Biblical Manhood and Womanhood at CBMW.org. https://cbmw.org/uncategorized/satisfied-and-complementarian/.

———. "Summaries of the Egalitarian and Complementarian Positions." Council on Biblical Manhood and Womanhood at CBMW.org. https://cbmw.org/uncategorized/ summaries-of-the-egalitarian-and-complementarian-positions/.

CBS News. "Gender-Neutral Bible Accused of Altering Message." CBS News (March 2011). https://www.cbsnews.com/news/gender-neutral-bible-accused-of-altering-message/.

Clement of Rome. *Epistle to the Corinthians*.

Clines, David J. A. *The Concise Dictionary of Classical Hebrew*. Sheffield, UK: Sheffield Phoenix, 2009.

Common English Bible. Nashville, TN: Christian Resources Development Corporation (CRDC), 2011.

Eldredge, John. *Wild at Heart: Discovering the Secret of a Man's Soul*. Nashville, TN: Thomas Nelson, 2011.

Eldredge, John, and Stasi Eldredge. *Captivating Revised and Expanded: Unveiling the Mystery of a Woman's Soul*. Nashville, TN: Thomas Nelson, 2011.

English Standard Version. Wheaton, IL: Crossway, 2001, 2007, 2011, 2016.

Euripides. *Electra*.

———. *Orestes*.

Foh, Susan. "What Is the Woman's Desire?" *The Westminster Theological Journal* 37 (1974/75) 376–7.

Fox, Everett, Translator. *Schocken Bible: The Five Books of Moses*. New York: Schocken Books, 1995.

Frymer-Kensky, Tivka. *Reading the Women of the Bible*. New York: Schocken Books, 2004.

Gilmon, Jean François. *John Calvin and the Printed Book*. Kirksville, MO: Truman State University Press, 2005.

Good News Bible. New York: HarperCollins, 1966, 1971, 1976, 1979.

Grudem, Wayne, (ed). *Biblical Foundations for Manhood and Womanhood*. Wheaton, IL: Crossway, 2002.

———. *Countering the Claims of Evangelical Feminism*. Colorado Springs, CO: Multnomah, 2006.

———. *Evangelical Feminism and Biblical Truth*. Wheaton, IL: Crossway, 2004, 2012.

———. "Over 100 Christian Leaders Claim that the TNIV Bible Is Not Trustworthy." *Journal of Biblical Manhood and Womanhood* 7, no. 2 (2002) 92–95. https://cbmw. org/journal/.

———. *Systematic Theology*. Zondervan, 1995.

Grudem, Wayne, and John Piper, eds. *Recovering Biblical Manhood and Womanhood.* Wheaton, IL: Crossway, 2006.

Gunter, J. D. "Men as Providers." Council on Biblical Manhood and Womanhood at CBMW.org. https://cbmw.org/topics/leadership-2/men-as-providers/.

Hacker, Carlotta. *The Indomitable Lady Doctors.* Halifax, Nova Scotia: Formac, 2001.

Hardesty, Nancy. "Paula: A Portrait of 4th Century Piety." *Christian History Institute* 17 (1988). https://christianhistoryinstitute.org/magazine/article/paula-a-portrait-of-4th-century-piety/.

Herodotus. *Histories.*

Holman Christian Standard Bible. Nashville, TN: Holman Bible, 2004.

Homer. *The Iliad.*

Hunt, Susan. "Defenders of Women." *Journal for Biblical Manhood and Womanhood* 13 no. 2 (2008) 24. https://cbmw.org/journal/.

Isocrates. "Against Callimachus." In *Isocrates with an English Translation in Three Volumes,* translated by George Norlin, 252–97. Cambridge, MA: Harvard University Press, 1980.

Kassian, Mary. "Female Beauty Matters." *Girls Gone Wise.* https://www.girlsgonewise.com/female-beauty-matters/.

Keil, C. F., and F. Delitzsch. "The Pentateuch." In *Commentary on the Old Testament in Ten Volumes,* Vol. 1. Grand Rapids, MI: Wm. B. Eerdmans, 1982.

Kostenberger, Andreas. "Saved Through Childbearing?" Council on Biblical Manhood and Womanhood at CBMW.org. https://cbmw.org/uncategorized/saved-through-childbearing-2/.

Kostenberger, Andreas, and David Jones, *God, Marriage and Family: Rebuilding the Biblical Foundation.* Wheaton, IL: Crossway, 2010.

La Sainte Bible–Nouvelle Edition de Genève. 1979.

Larsen, Iver. "Biblio Greek." http://lists.ibiblio.org/pipermail/b-greek/2009-May/049029.html.

Levenson, Alan. *Making of the Modern Jewish Bible.* Lanham, MD: Rowman & Littlefield, 2011.

Levine, Lee. *The Ancient Synagogue: The First Thousand Years* (Second Edition). New Haven, CT: Yale University Press, 2005.

Liddell, Henry George and Robert Scott. *A Greek-English Lexicon* (revised and augmented by Sir Henry Stuart Jones with the assistance of Roderick McKenzie). Oxford, UK: Clarendon, 1940.

Lucian. *Anacharsis,* translated by H. W. Fowler and F. G. Fowler. Oxford, UK: Oxford University Press, 1905.

Lucian of Samosata. *Zeus, the Tragedian.*

Luther, Martin. *On Translation: An Open Letter.* 1530.

Martin, Jay. "The Marks of a Godly Husband." *Southern Seminary Magazine* (Winter 2005) 17.

McKay, John P., Bennett D. Hill, John Buckler, Patricia Buckley Ebrey, Roger B. Beck, and Clare Haru Crowston. *A History of World Societies, Combined Volume.* London: McMillan, 2011.

Mindell, Cindy. *Jewish Ledger, Connecticut Edition* (July 2013). http://www.jewishledger.com/2013/07/conversation-with-dr-robert-alter/.

Mishkovsky, Zelda Schneurson (lyrics). *Le kol ish yesh shem.* c. 1950. http://www.hebrewsongs.com/song-lecholishyeshshem.htm.

Mohler, Al. "Men Not at Work: A Symptom of Manhood in Crisis." *Albertmohler.com.* https://albertmohler.com/2006/08/03/men-not-at-work-a-symptom-of-manhood-in-crisis/.

Moore, Russell. "Guest Editorial: O. J. Simpson Is Not a Complementarian: Male Headship and Violence against Women." *Journal for Biblical Manhood and Womanhood* (Fall 2005) 4. https://cbmw.org/journal/.

Mounce, Robert, and William Mounce. *Mounce Reverse-Interlinear New Testament.* Self-Published, 2011.

New American Standard Bible. La Habra, CA: Foundation Publications, 1971.

New English Translation. Richardson, TX: Biblical Studies Press, 2005. https://bible.org/netbible.

New International Version. Grand Rapids, MI: Zondervan, 1984, 2005, 2011.

New Living Translation. Carol Stream, IL: Tyndale House Foundation, 1996, 2004, 2015.

New Revised Standard Version. National Council of Churches, 1989.

Pagninus. *Veteris et Novi Testamenti nova translatio.* 1527.

Palladius. *The Lausiac History.*

Patterson, Dorothy. ""'Equal in Being, Unequal in Role': Exploring the Logic of Woman's Subordination" by Rebecca Merrill Groothuis." *Journal for Biblical Manhood and Womanhood* 10 no. 1 (2005). https://cbmw.org/journal/.

Pindar. *Pythian Odes.*

Plass, Ewald. *This Is Luther.* St. Louis, MO: Concordia, 1948.

Plato. *Hipparchus.*

———. *Laws.*

———. *Theaetetus.*

Poythress, Vern. "Gender Neutral Issues in the New International Version of 2011," Frame-Poythress.org. https://frame-poythress.org/gender-neutral-issues-in-the-new-international-version-of-2011/.

Poythress, Vern, and Wayne Grudem, *The Gender-Neutral Bible Controversy.* Nashville, TN: Broadman and Holman Academic, 2000.

———. *The TNIV and the Gender Neutral Bible Controversy.* Nashville, TN: B&H Academic, 2005.

Rainey, Dennis. "What Robs Men of Courage." https://www.oneplace.com/ministries/familylife-today/read/articles/what-robs-men-of-courage-15107.html.

Rashi. *The Complete Tanach with Rashi Commentary.* Judaica at Chabad.org. https://www.chabad.org/library/bible_cdo/aid/63255/jewish/The-Bible-with-Rashi.htm.

Revised Standard Version. National Council of Churches, 1952, 1971.

Schreiner, Tom. "Head Coverings, Prophesies, and the Trinity." In *Recovering Biblical Manhood and Womanhood,* edited by John Piper, Wayne Grudem. Wheaton, IL: Crossway, 2012.

Smith, Brandon. "4 Lessons I'm Learning as a Soon-to-Be Dad." Council on Biblical Manhood and Womanhood at CBMW.org. https://cbmw.org/topics/leadership-2/4-lessons-im-learning-as-a-soon-to-be-dad/.

Smith, Emily. *With Her Own Eyes: The Story of Julia Smith, Her Life, and Her Bible.* Knoxville, TN: The University of Tennessee Press, 2006.

Smith, Julia E. *The Holy Bible: Containing the Old and New Testaments; Translated Literally from the Original Tongues.* Self-Published, 1876.

Sophocles. *Electra.*

"Statement By Participants In The Conference On Gender-Related Language In Scripture." *Journal of Biblical Manhood and Womanhood* 2 no. 3 (1997) 7. https://cbmw.org/journal/.

"Statement of Concern about the TNIV Bible." http://www.bible-researcher.com/tniv2.html.

Stein, David E. S. "The Noun *ish* in Biblical Hebrew: A Term of Affiliation." *The Journal of Hebrew Scriptures* 8 Art. 1 (2008) 1–24.

———. "Part 1: The Initial Case for Reconsideration." *David E. S. Stein.* http://scholar.davidesstein.name/Memoranda.htm.

———. "What Does It Mean to Be a 'Man'?" *David E. S. Stein.* http://scholar.davidesstein.name/Memoranda.htm.

Stinson, Randy and Dan Dumas. *A Guide to Biblical Manhood* (Kindle Edition). Louisville, KY: SBTS, 2011.

Strachan, Owen. "Biblical Support for Women as Homemakers." *Owenstrachan.com.* http://owenstrachan.com/2006/09/20/biblical-support-for-women-as-homemakers/.

———. "The Genesis of Gender and Ecclesial Womanhood." *9Marks Journal.* https://www.9marks.org/article/genesis-gender-and-ecclesial-womanhood/.

Strauss, Richard. "Dad's Many Hats." Bible.org. https://bible.org/seriespage/dad%E2%80%99s-many-hats.

Strong, James. *Strong's Exhaustive Concordance of the Bible.* Peabody, MA: Hendrickson, 2009.

Svenska folkbibein. 1917.

Thucydides. *The History of the Peloponnesian War.*

Today's New International Version. Grand Rapids, MI: Zondervan, 2005.

Todd, Douglas. "British Columbia's 25 most influential spiritual leaders." *Vancouver Sun* (November 2010).

———. "Vancouver Sun Archives." *Vancouver Sun* (April 2000).

Tyndale, William. *The Obedience of the Christian Man* (edited with introduction and notes by David Daniell; first pub. 1528). London: Penguin Books, 2000.

Van Leeuwen, Mary Stewart. *Gender and Grace: Love, Work and Parenting in a Changing World.* Downers' Grove, IL: InterVarsity, 1990.

Walton, John H. *The NIV Application Commentary (Genesis 2:18–25).* Grand Rapids, MI: Zondervan, 2001.

Walton, Mark David. "Relationships and Roles in the New Creation." Council on Biblical Manhood and Womanhood at CBMW.org. http://cbmw.org/uncategorized/relationships-and-roles-in-the-new-creation/.

Ware, Bruce. *Big Truths for Young Hearts: Teaching and Learning the Greatness of God.* Wheaton, IL: Crossway, 2009.

———. "Male and Female Complementarity and the Image of God." Council on Biblical Manhood and Womanhood at CBMW.org. http://cbmw.org/uncategorized/male-and-female-complementarity-and-the-image-of-god/.

Weinrich, William. "Women in the History of the Church." In *Recovering Biblical Manhood and Womanhood,* edited by Grudem, Wayne and John Piper, 265–84. Wheaton, IL: Crossway, 2006.

Wendland, Ernst R. "Martin Luther—The Father of Confessional, Functional-Equivalence Bible Translation (Part 1)." *Notes on Translation* 9 no. 1 (1995) 16–36. http://essays.wls.wels.net/bitstream/handle/123456789/771/WendlandLuther.pdf?sequence=1&isAllowed=y.

Williams, Charles. *Translation of the New Testament.* 1937.

Wolters, Al. *The Song of the Valiant Woman: Studies in the Translation of Proverbs 31:10–31.* Carlisle, Cumbria, UK: Paternoster, 2001.

הלפת וכשמ: *A Reform Siddur: Weekdays and Festivals.* New York: CCAR, 2007.

Index

Manufactured by Amazon.ca
Bolton, ON

25998957R00122